Radicals, Resistance, *and* Revenge

ALSO BY JUDGE JEANINE PIRRO
PUBLISHED BY CENTER STREET

LIARS, LEAKERS, AND LIBERALS:
THE CASE AGAINST THE ANTI-TRUMP CONSPIRACY

DON'T LIE TO ME:
AND STOP TRYING TO STEAL OUR FREEDOM

Radicals, Resistance, *and* Revenge

The Left's Plot to Remake America

Judge Jeanine Pirro

CENTER
STREET®

NEW YORK   NASHVILLE

Center Street
Hachette Book Group
1290 Avenue of the Americas, New York, NY 10104
centerstreet.com
twitter.com/centerstreet

Originally published in hardcover and ebook by Center Street in August 2019
First Trade Paperback Edition: May 2021

Center Street is a division of Hachette Book Group, Inc. The Center Street name and logo are trademarks of Hachette Book Group, Inc.

The publisher is not responsible for websites (or their content) that are not owned by the publisher.

The Hachette Speakers Bureau provides a wide range of authors for speaking events. To find out more, go to www.HachetteSpeakersBureau.com or call (866) 376-6591.

Print book interior design by Timothy Shaner, NightandDaydesign.biz

Library of Congress Cataloging-in-Publication Data has been applied for.

ISBNs: 978-1-5460-8518-8 (hardcover), 978-1-5460-8601-7 (signed edition), 978-1-5460-8600-0 (B&N.Com Signed Edition), 978-1-5460-8517-1 (ebook), 978-1-5460-8519-5 (trade paperback)

Printed in the United States of America

LSC-C

Printing 1, 2021

This past April my rock, my inspiration, and my muse passed.

She taught me to stay true to my moral core, to fight
for the underdog, and to never fear taking a stand,
no matter how unpopular.

I dedicate this book to the woman who stands tall,
above all others in my life, and to whom I am eternally
grateful, my mom, Esther Ferris.

Contents

Radicals, Resistance, *and* Revenge

Chapter One

Here's My Open

A s we approach publication date, we are confronted yet again with a never-ending news cycle that seems to compete with the speed of light. No surprise, since Donald Trump himself is a nonstop, never-give-up, no-holds-barred human version of the speed of light. Even his terrific staff, many half his age, can barely keep up. Luckily for us, the Trump presidency has changed just about everything in record time. And thank God it has.

For over two years, the presidency of the United States has been under siege. Our commander in chief has been subjected to unprecedented maligning by the mainstream media, high-level Obama administration officials, and disappointed, disgruntled, and deranged Democrats. He has been accused of being an agent of a foreign government, a Putin puppet, and a treasonous dictator, all because they despise the president we put in the Oval Office.

The White House stands alone like an ancient walled city with barbarians storming the gates, looking to annihilate the man the American people put in that house in 2016. He was the outsider, beholden to no one, who promised to take back their government from the corrupt special interests who had stolen it from them in order to remake America into a borderless, multicultural, socialist wasteland they could then plunder and leave to rot.

That corrupt establishment—"the Swamp," as President Trump and his supporters call it—was not going to give up the Oval Office without a fight. They were determined to maintain their power regardless of any election results, regardless of the consent of the governed. They were not satisfied to fight honestly at the polls. If the people voted for change, they were going to nullify those results with phony investigations, all-out suppression of dissent, insurrection at our borders, and even violent "resistance." Their goal was to destroy the administration of the duly elected forty-fifth president by any means possible, legal or illegal.

The Mueller report exposed the Left's plot to remake America. Donald Trump's election interrupted the leftward, globalist course Barack Obama had set. It would have been full steam ahead under Hillary Clinton. So, they had to take Trump down if they were ever going to get back on course.

As a result, we stood witness to the biggest scandal in American history, bar none: an attempted elimination of a presidential candidate and then coup against the duly elected president of the United States from within the government itself. They conned us, they gamed us, and they lied to us, over and over and over, for three years. They destroyed lives, reputations, and families. And, in the end, no one connected with

Donald Trump or his campaign colluded, coordinated, or conspired with Russia. Not Donald Trump himself, not any member of the Trump family, not anyone on the campaign, not one American.

For two years, prosecutors savagely strove to indict the president and everyone in his orbit. For two years, the mainstream media, the talking heads, the networks, and the lying, liberal Hollywood hypocrites all tried to convince you that Donald Trump was an illegitimate president. And after all of that—there turned out to be nothing to any of it, just as I've always said. No collusion, no obstruction, nothing.

The president's enemies didn't care whose lives they destroyed. What mattered was that they destroy the outsider, the one we—the forgotten men and women of America—put in the White House. Businessman Donald J. Trump was that outsider who convinced us the status quo was a choice and he could do better. The perpetrators of this attempted coup were furious at the thought and chipped away with unending zeal, desperate for any connection, threatening families and witnesses and individuals' civil liberties to obtain their corrupt goal of removing the president of the United States from office.

The very people who scoff and laugh at the idea of a "Deep State" actually watched it shamelessly and repeatedly broadcast on prime-time television. These Swamp Scum were so arrogant they didn't even try to hide what they were doing. They lied to your face and dared you to call them on it, from Cardinal James Comey, Clueless James Clapper, and Pond Scum John Brennan on down. It was the first time in American history that people with unbridled power tried to eliminate a presidential candidate and then, when that failed, planted the seeds for the indictment and impeachment of the now-elected president, destroying the will of the American people who voted for change.

Where did this group get the confidence that this was okay? Who above them could possibly have given them the green light? It could only have come from the top, not just on the orders of the head of the CIA John Brennan, the head of the FBI James Comey, and the head of the Justice Department Loretta Lynch. Ultimately, at the very least, there had to be a wink and a nod from the commander in chief, if not full-on involvement of Barack Obama.

The unverified Steele dossier was the excuse and justification for this rogue intelligence operation. They used it as a basis to spy on an opposing candidate for the highest seat in the land. They knew it was a lie, they knew it was a political document—not an *intelligence* document—and they knew Hillary paid for it and yet this cabal of Trump-hating, Obama-loving sycophants followed their boss, doing everything they could to destroy Donald Trump's chances to become president of the United States.

The March 2019 Mueller report, delivered to Attorney General Bill Barr on March 22, was a turning point after two years of gut-wrenching, slanderous, hateful bile coming from the Left. They promised their teed-up special counsel investigation would deliver the goods after they themselves created the narrative of Donald Trump as an illegitimate president, who had no right to be sitting at 1600 Pennsylvania Avenue. But, like most of their baseless accusations, it backfired. The Russia collusion delusion was nothing more than an illusion straight from the Resistance movement that didn't want a Trump presidency.

So why did it take almost two years, with such a large staff, to figure out there was no "there" there (to use Peter Strzok's infamous words)?[1] In early 2018, reports suggested Mueller had already moved on from collusion to obstruction. Mueller outlines ten points he claims suggest obstruction, which came from a handful of witnesses. So, the question is, could this report have been issued before the 2018 midterms? Why did he wait another four months after that? Was Mueller stringing his investigation along, refusing to conclude it in order to help the Democrats who, in their dream of impeachment, needed to win the House? The answer to that last question tells us whether Mueller was a political operative or an objective special counsel. Maybe we'll get an answer when Mueller is scheduled to appear before Congress in mid-July.

After all that time investigating and prosecuting people like Paul Manafort who received what amounted to a life sentence for crimes unrelated to his investigation, Mueller couldn't figure out why he couldn't get anything on Donald Trump.

Maybe, Bob, there was nothing to get. Maybe the fact that you couldn't even get people to lie to save their own hides should tell you they couldn't even figure out a way to implicate him. You tried everything you could in your bag of dirty tricks to get Trump and you came up with nothing, nada, zip.

The more we heard about warrants based on unverified political documents paid for by Trump's opponent, the more it became apparent that there was no collusion and no obstruction, since, by the way, there was no crime to obstruct. No one looked at the corruption that led to the framing of a president. How and why did a counterintelligence investigation even begin? Mueller wasn't interested in investigating that.

So, the special counsel comes out with its thirty-four indictments and a final report. None of the indictments involved Donald

Trump, his family, the Trump campaign, or any American, for that matter, colluding with Russia. There was full cooperation by the White House, which never claimed executive privilege and handed over more than one million documents. Too many people in the Trump orbit were destroyed politically, financially, and emotionally for no reason by the Hillary-loving and Trump-hating attorneys and investigators. Team Mueller took down people with process crimes having nothing to do with Russia.

If after two years, 19 prosecutors, 40 investigators, more than 2,800 subpoenas, nearly 500 search warrants, several grand juries, and $34 million spent there was not a scintilla of evidence to the collusion claim, whose idea was it to start the investigation and why?

We still don't know with certainty the exact date the FBI's Peter Strzok began the counterintelligence investigation. There was a lot of dancing by Strzok when he was forced to testify before Congress. The generally stated date is July 31, 2016, but when asked for specifics of the genesis of his investigation, Strzok demurred, saying he didn't have clearance to discuss it. Then, when the FBI said that same day—during the same hearing—that there was no prohibition and gave him permission to answer, Strzok pivoted, shockingly, with an arrogant smirk on his face, and said he had no recollection.

To determine whether there was even a legitimate purpose behind it, the investigators need to be investigated. That includes James Comey, Andrew McCabe, Peter Strzok, Lisa Page, John Brennan, James Clapper, Samantha Power, Loretta Lynch, and the rest of the conspirators I talked about in my last book, *Liars, Leakers, and Liberals*.

Just a week before the Mueller report was released, former CIA director and Pond Scum John Brennan—who himself accused the president of treasonous behavior, a crime punishable by death—was on television saying there were pending indictments to be released imminently, even one against the president's own son.[2] It never happened.

Mueller and his nineteen lawyers, invested financially, philosophically, and ideologically in the Hate Donald Trump Movement, would have done anything they could to legally and politically deep-six Donald Trump, but they didn't have the goods, pure and simple. In the interim, along this tortuous two-year path of meritless accusations, our nation was fractured and in chaos. Mueller's investigation provided cover for a tsunami of lies and obfuscations from CNN, MSNBC, and the rest of the mainstream media. Even Nobel laureate Paul Krugman said in November 2017, "There's really no question about Trump/Putin collusion, and Trump in fact continues to act like Putin's puppet."[3] A year earlier, he had predicted the stock market would never recover from Donald Trump's election,[4] earning him first place in the president's hilarious "Fake News Awards."

What happened to him? If Krugman wasn't allowing politics to corrupt his intellect, then what the hell were they smoking over there at the Royal Swedish Academy of Sciences when they made him a laureate in Economic Sciences?

All the while, President Trump remained focused and determined to execute the mission to which he was elected. Have you ever seen a man face an onslaught of incoming like this, day in and day out and still forge ahead on America's behalf—our behalf—to make the economy stronger and the country safer?

For most of this ordeal, the president was surrounded by wimps like former attorney general Jeff Sessions, who hid under his desk. Contrast him with Barack Obama's attorney general Eric Holder, who was held in contempt of Congress in 2012 for withholding documents related to the Fast and Furious scandal.[5] You didn't see Holder recusing himself from anything. Barack loved his loyal, protective "wingman."

They even criticized the president's anger regarding these allegations. Of course he was furious. He was an innocent man! They took away his ability to enjoy a single moment of his presidency or do his job without someone accusing him of being an illegitimate president, a fascist, a sexist, a racist, a xenophobe, or a Russian asset. No one deserves that. And despite their allegations blowing up in their faces, the Left continues to relitigate the very issue that Mueller shut down. We can only hope their transparent hatred for our president and our country is punished by clear-thinking Americans at the polls in 2020.

I'm not going to dwell on the fact that the real collusion with Russia was perpetrated by the Bonnie and Clyde of American politics, Bill and Hillary Clinton, who sold 20 percent of America's uranium to a Russian company and pocketed $145 million through their trusty charity.[6] And of course Bill was paid $500,000 for a quick speech in Russia to a Kremlin-connected company shortly thereafter.

As for the Russians meddling in our election, everyone agrees that not one vote was affected. The Russians bought a few Facebook ads to try to influence Americans, which amounted to bubkes. Even Barack Obama said there was no way the 2016 election could be rigged by Russia.[7]

But the Left is not going to stand for the truth.

They continue to complain. They don't like the report and want to see all the redactions in this 448-page document, although such redactions are required by law.[8] And when given the opportunity to see the report in a SCIF (sensitive compartmented information facility), no Democrat bothered to do so. I guess they don't want the truth because they "can't handle the truth."

And their new public enemy number two is Attorney General William Barr. His summary of that 448-page report is not enough. The fact that the entire Mueller report is published is not enough. The Resistance will read, reread, and reinterpret every word to try to bring down the president.

Volume two of the 448-page Mueller report examines the obstruction of justice issue, and Mueller curiously refused to take a position on whether the president committed this crime. If there wasn't enough evidence to bring a charge that should have been the end of it. But no. In a show of political whoremanship, Mueller left crumbs for his fellow travelers in Congress. He added the statement that he couldn't exonerate Trump to give the Democrats something to work with. Now, we're about to get eighteen more months of this.

Mueller slamming the president on his way out was meant to satisfy his unsatisfied client, the Democrats. I've empaneled and presented to many grand juries. You don't come out and say, "I didn't indict him, but I couldn't exonerate him either." I've never seen that. If, as a prosecutor, you don't have evidence to indict you keep your mouth shut.

Shame on Robert Mueller. He could have made a decision on that, just as he did on collusion. But he had to give something to the Democrat House.

Little Adam Schiff, now chair of the House Intel Committee since the Democrats won the House in the midterm elections, should be hiding under a rock after all the doozies he came out with during the Mueller investigation. Instead, Mueller, with his nondecision on obstruction, has given him a chance to shamelessly continue his Hate Donald Trump Campaign. He just won't end it. He and many on the Left are not interested in doing the people's work. They are solely interested in getting Donald Trump out of the way, the people and their work be damned.

All nine Republican members of the House Intelligence Committee signed a letter asking Schiff to resign as chairman.[9] But for Mueller's safety-valve obstruction statement, he'd have no other choice.

Yet, instead of being smart enough to get off the collusion delusion and pivot to obstruction of justice, Schiff answered his Republican committee members by doubling down on the discredited collusion narrative. Citing Donald Trump, Jr.'s completely innocuous meeting with Russians in possession of absolutely nothing of use for his father's campaign, and Paul Manafort's completely unrelated convictions—many of which could have been hung on most of the lobbyists on K Street— Schiff defiantly responded, "And yes, I think it is corrupt," he added. "And evidence of collusion."[10]

Some people don't know when to quit. Kind of like those wackadoos at the annual running of the bulls in Pamplona, who think they're going to outsmart and outrun a 2,400-pound bull but end up with hoofprints on their skinny necks.

CHAPTER TWO

They Can Lie, but They Can't Stop Trump from Winning

They don't make movies like they used to. A couple of years back, one came out called *The Post*. It was about the *Washington Post* back in the '60s; you might have heard about it. The movie starred Meryl Streep and Tom Hanks. It was directed by Steven Spielberg. In other words, it was the Hollywood liberal elite making a film about the media liberal elite. A regular love-in. Though the plot concerned the leaking of the Pentagon Papers, the secret sordid history of America's involvement in Vietnam, you didn't have to be a Film Studies professor to see the underlying message of the movie was an indictment of President Trump—a poor little liberal newspaper battles a big, bad Republican president and wins the day. "The allegory is obvious," Spielberg himself said many times. Pure Hollywood horse crap.

There was one thing the movie got absolutely right, however, and that was the relationship between the mainstream media and the Left. Like *Dancing with the Stars*, the Democrats tell the media to jump, and the press says *How high?* They've gotten so good at the routine that fake news doesn't just smear the president with lies. Oh, no. It does even more damage than that. Allow me to explain.

Unfortunately, I have to listen to the mainstream media on a regular basis. It's part of my job. I need to keep myself apprised of what they're up to. Maybe it was my prosecutorial sixth sense, but a while back I began to notice a suspicious pattern in the liberal press. How many times over the past two and a half years did we hear Mueller was "closing in" on President Trump? Large segments of the American public likely believed indictments or at least articles of impeachment were imminent on so many occasions it's difficult to try to put a number to them. But at no time in the past two years did Mueller have enough evidence to bring a single indictment against any American for colluding with Russia to affect the 2016 elections. Still, there was no better story to lather up liberals than a Mueller-hot-on-the-trail tale, so it isn't unusual that the fake news ran so many different versions of the story. What was unusual, however, was the timing of those stories.

As far back as September 20, 2017, *Vanity Fair* ran a story titled "Robert Mueller Is Officially Closing in on Trump."[1] Why closing in? Because Mueller's office had requested a number of documents from the White House, a routine part of any investigation into anything. But for the seemingly hysterical media, this was a major development indicating Mueller was onto some

significant discovery. As you might imagine, the story dominated the mainstream news cycle.

The day before, on September 19, 2017, President Trump
had delivered an historic address to the United Nations. I say
historic because it was one of the first times the president had
spoken directly to the member nations on how his America
First policy would impact the rest of the world. "As president of
the United States, I will always put America first, just like you,
as the leaders of your countries will always, and should always,
put your countries first," said the president.[2]

The speech didn't represent a withdrawal from the world
by the United States, but it was a clear message to the other
nations that they could no longer take advantage of the United
States. The president called out member nations for continuing to trade with Iran and North Korea and called for support
against Venezuela's murderous socialist regime. He called it a
"massive source of embarrassment to the United Nations that
some governments with egregious human rights records sit on
the UN Human Rights Council."[3]

This was an early attempt by the president to redefine
America's relationship with its allies as one of fairer mutual
cooperation, a promise he'd made repeatedly on the campaign
trail. And yet, as great as the speech was, the Mueller "closing
in" crap, which was published the very next day, drew most of
the attention in the liberal press.

Then on January 24, 2018, Business Insider ran a story titled,
"The Russia Investigation Is Reaching a Pivotal Moment and
It Looks Like It's Closing in on Trump."[4] Why closing in this
time? Mueller had just interviewed former Attorney General

Jeff Sessions a few days earlier. It was also reported Mueller's team had interviewed Cardinal James Comey in late 2017. Supposedly, this was the reason the media believed Mueller to be "closing in" when he wasn't.

Or, was it because President Trump had signed the first of his tariffs on Chinese imports just three days before,[5] keeping another campaign promise and implementing a strategy that would become successful in reaching an agreement with China where so many previous presidents had failed? Not only had the president just imposed the first of his tariffs on Chinese goods, but he was leaving for Davos, Switzerland, to deliver another international address crucial to his economic platform.[6] The speech was scheduled for the very next day after the latest "closing in" articles appeared.

Newsweek ran another "closing in" article a couple months later, on March 6, 2018, titled "Is Mueller Closing in on Trump? Incidents Involving President's Lawyer and Russia Under Scrutiny, Report Says."[7] This story had to do with the Mueller probe's interest in Michael Cohen, a convicted perjurer who eventually testified to precisely nothing implicating Donald Trump or his campaign in collusion with Russia or obstruction of justice.

But on March 6, 2018, this was the latest evidence Mueller was "closing in" on the president, just a few days after President Trump announced his tariff on steel.[8] The move was controversial and debate on it was justified, but it seems at least some media would rather just shut that debate down by running the "closing in" fake news talking point.

In late November 2018, US Border Patrol agents were forced to use tear gas on a mob of illegal immigrants who rushed the border, temporarily closing down the San Ysidro port of entry, one of the busiest on our southern border.[9] President Trump threatened to close the border down permanently if Mexico didn't do something about the migrant caravans increasingly assaulting our southern border.

The tough talk paid off. Over that weekend, the president reached a tentative agreement with incoming Mexican President Andrés Manuel López Obrador to keep asylum applicants in Mexico while their claims are processed, rather than allowing them to wait for adjudication in the United States. This was yet another policy achievement his predecessors had failed to realize. Two days after the agreement was announced, on November 28, 2018, the Pentagon told the media the president would extend the deployment of US troops on our southern border, for obvious reasons.[10] The anti-American Left hates the idea of troops on the border, mostly because it works.

Right on cue, *The Nation* ran a headline the very next day shouting—you guessed it—"The Mueller Investigation Is Closing in on Trump—and the Next Congress Won't Protect Him."[11] Running out of ideas, the latest "closing in" hysteria was based on supposedly new developments in the Cohen investigation, which just happened to occur when the president was fighting to keep another key campaign promise to the people who elected him.

I could probably write a whole book on the "closing in" talking point, but I'll give you just one more example. On January 23 of this year, the situation in Venezuela had deteriorated to the point of constitutional crisis. Amid nationwide protests, Venezuela's National Assembly—its unicameral equivalent to our bicameral Congress—declared Juan Guaidó acting president of Venezuela.

President Trump joined Canada, Brazil, and several other Latin American countries in supporting Guaidó and opposing the tyrannical socialist Nicolás Maduro. Russia, China, and Cuba supported Maduro. The *Washington Examiner* called the president's resolute defense of freedom "bold moral leadership."[12] By February 6, all of South America, except Bolivia, and most of Europe supported Guaidó,[13] proof the president's international leadership going back to that first United Nations speech was taking hold.

You can imagine how problematic this was for the Left, on multiple levels. First, it called worldwide attention to the disaster of Venezuela's socialist "paradise." It was once extolled by the Left as proof socialism works.[14] These days, the Left tries to argue Venezuela never practiced "real socialism," contrary to their claims at the time.

Those who have lived under it tell a different story. Writing in *USA Today*, Daniel Di Martino, who came to the United States from Venezuela in 2016, said,

> Though so many of us Venezuelans fled to the USA to escape from the destructive consequences of socialism, liberal politicians like Sen. Bernie Sanders, I-Vt., and Rep. José Serrano, D-N.Y., have praised the same kind of policies that produced famine, mass exodus and soaring inflation in Venezuela.[15]

Worse even than the world seeing the results of the socialist policies they'd praised in Venezuela and now proposed for their own country was the dynamic of this conflict on the international stage. The supposedly "compromised by Russia"

President Trump had taken a firm stand for freedom *against* Russia yet again, as he had when he imposed sanctions against Russia and when he punished Russian ally and Syrian President Bashar al-Assad for chemical attacks on his own people with missile strikes on Syrian military targets.

The president had again made the right decision on the international stage and, right on cue, headlines repeating the absurd "closing in" talking point appeared almost immediately. On January 25, 2019, just two days after the president announced his support for Juan Guaidó, *The Week* ran its story, "The Mueller Investigation Is Closing in on Trump."[16] This time the "smoking gun" that would prove too much for the president to survive politically was the over-the-top arrest of Trump associate Roger Stone, an elderly man with a hearing-impaired wife, against whom the DOJ mobilized air, sea, and land forces as if they were laying siege to an ISIS stronghold.

Perhaps the media weren't as culpable as the Deep State on this occasion, as the DOJ made sure the arrest of this unarmed man accused of "process crimes" was as newsworthy as they could make it. Twenty-nine FBI agents bearing loaded automatic weapons arrived in seventeen different vehicles. CNN "just happened" to be on the scene. They say they weren't tipped off about the arrest in advance. According to CNN, they were at this man's house before sunup because of "reporter's instinct,"[17] which you and I both know is nonsense.

Given that all of Stone's alleged crimes resulted from the bogus investigation into Russia collusion and are the kinds of charges most defendants are allowed to self-surrender to answer, this was clearly a case of the DOJ trying to create a much bigger news story than there was, whether they tipped off CNN or not. Regardless, Stone's arrest in no way represented the special counsel "closing in on Trump." While Stone was a longtime friend of the president, he only worked on the campaign very briefly in 2015, long before even the dizziest Democrat claimed the president was "colluding" with Russia.

Maybe it was just coincidence that every "closing in" headline I've mentioned here dropped during a crucial moment for the president's policy agenda, especially his international agenda. Maybe I'm jaded after decades as a prosecutor who has good reason to be suspicious of coincidences that benefit bad actors. Even if I am, this much is true. Every one of these bogus headlines distracted from, diminished, impaired, or plain covered up a major policy victory by President Trump. And the two-year, completely false narrative that Mueller was "closing in on Trump" interfered with the president's ability to do his job.

Not on one single day was Robert Mueller closing in on the president. Not in September 2017, in January 2018, in March 2018, November 2018, January 2019, or a week before Mueller turned in his report, when former CIA director Brennan was on television saying the president's son would be indicted and arrested any day. Mueller was never closing in because there was nothing to close in on. This was weaponized fake news from beginning to end, and it was directed at you, the people. Can anyone wonder why the president calls the national media your enemy?

Winning Despite the Lies

Even as someone who knew all along that Russiagate was a fraud, it is startling even for me to look back at what the media accomplished as part of their revenge to bring down the president. Even more startling has been President Trump's achievements while they did so. While enduring one outrageous lie told about him after another, the president continued to do his job and establish his place in the world. Just as he promised he would, he put NATO on alert that we're not going to carry their baggage anymore and we might not even come to their aid unless they pay up. He went toe to toe with Rocket Man Kim Jong-un and with China. And nothing about his treatment of Russia was significantly different from the way he handled other world leaders.

Did he want to be able to talk to adversaries? Absolutely. But there was nothing in how he handled Russia that was in any way a reflection of his affection for Putin or his fear of Mueller. In fact, he imposed the toughest sanctions ever enacted against Russia. It was all just vintage Trump: try to make friends but make the lines very clear.

He has said conciliatory things about Putin when he has been able to because you can't get anywhere diplomatically without treating adversaries with respect. If nothing else, you must give them political capital they can use with their own people to be able to agree to your demands.

He treats Putin the same way he treats President Xi in China, Little Rocket Man Kim Jong-un in North Korea, and any other political leader with whom he must negotiate. Saying kind words about them when he can is just part of his salesmanship. That's what he does in business and in everything else. It lets an adversary know that when it's time to get tough, to draw a line in the sand, it's not personal. Professional and political adversaries can do their jobs while retaining personal respect. I know this from decades as a prosecutor. Do you think

I hated or disrespected every defense lawyer I ever opposed in the courtroom? Of course not.

His opponents can spin it any way they want, but Donald Trump is going to fight for this country. And if you haven't noticed, his style is *working*. When was the last time North Korea launched a missile over Japan? When was the last time Kim Jong-un walked over the DMZ and a sitting United States president actually stepped foot on North Korean land? Where has Putin shown any aggression in Europe or anywhere else? Just as in domestic affairs, liberals don't care about results, just their feelings. Donald Trump doesn't make them feel good while failing, like his predecessor did, so they hate him.

Still, he keeps soldiering on and winning, despite the most hysterical opposition to a president in American history. This is a man who four years ago was a billionaire, living a fairy-tale life, married to a beautiful, elegant, intelligent woman who speaks five languages, and the father of five wonderful kids, three of whom are already hugely successful in their own careers. He didn't need this. Unlike his predecessor, the presidency represented a financial step down for him. He's not only lost money being president. He doesn't even take a paycheck. He's losing money and his sons are losing money because they can't do any work internationally. And he's endured unjustified hatred he never would have encountered if he'd stayed in the private sector.

Americans need to understand this is nothing more than a plot to take down a guy who's got nothing to gain, receives no salary, and isn't beholden to anyone. No lobbyist put him in office. He's the one guy who's doing it for all the right reasons and that makes him a threat to everyone there doing it for the wrong reasons.

He sought the presidency and won because he loves this country enough that it was worth everything it cost him. And everyone who said otherwise for two years based on this bogus vengeful plot to redo the election owes him an apology for what they put him and his family through.

Being president isn't easy for anyone. But this president should have had at least one day in the Oval Office to focus on enjoying the job he's doing. That was impossible with the haters like Strzok and McCabe and sanctimonious Jim Comey. When you look at all the resources they had—more than 2,800 subpoenas, nearly 500 search warrants, 230 orders for communication records, 40 FBI agents, 19 lawyers, several grand juries, investigations touching 30 countries, costing over $34 million[18]—no investigation in history compares. Now, contrast that with how the investigation of Hillary Clinton was handled. No grand jury, no subpoenas, no search warrants—it was a complete joke.

While Mueller's report finally proves Putin didn't have a willing partner in Donald Trump, I can't say with certainty Putin would not have had a willing partner if Hillary Clinton had been there. She was certainly willing when she was Obama's secretary of state.

Hillary is the one who did the Uranium One deal with Russia and received huge "donations" from Kremlin-connected businesses to her so-called charity, with help from her fundraising husband. If anyone should have been investigated for being compromised by the Kremlin, Hillary was their man.

The Real Colluders

The crux of the matter is not so much the approval by the Committee on Foreign Investment in the United States (CFIUS), under which the State Department leads the decision-making process. It is the double standard employed by the intelligence community and the most prestigious law enforcement agency in the land. The latter was led in both investigations by the same guy, Jim Comey. You'd have to be one of those see no evil, hear no evil, speak no evil monkeys to believe Donald Trump and Hillary Clinton were treated equally by the FBI.

For Hillary, there were no real interrogations, just get-out-of-jail-free cards. Only in Third World countries do they run make-believe investigations like Comey did here. Comey was an evil actor in this situation, looking to protect Hillary, who had a lot of connections with Russia, and destroy Donald Trump, who had no connections with Russia.

Where is Christopher Steele? Maybe I missed it, but I don't think he was interviewed. I don't remember him being hauled up before Congress. Of course not. Steele has been hiding out in the UK since all this began. It was his phony dossier from which a phony warrant and phony extensions of that warrant were derived, and they used an innocent American, Carter Page, as a basis to infiltrate the Trump campaign. Don't forget, Carter Page is still walking around. Why? Because he didn't do anything.

When Russians look for assets, they don't look for political candidates; they look for people with military or cyber-security backgrounds whom they can use to their advantage. They typically try to get dirt on both sides, not help one and hurt the other. They're not looking to be friends with anybody. Friendship is not in the Kremlin's DNA. But since when is the truth relevant to politics? They needed Russia to be specifically interested in co-opting Donald Trump.

Just like a classic cheater, projection is always the Swamp's argument. If a guy is caught cheating on his wife, the first thing he says is "No, you're the cheater." Well that's what happened here. It was classic projection. Their projection was Donald Trump colluding with Russia, not the Clinton-Obama presidency with its "reset button" and everything else. This is how these corrupt individuals in the Department of Justice rationalize their corruption.

When the Mueller report was released, I actually heard some people talking about how the president should be *grateful* to the DOJ because they finished their investigation. Mueller concluded his investigation, but not, in my opinion, out of any sense of justice. He wasn't about to do the president any favors. Rather, I think he knew that if he recommended charging President Trump or any of his children, he would have to put his evidence where his mouth was. He would have to prove beyond a reasonable doubt they committed a crime, and he couldn't prove the hoax was real.

An Attempted Coup

So, where do we go from here? I want to know: why isn't the chief justice of the United States Supreme Court, John Roberts, reviewing what is painfully obvious to the nation—that a make-believe story paid for by Hillary Clinton and laundered through a law firm, written by a foreign operative, became the basis of a warrant to spy on a U.S. citizen in order to spy on the Trump campaign?

I want John Brennan—who tried to get out of this mess he's in by saying, "Oh, I got bad information." I want him investigated by a grand jury. And McCabe. And Strzok. And FBI lawyer Lisa Page, his girlfriend. And Loretta Lynch. And that pious, condescending, sanctimonious, holier-than-thou Cardinal Jim Comey.

When someone lies to you, do you just say, "Don't worry about it; I'll get over it?" Well, that's not how our system works. There must be accountability. There must be consequences, because as the president himself said, this should never happen again. And I can guarantee you it *will* happen again, unless we make an example of the traitorous, treasonous group that accused Donald Trump of being an agent of the Russian government.

Here are some more things I want to know: Who did the unmasking? Who did the leaking? If we don't have consequences, if people at the highest levels of government are not held responsible for this, it is a blueprint for future efforts to overturn election results with congressional hearings. And enough with the congressional hearings and inspector general reports. A well-focused prosecutor doesn't need either of them. A well-focused prosecutor only needs a grand jury and subpoena power. Although I am not saying congressional hearings are never needed, it's just that after a while they are nothing but a show for whichever side holds positive information to spin to its advantage. It is rare that these dog and pony shows are searches for the truth. They seem to be nothing more than political theater interrupting the work that should be done in the people's House.

So, should we all just move on? We cannot. There were people at the highest levels of our government, possibly going as high as the White House, who chose to change the rules, violate the law, leak information, unmask innocents, and seek warrants based upon unverified political opposition papers. America cannot afford to simply forget the crimes that were committed in order to frame the president of the United States.

The lies, the dishonesty, the perjury, the fraud, and the intimidation were weapons used by individuals who blatantly and openly hated the outsider. The Jim Comeys, Andrew McCabes, Peter Strzoks, and Loretta Lynches of the world need to feel the justice they tried to impose on an innocent man. They created the blueprint for a presidential coup. Lady Justice doesn't care about party affiliation, color, or gender. Lady Justice cares about corruption. She cares about law and order. Our forefathers did, too. That's why our Constitution must be respected.

For their own selfish purposes, these people worked to prevent Donald Trump from gaining the presidency and then, once he succeeded despite their efforts, worked tirelessly as a cabal to try to get him impeached. We cannot afford to let them walk away unscathed. You can laugh at us. You can laugh at opposing parties, but you cannot laugh at Lady Justice.

Bill Barr is a serious guy. He's a no-nonsense straight shooter who doesn't care what anyone says or thinks about him. He's a true warrior and I believe he will follow through on his mission as attorney general and at long last bring justice to the people who so deserve it.

Don't be satisfied with the Mueller report. What happened to Donald Trump is bound to happen again, because the arrogant, lying, condescending, leaking haters—and make no mistake, it's you and me they hate—are going to do it again, unless we stop them. And the only way to do that is with justice, true justice. And that's behind-bars justice.

CHAPTER THREE

Revenge Off the Rails
The Resistance Attacks Barr

After the Mueller report was released confirming there was no collusion between the Trump campaign and Russia, the Washington, DC, Swamp officially entered surreal territory. The Democrats became the kind of angry, unreasonable mob one usually sees only in the movies; a real-life bunch of crazies, so desperate to hang on to a narrative dispelled by their own team that they're running around like chickens with their own heads cut off.

Their one mantra: impeach anyone who gets in their way.

Attorney General Bill Barr isn't just in their way. He's on their trails with an investigation into the origins of this attempted presidential coup. The Democrats were already concerned about how Barr would handle the Mueller report before he was even confirmed.[1] But once the Mueller report was released and Barr wrote his four-page memo describing the report's conclusions, the Democrats completely left the mother ship. Their hysteria over Bill Barr was so intense that for a while it seemed like they forgot Donald Trump was the man they hated. It was like a mini-Resistance within the main Resistance. They became desperate because they understood what Bill Barr is capable of.

Not Trump's Attorney General?

The Left continues to accuse anyone associated with Trump of being in the Trump camp and incapable of objectivity. Apparently, within the alternate reality they've created for themselves since Donald Trump was sworn in as president, no one who works in the executive branch is supposed to follow the direction of the president. Suddenly, they're all supposed to be "independent" of the elected president for whom they work.

Folks, that sounds an awful lot like a "Deep State."

It's no surprise this cockeyed principle has been applied to the attorney general since the Democrats now want to undermine Barr. Apparently, they want the American public to believe—contrary to 230 years of American history—that an appointed attorney general should have no political affiliation at all to the president he serves. Any sign of loyalty to his elected superior supposedly renders the attorney general unable to faithfully execute his office.

Writing for *The Nation*, John Nichols went so far as to say, "The United States does not currently, in any practical or realistic sense, have an attorney general."[2] Say, what? As if we had one with Jeff Sessions, who hid under his desk during his entire tenure. That's not just fake news. That's batshit crazy news.

You don't have to go back to George Washington's attorney general, Edmund Randolph, to debunk this novel claim. You need only go back to the Obama years, when Eric Holder said he was President Obama's "wingman."[3] Does anyone believe Loretta Lynch, who stayed quiet while Jim Comey let Obama's secretary of state off the hook, wasn't also a political ally of Obama's? John F. Kennedy appointed his own brother, Robert Kennedy, as AG. Would the Democrats try to argue Bobby Kennedy had no loyalty to his brother's administration?

AGs defend their bosses. It's what they have done historically. Jeff Sessions was atypical in this regard. In him, Trump appointed an attorney general who not only didn't defend the president but also wasn't terribly interested in doing the job at all, based on his self-recusal from the most important investigation his office would undertake during the first two years of Trump's term. President Trump was saddled with a guy who not only didn't like him, but who enabled the other side.

It's hard to tell what happened with Sessions, who was such a strong supporter during the campaign. He was the first senator to endorse candidate Trump. But something happened once he got into office and the Trump-Russia collusion narrative became public. He either had some skeletons in the closet the Left knew about or he just turned lazy after ten years in the Senate doing nothing. Think about how hard the Senate works on what they're elected to do. Fundraising is the "number one job of any member of Congress," according to former Congressman David Jolly.[4] Over $33 million has already been raised just for U.S. senators seeking reelection in 2020.[5] Meanwhile, our borders remain in crisis, healthcare remains broken, and infrastructure unfunded.

Or maybe Sessions just didn't have the balls, certainly not the prosecutorial balls, to be attorney general. Being a prosecutor isn't always a glamorous job. Quite the opposite. A prosecutor does his or her job without fear or favor. A prosecutor puts a stake in the ground and keeps it there no matter the public outcry.

So, they were either threatening Sessions or he was such a simpleton that they convinced him he had to recuse himself. Every time he issued a press release it was about drugs. Thank you, Jeff, but local prosecutors investigate and prosecute drug dealers every day. Donald Trump, for all intents and purposes, was without an AG for the first two years of his presidency because the guy who begged him—and these are the president's words, *begged* him—to appoint him attorney general decided not to do the job.

The president offered Sessions other positions, but he wasn't interested. He said, "Please, this is what I want! I was a US attorney 150 years ago!" Many believe Sessions knew at the time he was taking it that he was going to recuse himself from the most controversial investigation of the Trump presidency.

So, President Trump's attorney general was more like an enemy in his own camp, while Obama had a wingman, Holder, followed by Loretta Lynch who met with Bill Clinton on the tarmac of an airport just before Lynch and Comey let Clinton off the hook for her crimes. And then, within a few days, Hillary announced that if elected, she would appoint Loretta Lynch to be her attorney general. But I'm sure she and Bill didn't talk about that.

Yet, just two years later, the Democrats have suddenly discovered the attorney general should act completely independent of the president's wishes or direction? Preposterous!

Who Cares If It's Legal or Ethical?

"Release the whole report!" was the first rant the Democrats went on after Barr's conclusion.[6] While it was clear early on Barr intended to release the report, it's important to remember he was not legally obligated to do so. Mueller worked for the attorney general, Bill Barr. He was investigating on behalf of the attorney general. His job was to write a report to the attorney general—nothing more and nothing less. In fact, Barr didn't even need to write a report. All he was required to do after the investigation was say whether or not there was sufficient evidence to go forward with criminal charges. But of course, there wasn't. Everything Barr did with the Mueller report beyond that announcement he did at his discretion.

Then, he decided to release the report. Understand there were certain legally required redactions, such as grand jury testimony, referred to as "6E material." Repeat. Barr was *legally required* to redact those parts of the report that quoted grand jury testimony. Had he not done so, he would have been subject to prosecution himself. I have actually indicted people for leaking grand jury testimony. It's against the law for very good reasons.

Grand jury testimony is considered secret testimony. This principle has a basis in common law going back hundreds of years. There is nothing in the grand jury that can ever be released to the public unless it is used in trial or as a basis for some other legal document. A grand jury is the one place where you're allowed to go and not fear that there will be public recriminations for what you've said or what you haven't said. Grand jury minutes have always been secret. That's a truism.

This doesn't just protect the witnesses; it's for everyone. Besides witnesses who may not want to testify in public, secrecy protects innocent third parties and the accused, who is legally presumed innocent until proven guilty in open court. If the grand jury doesn't return an indictment, you don't want pieces of what was disclosed there taken out of context and used to attack people in public, not even the accused. This is a centuries-old legal principle as basic to our system as due process itself.

Even when there is no grand jury convened, police or other law enforcement agents do not release information gathered about a target when the investigation fails to produce enough evidence to secure an indictment. It's just not done.

Rod Rosenstein cited this principle in his letter recommending the termination of Jim Comey, based on his handling of the Hillary Clinton email investigation. Comey publicly disclosed information gathered during an investigation that did not result in an indictment. As Rosenstein wrote,

> The Director ignored another longstanding principle: we do not hold press conferences to release derogatory information about the subject of a declined criminal investigation. Derogatory information sometimes is disclosed in the course of criminal investigations and prosecutions, but we never release it gratuitously. The Director laid out his version of the facts for the news media as if it were a closing argument, but without a trial. It is a textbook example of what federal prosecutors and agents are taught not to do.[7]

All of these basic pillars of our justice system go right out the window where Donald Trump is concerned. Forget hundreds of years of common law, the Constitution, federal statutes, the presumption of innocence, or due process. For Donald Trump and, increasingly, any conservative, it's mob rule and vigilante justice. Brett Kavanaugh is another shining example of how the Left strips away individuals' rights when they engage in their revenge.

So, regardless of these longstanding legal principles, the Left is trying to convince the public there is something sinister about the Mueller report redactions, that they're part of a cover-up.[8] The want you to believe the redacted material will prove Donald Trump colluded with Russia or committed a crime. It's just more noise. Anyone who reads the report can guess what most of the redactions are about. They're about pending or ongoing investigations or prosecutions of "process crime" cases, like Roger Stone's, that have been trumpeted by the media as supposed proof of the nonexistent collusion for the past two years. There isn't anything there the public hasn't already heard about from the media.

Some redactions also protect sources and methods used in intelligence gathering or suppress material that would "unduly infringe on the personal privacy and reputational interests of peripheral third parties."[9] No one would have considered these types of redactions controversial in the past and no reasonable person would expect to find information within that redacted material that would substantially change a finding of no collusion and no obstruction. But these provide fodder for hysteria, too, for the vengeful, radical Democrats.

We're not talking about a lot of redacted information. Just to put this in perspective: only 8 percent of the publicly released version of the report and only 2 percent of the version made available to Congress is redacted. Of that 2 percent, most of the redactions are in volume one of the report, which deals with the Russia collusion materials and these are no longer at issue. Only one-tenth of 1 percent of volume two, which deals with possible obstruction of justice is redacted.[10] That means *99.9 percent* of the report is available to the Democrats and they haven't even bothered to read it!

Barr gave access to this almost fully unredacted report to the Senate Judiciary Committee, comprised of six Republicans and six Democrats. No Democrats took advantage of Barr's offer to look at it.[11] They didn't even want to see it. But when Barr voluntarily testified before the Senate Judiciary Committee regarding his four-page conclusion of Mueller's 448-page report, the show put on by these hysterical, hyperventilating, histrionic, frenzied Democrats, dripping with hate and venom, was must-see TV. Barr, on the other hand sat staring at them in what appeared to be disbelief, listening to their pontifications, and trying to understand what the hell they were asking him. In spite of all that, he was lucid, focused, and unflappable. I can only wonder what was going on in his mind as they attempted to harass and demean him.

Barr's Senate Testimony

Barr appeared before the committee on May 1, ostensibly to answer questions about his four-page letter and handling of the Mueller report in general. Of course, his ability to answer questions on any topic requires that questions be asked. Instead, Democrat Mazie Hirono opened her "examination" of Barr with this hate-filled diatribe: "Mr. Barr, the American people know you are no different from Rudy Giuliani or Kellyanne Conway, or any of the other people who sacrifice their once decent reputation for the grifter and liar who sits in the Oval Office."[12]

Hirono then went on for over three more minutes spewing similar invective without managing to formulate a single question for Barr. Along the way, she made the ridiculous claim that Barr had previously lied to Congress, which I'll get to momentarily. But her unhinged rant was a perfect example of why so many members of Congress admit open sessions of this type are practically worthless. They turn out to be nothing but grandstanding and get Congress nowhere closer to the truth.

Kamala Harris managed to ask Barr some questions but pursued several ridiculous and irrelevant lines of inquiry. One was to establish that Barr and Deputy Attorney General Rosenstein had made their decision not to charge the president with obstruction of justice based purely on Robert Mueller's report and not on the underlying evidence that supported Mueller's conclusions. The Left-wing media was atwitter with delight over Harris's supposed bombshell revelation, but this is a nonissue. In Barr's own words:

The evidence represented in the report. This is not a mysterious process. In the Department of Justice we have pros-memos [memos recommending prosecution] and declination memos [memos recommending the

attorney general decline to prosecute] every day coming up. And we don't go and look at the underlying evidence. We take the characterization of the evidence as
true.[13]

I have to give Senator Harris credit for making nothing sound like something for the benefit of her political allies
in the media. Perhaps, in a vacuum, a layperson would hear,
"He decided not to prosecute without looking at the underlying evidence" as something outrageous. As a lawyer, judge,
and former prosecutor, I can tell you this is less than a nothing burger. Think about what Harris is really saying. Special
Counsel Mueller spent two years interviewing people, executing search warrants, and performing other forms of investigation. No attorney general would be expected to go through
every word of testimony, the reports on every search warrant
and FBI interview, and draw his own conclusions. That would
constitute redoing all the work Mueller just finished in formu-
lating the report!

If an attorney general were expected to review every piece
of underlying evidence federal prosecutors gather during often
years-long investigations to either recommend prosecution or
declination, no one would ever be prosecuted. As Barr said,
examining the underlying evidence was Mueller's job.

Besides its silliness, the irony and hypocrisy of this line
of questioning is too rich for words. Barr had made a far less
redacted version of the Mueller report available to Congress
and not a single one of them bothered to examine it. But they
are now criticizing Barr for accepting Mueller's representation
of the evidence in his own investigation, conducted by an over-

whelmingly Democrat panel of lawyers.[14] Don't they realize how ridiculous they look?

Next, Harris asked a series of questions the purpose of which was to—get this—suggest Deputy Attorney General Rod Rosenstein should not have participated in the decision not to charge President Trump with obstruction of justice because he was also a witness in the matter of the firing of James Comey. Harris asked Barr if he had consulted with DOJ ethics officials before enlisting Rosenstein to participate in that decision to ensure Rosenstein was not seen to have a conflict of interest.

I must admit I burst out laughing when she went down this road. Conflict of interest? If anything, Rosenstein's conflict would be against the president, not for him! This is the man widely believed to have offered to wear a wire when talking to President Trump to try and establish a case to remove the president from office based on Article 25.[15] Was Harris seriously trying to suggest Rosenstein might be too biased in favor of the president?

But let's get to the heart of what all this attempted smearing of Barr is really about. It's about the ongoing inspector general investigation of the origins of this whole attempted coup. Harris opened her segment of this sideshow by asking Barr, "Attorney General Barr, has anyone at the White House ever asked or suggested that you open an investigation of anyone?"

Asked or suggested? Anyone? This was an obvious attempt to get Barr on the record saying "no" and then later claim he lied to Congress, having perhaps forgotten a conversation with some insider at the White House that never went anywhere. Perhaps Harris was attempting to "trigger" Barr by exhibiting such open hostility toward him.

No such luck. Barr's blood pressure didn't rise one beat. He hesitated in answering, but any objective observer would conclude his only hesitation was his own good faith effort in attempting to answer Harris's question with a "yes or no," as requested, without misleading the other members of Congress. Barr admitted, "I'm trying to grapple with the word 'suggest,'" and then continued, "There have been discussions of matters out there that . . . they have not asked me to open an investigation."

"Perhaps they've suggested?" replied Harris. "Hinted? Inferred?"

Give it a rest, Kamala. You know you're reaching and so does the American public, or at least that part of the public that doesn't desperately need to believe there is some reason to end the Trump presidency without actually winning an election. If there is a scandal here, it's that Comey, Brennan, McCabe, Clapper, and the rest of the coup conspirators weren't even investigated by Mueller's team of Trump-hating lawyers.

Luckily for Harris and the Democrat smear brigade, the media are on their side, as always. After Harris melodramatically marched out of the Senate hearing to mug for the cameras and call for Barr's impeachment, *Vanity Fair* proclaimed "Kamala Harris Guts Barr Like a Fish, Leaves Him Flopping on the Deck."[16] Greg Sargent at the *Washington Post* claimed Harris had "roasted" Barr while falsely stating Barr refused to answer Harris's question of whether anyone had asked him to open an investigation.[17] Barr was forthright in stating he hadn't been asked but "matters out there" had been discussed.

That bastion of hard-hitting journalism, CNN, ran video of Barr's testimony with the headline, "See Kamala Harris Stump William Barr During Hearing." That's classic CNN. It's technically true that Barr was stumped, but it was over Harris's deliberately problematic wording of the question, not because Barr was fraught over having been caught red-handed regarding something improper. Again, the AG's office *should* be investigating a lot of people involved in trying to overturn the 2016 election.

With the avalanche of uncritical media trumpeting the Democrats' newest fantasy, it's no surprise that calls for Barr's resignation or impeachment were immediate. They were simply the latest outrage and unsupported demands of the loony Left. But then to add more drama to the report that defeated the mainstream media's Trump-Russia collusion fiction, the Left weaves yet another new web: that Barr misrepresented the Mueller report.

A letter written to Barr on Mueller's letterhead suggests that Barr's conclusions did not "fully capture the content and substance" of findings by Mueller. The Left does its crazy dance again. The truth? Barr called Mueller immediately after seeing the letter.

Barr said that the letter was received on a Wednesday night in the White House. Apparently, it goes through a screening process, so Barr got it on Thursday morning. He immediately called Mueller and, according to his testimony in Congress, "I asked him if he was suggesting that the March twenty-fourth letter was inaccurate and he said, 'No,' but that the press reporting had been inaccurate."

Did you get that? Mueller himself said Barr's letter was accurate. But he was frustrated with the press's inability to capture certain nuances, i.e., prejudicial evidence that Mueller thinks makes the president look bad but which doesn't indicate any criminal wrongdoing. In other words, Mueller is upset Barr didn't help the Left-wing media spin the report for political reasons, since there was no basis for legal action.

You have to love the irony here regarding Mueller's disappointment in the media and his implication Barr had something to do with it. Since when is Barr, a Republican, able to convince the media of anything?

Hey, Bob, go complain to your Deep State pals. Start with Jim Comey. Have Comey call his pals at the *New York Times*, CNN, and MSNBC. He's proven he's good at that. He'll tell the media what you want them to hear; he doesn't have Barr's commitment to the truth. And next time, Bob—let's hope there never is one for you—don't write a 448-page report and expect everyone to get it just the way you wanted in four pages.

Barr Didn't Lie

Mueller's whining letter to Barr and their subsequent conversation became the supposed basis for the next baseless attack on Barr—that he lied to Congress during a previous appearance in April. While I agree with *National Review*'s Andrew McCarthy—a onetime "Never Trumper" who contributed to *NR*'s January 2016 issue wholly devoted to opposing Donald Trump[18]—that this allegation may be "too stupid to write about," the media have made it necessary to debunk this whopper.

It's important to remember the timeline to understand what the Democrats are alleging. Barr released his four-page letter on March 24 of this year. Mueller writes his letter to Barr on March 27, which Barr sees on March 28, after the screening process. On April 9, Barr testifies before Congress. During that testimony, the following exchange occurred between Barr and Democrat Congressman Charlie Crist of Florida:

CRIST: Reports have emerged recently, General, that *members of the special counsel's team are frustrated* at some level with the limited information included in your March twenty-fourth letter . . . that it does not adequately or accurately necessarily portray *the report's findings.* Do you know *what they're referencing with that?*

BARR: *No, I don't.* I think—I think . . . *I suspect that they probably wanted more put out,* but, in my view, I was not interested in putting out summaries or trying to summarize because I think any summary, regardless of who prepares it, not only runs the risk of, you know, being under-inclusive or over-inclusive, but also, you know, would trigger a lot of discussion and analysis that really should await everything coming out at once. So I was not interested in a summary of the report. . . . I felt that I should state the bottom line conclusions and I tried to use Special Counsel Mueller's own language in doing that.[19]

As juvenile as this sounds, the Democrats are claiming this answer was a lie because Barr already had Mueller's March 27 letter, so when he said, "No, I don't" in answer to Crist's question, "Do you know what they're referencing with that?" he was not telling the truth. Supposedly, he knew what Mueller's staff was "referencing" because he had the letter.

First, as Barr later pointed out, he wasn't talking to unnamed members of Mueller's staff; he was talking directly to Mueller, whom he has known for decades. And it obviously would not be true to say Barr knew what the staff was concerned about, because after reading the letter, he didn't even know what Mueller was concerned about. That's why Barr called Mueller to ask!

To which Mueller answered that he wasn't concerned about what Barr did, but rather how the media reported it. As Mueller said this directly to Barr on or about March 28, it would stand to reason Barr would not know what Mueller's staff might be concerned about twelve days later on April 9. Given that Barr was not required to do anything at all with the Mueller report except decide whether or not to prosecute, I'm not sure why anyone thinks Barr should even care what Mueller's staff thinks about his handling of the report.

Yet, Barr again goes the extra mile in trying to be cooperative with a hostile Congress and speculates, probably based upon the cryptic statements in Mueller's March 27 letter, that he suspects they "may have wanted more put out." Barr is uncharacteristically speculating here in an attempt to provide an answer; Mueller's letter said nothing about putting out more information. It merely said Barr's letter "did not fully capture the context, nature, and substance of this office's work and conclusions."

What Barr is very obviously not doing is lying. You can tell that from his demeanor during the exchange, in addition to examining the facts. The only truthful answer Barr could have given Crist about why Mueller's staff might be frustrated with Barr's March 24 letter was "I don't know." There was no reason for Mueller's staff to be frustrated, other than that their two-year, $34 million revenge investigation didn't achieve its primary goal—to overturn the 2016 presidential election.

I have to give the devils their due. The Democrats are the best chess players out there. They're demonizing Barr without even having anything to demonize him for, but Barr has remained very calm. He wasn't flustered by Mazie Hirono's unhinged attack or her false allegations. This is the woman who says all men should just shut up, all women accusers must be believed, and there is no presumption of innocence—if you're a Republican male. That's where we are in this country.

Resistance and Revenge Are Futile

There isn't anything left to accuse Barr of at this point. The Democrats won't be able to stop him from doing his job. Barr will get to the bottom of the origins of the counterintelligence investigation on the Trump campaign, including when it really started and why. He will find the truth about the FISA warrant to surveil the campaign, especially now that the president has decided to declassify (sooner than originally thought), and whether or not there was any new evidence in subsequent FISA warrant applications that justified continuing wiretaps.

Barr is the Democrats' worst nightmare. He's a veteran prosecutor with no discernible ego. He's not looking to write a book. He appears impervious to politics. When he's asked questions by grandstanding politicians, he doesn't take the opportunity to grandstand himself. If he can answer the question with a "yes" or "no," he does. It even catches me by surprise at times. For the Deep State actors who attempted to take down the duly elected president, knowing a man like this is on their trail must be terrifying.

It all comes down to twenty-eight little words Barr uttered during his Senate testimony:

"I think spying did occur. The question is whether it was adequately predicated. And I'm not suggesting that it wasn't adequately predicated. But I need to explore that."[20]

Explore it he will and it's unlikely to end well for the Comeys, Clappers, and Brennans of the previous administration. I believe justice is coming.

Meanwhile, the Left simply refuses to accept that the Mueller investigation is over. They are fixated on obstruction of justice but make no mistake. If Mueller wanted an indictment for obstruction, he would have recommended one.

Mueller tried to make that case for two years. He had an army of investigators, search warrants, subpoenas, and grand juries. He came up empty. His leaving the obstruction question open was political whoremanship. It was Mueller's attempt to satisfy an unsatisfied client by leaving crumbs the Democrats could fight over. This whole thing has been the biggest political con job and the closest thing to a successful coup in American history. Everything I said in my book, *Liars, Leakers, and Liberals* was right.

They hate Trump and they'll do anything, including subjugating the Constitution and our system of justice, to try to destroy the man. Their desperation to hang on to a narrative so torn up, worn out, and destroyed isn't even entertaining anymore. It's almost not even worth talking about.

What is worth talking about is how the tables will turn. Pursuant to his statement to the US Senate, Barr has appointed John Durham to "determine if intelligence collection involving the Trump campaign was lawful and appropriate."[21] Durham is another one the Democrats will find impossible to discredit.

He has experience investigating law enforcement corruption, including at the FBI and CIA. He was confirmed unanimously by the Senate and was described by the two Democrat senators from Connecticut as a "fierce, fair prosecutor" who knows how to try tough cases.[22]

Even CNN admits Durham is "known for bringing independent rigor to challenging and politically sensitive cases."[23] Like Barr, Durham has never run for elected office. He's not a politician. It's not in his blood. He's a truth seeker, pure and simple. And he appears to be cut from the same cold, relentlessly logical cloth as Barr.

God help the real conspirators in this case.

Grab your popcorn, Junior Mints, or whatever makes you happy. The real show is about to begin. Multiple criminal leak investigations are underway. The FISA warrants are being reviewed. The investigation Peter Strzok tried so hard to avoid is beginning and the inspector general's report, expected to be damning to Comey's FBI and Lynch's DOJ, will be out soon. Then, it's showtime for Obama, Brennan, Clapper, Lynch, Rice, Strzok, McCabe, and the whole Cardinal Comey crime family, who devoted themselves not only to obstructing the will of the American people but also the very foundation of justice in this great nation.

This will be true reality TV. No scripts, no rehearsals, just a gang of criminals pointing fingers at each other to save their own hides. It will be like a combination of true crime and the reality show *Survivor*. The Deep State Exposed.

They are not going quietly into the night and it will be a joy to watch.

CHAPTER FOUR

Rats Desert the Ship

I've said for the better part of two years that holier-than-thou former FBI director Cardinal James Comey was the head of his own crime family. The upper echelon of the FBI under his direction operated like an organized criminal enterprise. But only the upper echelon: the rank and file wouldn't have tolerated this. Even Bill Barr questioned it.

"The thing that's interesting about this is that this was handled at a very senior level of these departments," Barr told Fox News. "It wasn't handled in the ordinary way that investigations or counterintelligence activities are conducted. It was sort of an ad hoc small group and most of these people are no longer with the FBI or the CIA or the other agencies involved."[1] Barr is absolutely right. Field offices generally handle investigations and these investigations are reviewed at the upper levels.

For over two years, Comey and his gang—McCabe, Strzok, Baker, Page, Brennan, Clapper, and others—all riffed on how horrible President Trump was, calling him treasonous, a

Russian puppet or a Russian asset. They got away with it primarily because the mainstream media were receptive to their hateful narrative. After all, these were men in high positions in our government protecting us from Russia and those positions demand respect. Just as the office of the presidency demands respect, but not from this biased group.

If the truth be told, they were selling our democracy down the river so they could avenge Hillary's loss and remake America to benefit themselves. They were skilled at their jobs, leaking information to the media to get news stories to not only poison public opinion, but to undermine candidate Trump and to later create the basis to support a bloodless coup against President Trump.

Now, as with any criminal conspiracy, the players are arrogant and think they are above the law. But mistakes are always made. Also, like any conspiracy, the conspirators can never keep their stories straight. Here's one example: Comey told the president-elect the Steele dossier was unverified in January 2017. But he had already told the FISA court in October 2016 the dossier *was* verified when he used it to obtain a FISA warrant to spy on Trump's campaign.[2] We now know he knew the truth about the document long before that FISA application. He knew it was a political document, not an intelligence document, but used it to get a FISA warrant anyway.

That, friends, sounds like a felony.

Andrew McCabe, former deputy director of the FBI, is already under criminal investigation as a result of a referral by the inspector general. He claims that he's a victim in all of this and that his firing is the result of attacks designed to undermine him—as if anyone knows or even cares about Andrew McCabe.

McCabe lied under oath to both the FBI and to the inspector general.[3] It appears he leaked like a faucet, then when given a chance to come clean, he blamed Comey, another leaker. It's no wonder Attorney General Barr can't get his arms around any of this.

As I said, Barr is a cool cat. When the Mueller investigation came up empty, the Democrats hyperventilated and immediately pivoted to attack Barr, hysterically accusing him of everything they could think of, and holding him in contempt of Congress. Since there was no basis for their attack, Barr remained unphased.

"I thought that when I came in from the outside that all of the questions that I had and many other people had would be readily answered, once I got in. But I haven't found that to be the case," Barr told Fox's Bill Hemmer.[4] He went on to say that not only have the answers he's received been inadequate, but that some of the explanations he has been given "don't hang together."

Let me translate that for you. He knows at least some of the conspirators are lying. He hasn't said that explicitly because he's proceeding slowly and analytically, and the investigation is not yet over. But James Comey certainly knows what he means. So does Clapper, Brennan, and the rest of the conspirators.

Let me tell you something: I was a pretty tough prosecutor myself and I'd be terrified to have Barr on my trail. He's like a locomotive moving two miles per hour that you can't knock off its track. You can call it names, accuse it of partisanship, or hold it in contempt. It doesn't speed up or slow down. It's going to keep rolling until it gets to its destination and God help anyone who gets in its way. It's inevitable Barr will revisit the players and the whole purpose of the Trump Resistance and the attempt to drag Hillary Clinton across the finish line. The investigation will certainly have to address Hillary's role in all of this.

Plotters Pointing Fingers

Barr has all the conspirators pointing fingers at each other to save their own butts. Comey is now trashing Rod Rosenstein, saying Rosenstein didn't have anywhere near the "inner strength" to stand up to Donald Trump.[5] Comey claims those in the White House feel a sense of duty to protect the American people and says they compromise their values and praise the president insincerely to remain in the Trump administration. "And then you are lost," Comey added. "He has eaten your soul."[6]

Jim, I don't know if you were smoking something out in the woods looking for Hillary, or if you just got too much fresh air, but you've lost it. Eaten your soul? Maybe you rediscovered your inner communist in the wilderness, answering the question you were unable to answer back in 2003. "I voted for Reagan—I'd moved from Communist to whatever I am now. I'm not even sure how to characterize myself politically. Maybe at some point, I'll have to figure it out," you told reporter Chris Smith of *New York*.[7] You certainly sound as loony as the looniest of the far Left when you say the president eats souls.

Rosenstein responded by calling Comey "a partisan pundit, selling books and earning speaking fees while speculating about the strength of my character and the fate of my immortal soul." He added, "That is disappointing. Speculating about souls is not a job for police and prosecutors. Generally, we base our opinions on eyewitness testimony."[8]

Comey is also in a finger-pointing duel with former CIA Director John Brennan. This one I can't wait to watch play out. They're both accusing each other of being liars and being the first to put the fake dossier into the intelligence community. Brennan says the Barr investigation into the investigators of the Russia collusion delusion is "crazy." It's nothing more than a fishing expedition. Can you believe the irony? The fishing expedition is what he and his Deep State comrades have been conducting against President Trump for the past three years. And even after the Mueller report cleared the president, they don't have the good sense to take their lines out of the water and paddle their leaky boat back home. Forget about an apology.

Two months after Mueller turned in his report saying there was no collusion with Russia by the Trump campaign, California Democrat representative Eric Swalwell was on *Fox News Sunday* saying Mueller was wrong, as if this guy Swalwell had done anywhere near the investigation Mueller did. He resurrected the ridiculous claim that a joke the president made while campaigning—that "if the Russians want to find those thirty thousand emails that Hillary Clinton deleted, I'm sure the media will be interested in that"—amounted to colluding with the Russians on hacking the DNC email server. Even Chris Wallace, who hasn't shied away from criticizing Bill Barr's handling of the Mueller report, scoffed at that one.[9] But then again, if you're at the bottom of twenty-four radicals running for president, I suppose you have to say something radical yourself.

Maybe John Brennan will start calling the president a traitor again, something he did for two years, until the Mueller report was released, and he got called out for the buffoon he is. "Well, I don't know if I received bad information, but I think

I suspected there was more than there actually was," Brennan told *Morning Joe*. "I am relieved that it's been determined there was not a criminal conspiracy with the Russian government over our election."[10]

Have you noticed that John Brennan always uses the excuse "I had bad intelligence?" This guy was the head of the CIA! It's called the Central Intelligence Agency for a reason. Maybe its director should have been focusing on intelligence instead of trying to overturn an election. Who knows? Maybe then the Obama administration would have succeeded at something: preventing Russia from meddling in the election, effectively or not. Then again, maybe Brennan and Comey, who are accusing each other, are both right about one thing. They're both lying.

One amazing part of all this is that there is no more denying the existence of a "Deep State." Instead, its members are saying, "Hey, it wasn't me. The Deep State is over there. I'm not one of them."

There are a lot of people saying Brennan was the ringleader of this coup attempt and he very well may have been. As director of the CIA, he was arguably the most powerful person involved in the plot, although the Director of National Intelligence, Clueless James Clapper, is technically over the CIA director on the official organizational chart. But like so many others, Brennan points his finger at Comey and makes one wonder if maybe they're onto something.

Even James Baker, the former FBI top lawyer accused of illegally leaking to authorities, subtly directed attention at Comey with a Left-handed compliment that sounded like it was inspired by my last book, *Liars, Leakers, and Liberals*. I called the former FBI Director "J. Edgar Comey" because his dirty tactics were so similar to those of the corrupt former FBI director J. Edgar Hoover. Baker went on the Yahoo! News *Skullduggery* podcast and made a similar reference, although he tried to spin it as if he and Comey were trying to avoid the appearance of Hooveresque blackmail tactics:

> Jim and I had talked many times over the years about the Hoover days, especially the investigation of Martin Luther King, Jr., what was done there, the blackmailing of Dr. Martin Luther King. And, so, yeah, we were quite worried about that, quite worried about how that would come off and so we wanted to try to make sure to convey to the president-elect that that's what we were not doing.[11]

I'm not sure if Baker is delusional or if that is a coded message to Bill Barr: "Hey Bill, here's a narrative that will sound good at Comey's trial. He was blackmailing the president-elect, just like former FBI Director J. Edgar Hoover. Call me, I'm ready to make a deal."

Maybe Baker can use my last book as a reference.

Even Loretta Lynch is looking for a life raft, although she shouldn't need one. Rats can swim. She told a joint closed-door session of the House Oversight and Judiciary Committees last December that Comey's repeated statements, under oath, that she directed him to refer to the Clinton email investigation as a "matter" rather than an investigation were untrue.[12]

Folks, they can't both be telling the truth. At least one of them lied under oath to Congress, which constitutes two separate felonies, and for which others have been convicted or indicted. If they don't indict either Comey or Lynch for these contradictory statements, are they going to drop the charges against Roger Stone and let Lying Michael Cohen out of jail? Lynch and Comey have lied so often, it's hard to tell if they have any familiarity with the truth. Loretta Lynch, after she met Bill Clinton on the tarmac and refused to let anyone make any reports or take pictures, denied she talked to Bill Clinton about Hillary's case.

Gee, do you think Loretta told Bill what he and Hillary wanted to hear on that airplane? Loretta Lynch denied there were any communications between the Justice Department and the FBI regarding that conversation, but we later found out there were, using different emails, and Loretta Lynch in fact had her own pseudonym that she used to email about this.[13]

Here's the bottom line. This finger-pointing is not happening between lawyers in private rooms. It's happening in the public square for all to see. They know that Bill Barr is a serious prosecutor who has appointed another serious prosecutor, John Durham, to review the origins of the Trump-Russia investigation.

Indictments are his stock-in-trade. He is looking into the CIA's role and the FBI's role, which will inevitably lead him to the roles of Susan Rice, Samantha Power, and good ol' Loretta Lynch—all compromised by their political agenda to destroy Donald Trump, America be damned.

And get this. Comey says the guy he most admires in government is Clueless Clapper, another liar and leaker. This bozo, like Comey, flatly denied leaking the dossier. Back in January 2017, he even issued a statement that assured the incoming president that neither he nor anyone in the intel community was responsible for the leak.[14]

When Clapper appeared before a congressional committee, he stuck to that story at first, flatly denying leaking the dossier to the media. But later, he admitted he told CNN's Jake Tapper and possibly other news outlets about it, according to a report on his testimony from House Republicans.[15]

Is this guy incapable of telling the truth about anything? And why is he still walking the streets a free man, while so many others have been prosecuted for the same thing? Members of the Deep State have an automatic get-out-of-jail-free card.

As I said in the last chapter, this is the reason for the otherwise inexplicable disinformation campaign against Bill Barr. The Deep State and its media allies spent two years trying to bring down the Trump presidency based on a phony theory that many people broke laws to concoct and then broke laws to cover up. Now, the coup has failed, and the perpetrators are trying to discredit the lawman who has picked up their trail. If they can't discredit him, they'll all rat on each other to save their corrupt skins.

Prosecuting the Resistance

Conspiracies are by their very nature secret. But even their own testimony to Congress creates a slew of possible charges that could be brought against the conspirators.

For the record, eleven Republican members of the House of Representatives wrote a criminal referral to then-Attorney General Jeff Sessions way back in April 2018, recommending key members of the plot to overthrow Trump be prosecuted.[16] Maybe the problem was it landed on Sessions's desk. He wouldn't see it there because he was hiding under his desk from the Democrats or whatever scared him silly enough to recuse himself from the entire Trump administration.

Now, as opposed to the Russia collusion delusion, fabricated out of thin air and the fever dreams of vengeful radical Democrats, the evidence against Cardinal Comey and his pals is largely public knowledge. It is based on their own words, both written and verbal, and in some cases in testimony to Congress or in official documents written by them on government time.

We all remember Cardinal Comey's melodramatic press conference of July 5, 2016, during which he tried to use deceptive language to justify not charging Hillary with the mishandling of classified information. He avoided saying she'd been grossly negligent in her handling of classified documents, instead calling it "extremely careless," even though *grossly negligent* and *extremely careless* mean the same thing. In fact, an early draft of the memo exonerating Clinton used the words *grossly negligent*, but Comey's co-conspirator Peter Strzok changed them to *extremely careless*, because *grossly negligent* are the words used in 18 US Code § 793 to describe one way a person might illegally mishandle classified information.

Comey went on to say the so-called investigation of Crooked Hillary failed to find intent to mishandle or disclose classified information, even though the same statute clearly states intent is not a necessary element of the crime if the perpetrator is grossly negligent. In a nutshell, Comey explicitly announced to the world that Hillary had violated 18 US Code § 793 and then usurped the power of the attorney general by announcing his agency was not recommending prosecution, one of the key reasons he was ultimately fired.

If all that weren't bad enough, it turns out Comey drafted the memo exonerating Clinton months before she was even interviewed by the FBI![17] We found out about this through the emails, text messages, and congressional investigations. Comey was forced to admit that he did so in his own book, but tried to justify doing so by saying, "competent people think ahead."[18] Sure, competent people think ahead, but they don't waste their time drafting memos with a conclusion until they've investigated to the point of conclusion.

Yes, he had a plan all along to cut Hillary loose. To the extent this was done to try to affect the outcome of an election, it's un-American. But let me tell you what else it is for a sworn officer of the law to act in this manner: it's illegal. The House GOP criminal referral recommended investigating whether Comey violated 18 US Code § 1505 and 18 US Code § 1515(b) based on his conduct in this matter, both having to do with whether or not Comey obstructed federal proceedings.

He didn't just break the law by getting Hillary off the hook. Remember those infamous memos Comey wrote about his private meetings with President Trump? These are the memos that Comey told a Senate Select Committee on Intelligence he "asked a friend of mine to share the content" to the *New York Times*. We later found out the friend was Daniel Richman, a professor at Columbia Law School. What Comey was reticent to admit until much later, was that Daniel Richman was a nongovernment employee who had access to information and should have been briefed on the illegality of leaking classified and other government documents, meaning Richman, too, could be charged with a crime.

Well, it turns out that at least some of the information in the memos Comey leaked was classified, meaning he could be charged under 18 US Code § 641, 18 US Code § 793 and 18 US Code § 1924(a)—the same statutes that should have formed the basis for charges against Crooked Hillary for putting classified information on her private email server!

Maybe Cardinal Comey had become so arrogant or so delusional that he believed he could abolish these statutes by fiat. Or, more likely, it's just another example of how those in the Washington Swamp believe the rules don't apply to them. They're not just above the law; they're above the results of elections, above any scrutiny by the public, and above all reproach.

Two of the laws all these Swamp creatures believe themselves above are 18 US Code §1621 (perjury) and 18 US Code §1001 (lying to Congress). James Clapper seems to have an outright compulsion for the latter, but Comey also likely lied to Congress on multiple occasions. The House GOP criminal referral cites his misrepresentation of the FBI's relationship with Christopher Steele, but he may have also lied to Congress when he said the FBI and the Justice Department weren't coordinating with each other on the Clinton email investigation.[19]

He could be charged under the same statutes for his false testimony about Loretta Lynch's directing him to call the Clinton investigation a "matter," unless it turns out she's the one lying, in which case that count would be charged against her, not him.

The Deep State continues to point fingers at each other: Comey at Brennan, Brennan at Comey, Comey at Rosenstein, Rosenstein at Comey, Comey at Lynch, Lynch at Comey, and of course, Comey and former Acting Director of the FBI Andrew McCabe pointing the finger at one another.

McCabe remains under investigation for lying under oath about how an FBI investigation into the Clinton Foundation ended up in the *Wall Street Journal*.[20] He also told the Office of the Inspector General that Comey approved of his leaking the story to the media, which Comey denies. So, one of them is lying about that, too.

McCabe's allegedly false statements expose him to charges under 18 US Code §1621 and 18 US Code §1001. He can do all the whining he wants, write all the self-aggrandizing books and editorials he wants, and point the finger at as many of his co-conspirators as he wants. The bottom line is he lied under oath, not once, but on at least three separate occasions.[21] The only question regarding this liar and leaker is: Why is he still walking the streets while Michael Cohen rots in jail and Roger Stone awaits trial?

Let's not forget about our Trump-hating—Trump voter-hating lovebirds—Peter Strzok and Lisa Page. They didn't just demonstrate conflicts of interest by texting their hatred of Donald Trump to each other while Strzok led the collusion hoax investigation and Page was an FBI lawyer assigned to the case. They also may have materially interfered with the investigation into the Hillary Clinton email server. The House Republicans' criminal referral alleges they "eliminated evidence that Mrs. Clinton compromised high-level communications."

Strzok also told Page via text that "senior officials" had decided to obscure President Obama's role in the investigation by calling him "another senior government official." But by the time Comey delivered his infamous press conference on July 5, 2016, all references to that senior government official had vanished from the report.[22]

All of this exposes Strzok and Page to 18 US Code §1505 and 18 US Code §1515(b), which deal with obstruction of proceedings before departments, agencies, and committees and acting with an improper purpose, personally or by influencing another, including making a false or misleading statement, or withholding, concealing, altering, or destroying a document or other information, respectively. What that means in plain English is Strzok and Page tried to prevent Congress from finding out the Hillary Clinton investigation was a sham and Obama was involved in seeing it didn't go anywhere.

The DOJ and FBI leadership never seriously considered bringing charges against Hillary. Their investigation was a joke, done only to promote the appearance of justice for a public outraged at the latest Clinton crime to go unpunished. Thanks to additional Strzok-Page emails obtained by Judicial Watch via a Freedom of Information Act (FOIA) lawsuit in June of this year, we can now confirm the FBI was only going through the motions investigating her.

The FBI doesn't record most interviews it conducts. Before 2014, it never recorded them.[23] When the FBI conducts an interview with a subject, the agent takes notes and then produces an official record of the interview on Interview Report Form FD-302, universally referred to simply as a "302." Well, these newly obtained emails show that not only did the FBI give Clinton special treatment by giving her lawyers advanced notice before filing the 302 of Clinton's interview and rushing its release in advance of the election, but that as late as August 5, 2016—a month *after* James Comey's press conference indicating the FBI would not recommend charges against Clinton—at least four other 302s related to the case *had not even been written.*[24]

Don't let the official jargon and mundane-sounding government form numbers distract you from the importance of this new information. Based on my own experience as a prosecutor on cases in which FBI agents have been involved, I know how important that 302 report is in terms of evidence at trial. It is the document that will be entered into evidence and will back up the agent's verbal testimony. An FBI agent can expect to be asked by defense lawyers on cross-examination very precise questions about the process of producing a 302, particularly whether the 302 was written soon after the interview, while the agent's recollection would presumably be freshest.

Suffice it to say a defense lawyer would have a field day with a document produced a month after the interview, after the agent(s) who conducted it had presumably interviewed many other subjects during their normal course of business. Why would an FBI agent be so careless about producing arguably the most important documents in his or her investigation?

Answer: they knew all along Hillary Clinton would never be indicted.

Of course, there was long precedent in letting Hillary Clinton slide in the Obama Department of Justice. Let's not forget Loretta Lynch threatened a former FBI informant with legal action if he testified to Congress about his knowledge of fraudulent dealings connected to the Uranium One deal. This is the deal Secretary of State Hillary Clinton signed off on, allowing a Russian government–owned company to buy up 20 percent of US uranium production capacity after several shady contributions to the Clinton Foundation, which can be traced directly to Russia.[25]

House Republicans want Lynch investigated for possible violation of 18 US Code § 1505, which makes "by threats or force, or by any threatening letter or communication influences, obstructs, or impedes or endeavors to influence, obstruct, or impede" an inquiry or investigation by either House of Congress a felony. That would be in addition to lying to Congress about her instructions to Comey regarding calling the Clinton investigation "a matter," if it turns out Comey is telling the truth for once about that.

They were all protecting Hillary Clinton, whose crimes over the past several decades put them all to shame. How many times will this woman violate the law in the light of day and walk away unscathed with that ear-to-ear grin? One has to wonder if Hillary's smiling because she got away with it or laughing at our stupidity. That she violated federal law in putting classified information on her email server pales in comparison to her role in the Uranium One deal. And we now know it was Hillary Clinton and the DNC who colluded with the Russians to influence the 2016 elections. They paid laundered money through Fusion GPS to hire foreign agent Christopher Steele to get dirt on candidate Donald Trump from . . . the Russians!

It is noteworthy that Steele has not set foot in the United States since all of this began. The prosecutor in me tells me he fears an arrest. Reports are that US investigators will go to London to interview him there within weeks of this writing.[26] But where is Glenn Simpson of Fusion GPS in all of this? I want to know what he paid Nellie Ohr to do while her husband former Associate Deputy Attorney General Bruce Ohr, was having back-alley discussions with Christopher Steele, while the FBI had already cut ties. Also, what trips did Nellie take while working for Fusion? What is the backstory here? While we investigated Trump and dragged his son before congressional committees over and over, the key players in this are not on record. Christopher Steele hasn't been heard from.

Finally, we have the most egregious crime committed in furtherance of this conspiracy, submitting Steele's unverified and false dossier to the FISA court to obtain warrants to spy on Carter Page. This is something every member of the conspiracy had a hand in, including but not limited to former FBI Director James Comey, former Acting Director of the FBI Andrew McCabe, former Acting Attorney General Sally Yates, and former Acting Deputy Attorney General Dana Boente, according to the House's criminal referral.

For the record, knowingly submitting false evidence to the FISA court, not once, but again and again to get the warrant renewed, exposes these criminals to indictment under 18 US Code § 242, 18 US Codes §1505 and 1515b. But it's much more than just violation of a statute on the books. This was a direct attack on our democracy and our system of justice. Both the means used and the end to which they were employed constitute a danger to everything that makes America the freest country in the world.

Is This Still the Land of the Free?

Step back and think about what these people did and imagine it wasn't done to Donald Trump or any other high-profile person. They took a phony dossier filled with allegations so ridiculous that any reasonable person would be suspicious of them and submitted it to a secret court—which we've already seen is teed up for corruption—in order to obtain a warrant to conduct surveillance on an American citizen. They used this obviously phony evidence from a source they knew to be unreliable—had been told by our own State Department he was unreliable—when the law required them to verify their evidence and disclose any exculpatory evidence to the court.

This is the kind of thing the KGB in the former Soviet Union or Kim Jong-un's Ministry of State Security (his secret police) would do. You don't have to like Donald Trump to find this alarming. Can you imagine living in a country where precedents like these are allowed to stand? Forget the "land of the free." This is the stuff dystopian nightmares are made of.

You don't have to support President Trump to condemn the end to which Comey and team employed these corrupt means. They sought to determine who sits in the Oval Office themselves, regardless of the wishes of the people, in whom all power ultimately resides. Even the most virulent anti-Trumper should fear for our country if this conspiracy is allowed to go unpunished. If these Deep Staters are allowed to walk away after attempting to nullify a presidential election, it is not an exaggeration to say this will no longer be a government of the people, by the people, or for the people. This will literally be a blueprint for the next coup.

Donald Trump was elected because a critical mass of Americans understood they had lost control of the government that was supposed to serve them. They gave Trump the most shocking victory in American history in order to stop those trying to remake their country into something other than the free republic our founding documents say is our birthright. They exercised their ultimate power to restore protection of religious freedom, secure our borders from the Left's overt attempt to artificially change the demographics of our country, end unnecessary and counterproductive military interventions and confront the real threats from abroad, both economic and military.

Before and after Donald Trump's election, this cabal of unelected, elitist conspirators attempted to usurp that power from the people, destroy their duly elected president, and allow the remaking of America to continue, election results be damned. They must be brought to justice or they are going to do it again. Next time, they may succeed.

CHAPTER FIVE

Open Season on Conservatives

I don't know where you're reading this book. But if it's a public place, prepare to duck. These days, you might get something thrown in your face just for owning a copy.

This is because my picture is on the cover, and I am viewed as a conservative. I support President Donald Trump, and I make no apologies for that. If you're reading my book, you probably do, too.

That makes us both targets.

All over the country, the radical Left has decided that it's open season on conservatives like us. They now believe that they are allowed to punch us, scream at us, and throw things in our direction without consequence—all for the crime of supporting the President of the United States. They kick us out of their restaurants. They spit on us over the counters of their bars. They declare openly that we are not welcome in their small businesses. And if we dare fight back against *them*, they call it a hate crime.

Why, you ask?

Because we don't believe babies should be killed after they've left their mothers' wombs. Because we don't believe we should sit back and do nothing while our country is overrun with criminal illegal aliens. Because we think that the United States of America is a good country full of decent, hardworking people, not a nation full of racists and white supremacists. But most of all, it's because we have refused to abide the crazed lunatics on the anti-Trump Left—the ones who have been attacking this president at every turn since learning they blew it in 2016.

While they've been rocking back and forth in their padded cells, bouncing off the walls with their straitjackets on, whispering *I'm with her*, and babbling about Russia collusion, President Trump has been winning, just like he promised he would. Since being elected in the biggest political upset in history, he has made our country safer, richer, and more respected than it has been since World War II. He's accomplished what no president in history ever has. He has kept his promises and gotten things done.

For example, President Trump has nominated more conservative judges to the federal bench than any president in recent history. In fact, the only president who ever nominated more was George Washington, and that's only because he had none to begin with!

So, when Justice Anthony Kennedy retired and it came time for President Trump to fill his second vacancy on the Supreme Court, liberals lost their minds. Putting Neil Gorsuch on the

Supreme Court was fine; they couldn't stop him from doing that. But *two* Supreme Court justices? That was simply too much for their addled minds to handle. President Trump could have nominated Mother Teresa to fill that seat and liberals would have complained that she hung out with the wrong people. They would have objected to Jesus Christ himself. Whoever sat behind the desk during that confirmation hearing was in for an all-out assault.

So, President Trump nominated Brett Kavanaugh, a kind, mild-mannered former lawyer with the Bush administration. He was a shoo-in, already on the Circuit Court of Appeals, just below the Supreme Court. The man's record was impeccable. He was a beloved coach for his daughter's softball team. For him, a seat on the Supreme Court would be a well-deserved capstone to a long and prestigious career. You'd have to be a complete psycho to find something wrong with this man.

Wouldn't you know, "complete psycho" is the unofficial job description of today's Democrat party. By the end of Judge Kavanaugh's confirmation hearing, the loony liberals of the Senate had picked him apart like lions. The media immediately found him guilty in the so-called court of public opinion and demanded that he either give up his nomination or the Senate refuse to confirm him. Brett Kavanaugh was not entitled to the presumption of innocence. He was guilty, for no other reason than the Left did not want another Trump Supreme Court nominee confirmed. Because of their tactics, half the country truly believed that this man was a monster, a raging alcoholic, and—in a development that made my blood boil—a gang rapist.

Where I come from, that is a serious accusation. I have seen people who really do abuse women in the sick, horrific ways that Brett Kavanaugh was accused of—and worse. I've actually spent my life fighting for the rights of abused women and crime victims, long before the #metoo movement.

When I was an assistant district attorney in Westchester, my first homicide duty call involved a guy (an alleged drug dealer) who was run over three times in the woods. I was the first woman assigned to homicide duty and to make me feel nice and welcome, the cops didn't even want me at the crime scene. For the next thirty years, I saw darkness and fear. I saw women who were raped and had tree branches or other objects inserted into their vaginas, which had to be surgically removed. I had a little girl cry "Don't let daddy put his pee-pee in my peachy pie." I had girls trying to commit suicide by cutting their wrists.

As a prosecutor, I tried cases of children being thrown up against walls, beaten with baseball bats, and killed. Battered child syndrome, women stabbed to death or decapitated. I watched the skins of babies in hospitals burst like overcooked hot dogs because they had been immersed in scalding water as punishment. My job was to settle their scores.

And you wonder why I'm a tough bitch? I had to be.

It can be a very harsh world out there and I, for one, felt it was important to say that victims are people. It's crazy that it even needed to be said. I even had buttons made that said: "Victims Are People." I needed to stand up for those who never made the decision to harm another human being or to involve another person in the justice system. I wanted to be part of seeing impartial justice done for them, to help uphold the rule of law to protect the innocent. One of my mantras as the elected Westchester County District Attorney was, "People don't take crime personally enough." I wanted jurors to take it personally.

I wanted them to feel the pain of what the victim went through, the person who didn't deserve it or ask for it.

Yet, despite all that, I know how important it is to maintain the rule of law and let facts, not passion, not emotion, determine the course of justice. Every state constitution, as well as the federal, contains a bill of rights. Every defendant is entitled to a legal presumption of innocence, to not be deprived of life, liberty, or property without due process of law, to be protected from unreasonable searches and seizures, as well as from involuntary admissions or confessions.

When I watched Dr. Christine Blasey Ford testify about the terrible things that had been done to her all those years ago, I was moved. I don't know how you couldn't be. She seemed to be a credible witness, and most were tempted to believe every word she said.

Perhaps Dr. Ford believes the assault happened the way she said it did. But did it? Of course not. There were simply too many inconsistencies to ignore. Had I been a prosecutor presented with Ms. Ford's complaint, I doubt I would have taken her case to trial. There were too many problems. She couldn't remember the fundamentals: whose house it was, where it was, when the party was, how she got to the house or how she got home. She waited thirty years without telling her mother, a friend, a high school counselor, or anyone else, before now. When she did tell a therapist in 2012 that something happened to her, it appears she never mentioned Brett Kavanaugh's name, despite her later claim that she had. At the time, Brett Kavanaugh's name was everywhere in the press.

Remember also, this wasn't a case of "he said, she said," as it would have been if she claimed the incident happened when she and Kavanaugh were alone in a parking lot somewhere. Once she chose to say there were four additional people at the house, it becomes a "they said." And all four, including Leland Ingham Keyser, a classmate of Ford's at the all-girls school Holton-Arms, said they weren't at the party she describes and don't know what she's talking about.[1]

What would this tell me as a prosecutor about Ford's memory? If they weren't there, it's possible Kavanaugh wasn't there, either.

Ford's 2012 therapy session is crucial to this case, in my opinion. Ford now says she mentioned Kavanaugh's name during that session, for the first time since the alleged assault. That Ford's lawyers wouldn't hand over the notes taken by her therapist spoke volumes to me.[2] Ford herself was evasive when questioned by the prosecutor on this issue. It turned out she didn't mention Kavanaugh's name in therapy when she had a chance and that makes me wonder whether they may have done some hypnosis to refresh Ford's memory. In a courtroom, judges and juries are entitled to know if hypnosis is used, because it is an unreliable means of refreshing one's recollection. There is a risk of confabulation of recent events reported on television and in newspapers that impact one's memory.

There were other problems with her story not directly related to the alleged events in the 1980s. We were told she hesitated to come to Washington to testify because she was afraid to fly, then found out she'd had an internship in Hawaii that required her to fly there regularly. In fact, it was later revealed that she wasn't afraid to fly at all. The woman has flown all over the country, to the South Pacific and Hawaii! So unless she was paddling in a canoe, one must assume she was flying in an airplane.

As a prosecutor, I would only bring a case to trial if I thought I had a good chance to win. I don't want to go into court against a defendant who might well be acquitted if I don't think my victim's story is going to hold up under cross-examination. It's the defense attorney's job to defend his client to the best of his ability, meaning he's going to challenge the victim's claim with the same vigor as he would a woman who was making a false accusation. An acquittal for the defendant in a case where the woman was telling the truth can feel like the jury found her guilty. And that can do even more harm.

In Ford's case, I would never have gone to trial because she was contradicted by her own witnesses, and she showed none of the signs I typically saw in victims. Ms. Ford may have believed what she was saying, but she didn't convince me her story was true.

The people who manipulated her into going public with the accusation against Kavanaugh didn't care about any of that. They didn't care about her, about justice or the precedents they were setting. Ranking member of the Senate Judiciary Committee Dianne Feinstein could have proceeded with a confidential investigation upon learning of Ford's allegations, but she chose not to for political reasons. Instead, she referred Ford to attorneys partially funded by Left-wing activist billionaire, George Soros, who failed to inform Ford of the Senate Judiciary Committee's investigators' offer to interview Ford at home instead of in front of the whole world.[3] They were out to wring maximum suffering out of Ms. Ford, solely for political purposes.

They were desperate to win at all costs. Take a man and his family down? No problem. Destroy the principle of presumption of innocence? So be it. Democrat Senator Mazie Hirono all but said this explicitly. When asked directly if Kavanaugh was entitled to the same presumption of innocence as anyone else, she replied, "I put his denial in the context of everything I know about him in terms of how he approaches his cases."[4]

In other words, Hirono makes judgments about the accusations against Kavanaugh based purely on what she perceives as his political beliefs, not his innocence or guilt, or the merits of the evidence for or against him. For the Democrats, this is a political fight to the death—of our country and our liberty, if necessary.

Looking back, I'm just glad that the Senate voted to confirm Kavanaugh in spite of this painful three-ring circus. If things had gone a bit differently, we might well have had to witness a whole parade of fake Kavanaugh accusers coming through the Senate, telling their BS stories to get their fifteen minutes of fame. I can only imagine what it would have been like if Michael Avenatti, a man who has since been indicted for multiple felonies and narrowly escaped domestic abuse charges, had been allowed to bring his crew of crazy clients in to accuse Judge Kavanaugh of "gang rape," an accusation so absurd that even Lindsey Graham couldn't keep his cool when bringing it up during his closing statement. As usual, we were saved from the Left by their own incompetence.

The Use of Violence

In June 2018, Democrat Congresswoman Maxine Waters stood on the steps of a courthouse in Los Angeles and gave a gang of her liberal followers these marching orders: "Let's make sure we show up wherever we have to show up. And if you see anybody from that Cabinet in a restaurant, in a department store, at a gasoline station, you get out and you create a crowd. And you push back on them. And you tell them they're not welcome anymore, anywhere."

They got the message.

That same month, Kirstjen Nielsen, President Trump's former Homeland Security Secretary, went to a Mexican restaurant with her family and was met by a crowd of self-described "democratic socialists," who started screaming insults at her. The main chant consisted of one word: "Shame!"

Seriously? What is this? *Game of Thrones*? Were they going to hold some kind of witch trial out on the sidewalk?

Then, as if the heckling wasn't enough, these idiots followed her *inside* the restaurant and crowded around her table. The restaurant did nothing to stop them. "We will not let her dine in peace," said one of these hippie lunatics. After ten minutes of listening to the Batty Bernie Sanders Brigade screaming their nonsense, Nielsen left the restaurant. (For protection, she probably should have walked into a history classroom. Lord knows how much democratic socialists hate those.)

And what exactly was her crime?

Doing her job. Faithfully executing the orders of the President of the United States, and following the laws as written as she had sworn she would when she accepted that job. For that, she was called a white supremacist, a Nazi, and a purveyor of hate.

It didn't stop with Nielsen.

Later that month, the president's former press secretary, Sarah Sanders, was rudely asked to leave a restaurant in Alexandria, Virginia, just because she worked for Donald Trump. Just this last June, Eric Trump walked into a restaurant in Chicago and a waitress walked up and spat on him.

Although the Secret Service took the waitress into custody immediately, Eric took the high road and chose not to press charges. He called the incident "a disgusting act by somebody who clearly has emotional problems." Even the liberal mayor, Lori Lightfoot, said it was "very gracious" of him.

As of July 2018, John Nolte at Breitbart had compiled a "rap sheet" of 639 cases[5] of violence and public harassment against Trump supporters, which are increasingly condoned by the media—including the "new media," social media—which I will discuss in more detail later. You've already heard about the high-profile cases of Republican legislators or media figures being chased out of restaurants by angry leftist mobs. But it gets much worse than that.

A boulder was thrown through the window of House Majority Leader Kevin McCarthy's office last year.[6] Less than a week later, shots were fired into a Republican Party office in Florida.[7] Minnesota House of Representatives candidate Shane Mekeland was punched in the face by an angry leftist in a bar[8] and a Tennessee restaurant owner endured threats against his life for renting a room for a breakfast meet-and-greet campaign event to a Republican U.S. Senate candidate.[9]

These are just a few incidents from a *single month* in 2018, which was hardly atypical. Virtually every day since Donald Trump announced his campaign, anyone even suspected of supporting him has been subject to harassment, public intimidation, threats, beatings, assaults, and even arson. Yet, if the media mention any of this, they blame President Trump! The president is so provocative in his speech, they say, that unhinged leftists cannot help themselves in committing violent acts against his supporters.

The deranged Left doesn't limit their aggression to supporters of the president. My colleague Kat Timpf was forced to leave a bar in Brooklyn, New York, after being chased around and screamed at by a woman who recognized her as a Fox News contributor.[10] Kat leans more libertarian than conservative and has been outspoken in her criticism of President Trump's immigration policies on the very channel that seems to have inspired so much rage in this woman. No matter, Kat was found guilty and exiled from an establishment serving the public based on one unhinged Leftist's delusions about who she is and what she believes—all of which were incorrect.

For all their crying about being triggered, "microaggressions," and needing safe zones, it is the Left that commits real violence and harassment for political reasons. You can bet it's going to get worse as we approach the next election, with any attempt by the Trump administration to enforce law and order portrayed as fascist suppression of dissent by a media hostile to Trump and receptive to the political heirs of the Yippies, the Weather Underground, and other violent Left-wing groups of the 1960s.

Two Sets of Rules

As I said, the rule of law doesn't begin at a criminal trial. There are rules for the investigators into a crime as well. The Fourth Amendment protects us from unreasonable searches, the Fifth against being compelled to be witnesses against ourselves, and the Sixth guarantees we have the benefit of a lawyer for our defense. Based on these fundamental protections, other rules have been established to ensure those suspected of a crime are treated fairly by government investigators.

While no system is perfect, I never had reason to doubt these principles were generally being followed during my over thirty-year career as a prosecutor, judge, and district attorney. As I said, on the rare occasions where even the hint of impropriety existed in the gathering of evidence presented to me on the bench, I threw it out, even if I believed the accused to be guilty of the crime. It goes without saying that it didn't matter if the defendant was a Republican, a Democrat, an Independent, or even a communist. If the rules said they should walk, they walked.

Now consider the way the FBI, the highest law enforcement agency in the land, handled two cases: Michael Flynn's and Hillary Clinton's. Were the same principles of impartial justice applied to both of them?

The fundamental question: On January 24, 2017, was Michael Flynn treated as per the rules, like any other FBI target? The answer is a resounding no. He was treated differently, which brings us to the question: Why? The facts of this story are simple. Flynn was in the crosshairs of the FBI, targeted by the same players who we already know from publicized text messages and emails, tried to prevent a certain candidate from becoming president and promoted another. They were dirty. They lied, some under oath. They were leakers. And they were corrupt.

First, they leaked a story that Flynn had called Russian Ambassador Sergey Kislyak several times on December 29, 2016, leading the public to believe there was something improper about these calls because Obama was still president[11] and any contact with Russia was considered suspect. They then put out a story implying Flynn would testify against Trump in exchange for immunity. Anyone following these reports in the media could have assumed nothing other than that Flynn broke the law by contacting the Russian government before Trump became president and that he was going to implicate Trump with his testimony.

There was only one problem with this phony narrative: The conversation Flynn had with the Russian ambassador during the transition was legal. Perfectly legal. Take that to the bank. It is what is done in every new administration.

Michael Flynn was set up. Not only was he unmasked, he was told by FBI Deputy Director Andrew McCabe that the FBI wanted to talk to him about the Russians, and the quickest way to do it was to keep the lawyers out. Comey recently reveled in saying he took advantage of the White House being too new to require the normal procedures when interviewing someone of Flynn's stature. "Something we've—I probably wouldn't have done or maybe gotten away with in a more organized investigation—a more organized administration. In the George W. Bush administration, for example, or the Obama administration," Comey said.[12]

This was a clear violation of protocol, White House rules, and ultimately Flynn's constitutional rights. We know this because US District Court Judge Emmet Sullivan ordered prosecutors to hand over FBI files of the Flynn interrogation instead of sentencing him as scheduled. Forty-eight hours later, the files were sent to the judge, although incomplete and redacted.

Those files confirmed what Director Comey himself admitted and what the judge may have suspected, despite his later negative comments about Flynn: the DOJ and FBI intentionally avoided protocol and standard operating procedure in questioning Michael Flynn without an attorney present. Even Comey admits this when he pulls off his Cardinal Comey mask to reveal the face of a hardened political operative.

Contrast Comey and the FBI's treatment of Flynn with their treatment of Hillary Clinton, who, when questioned in July 2016, was accompanied by a small army of lawyers, including her personal attorney David E. Kendall.[13] Clinton was investigated for committing a serious crime—the mistreatment of classified information—as compared to Flynn's having a perfectly legal phone conference with a foreign diplomat. Yet, despite announcing to the world during an unprecedented news conference that Clinton had perpetrated every element of the crime, Comey went on to say that "no reasonable prosecutor would bring such a case" against her.[14]

Part of Comey's reasoning was that the FBI didn't find criminal intent on Clinton's part. Hillary's behavior so established intent on her part that you could do a law review article on it. But here's the rub: in determining guilt under the relevant federal law (18 US Code § 793—Gathering, transmitting, or losing defense information) intent is not a necessary element of the crime! Only *gross negligence* in handling classified information is necessary for a person to be guilty of that crime. The perpetrator need not have had criminal intent to mishandle, which makes a lot of sense. As Andrew McCarthy astutely observed in *National Review*, "People never intend the bad things that happen due to gross negligence."[15]

To add insult to injury, Comey also stated Clinton was "extremely careless" in handling classified information. Now, any legal dictionary—any dictionary, for that matter—defines negligence as "failure to take reasonable care" or words very close to those. In other words, being "careless." Negligence and being careless are virtually synonymous, legally and in everyday usage, so "extremely careless" and "grossly negligent" mean the same thing. By using the words he did, Comey all but said, "We have proof Hillary Clinton committed a felony, for which others have gone to jail, but we aren't going to charge her. We decide whom the rules apply to and to whom they don't."

In the end, Michael Flynn plead guilty to a felony, lying to the FBI. Curiously, he has not been sentenced and has recently hired a spitfire, FBI-hating lawyer to attack his conviction as well as the actions of the investigators in his case. His reasons for pleading guilty are his own, although they may have included threats of prosecution against his son or other family members, bankruptcy and other consequences not related to his guilt or innocence. The government can bring an awful lot of pressure on someone to plead, even when they follow the rules. Whether that is right or wrong is a discussion for another day.

What should concern us all right now are the two sets of rules applied to Flynn and Hillary Clinton. On the one hand, they used the most aggressive tactics and the strictest application of the law to railroad Michael Flynn, who stands convicted merely of lying to an agency that has been taken over by the biggest liars in the world. In fact, there are several members of the FBI who don't believe he lied to them. On the other hand, they applied the most lenient standards possible, rewriting the law to include an element of intent it does not contain, in order to avoid prosecuting Hillary for one of many crimes of which I believe she is guilty. This is not American justice as we have known it for the past two centuries.

The Most Barbarous Ages

If you're a liberal who generally votes Democrat, you may not be overly bothered by anything I've told you in this chapter. But you should be. The erosion of equal justice under the law, selective abandonment of the government's fundamental duty to protect life and property, and the disregard of the protections of rights of the accused are all swords that cut both ways. These principles have been established by trial and error over thousands of years to produce the highly civilized society we live in today.

We joke about "banana republics." We even have a clothing store chain named after them. But they're no joke. In countries without our long traditions of equal justice, liberty, and property rights, people can't depend upon the freedom and security we take for granted. These are countries where justice is not dispensed impartially and bribes, bullying by local bureaucrats and police, and politically motivated prosecutions followed by harsh punishments are a way of life—where the rule of men prevails over the rule of law and every citizen is a slave, forced to kowtow to the local commandant or face victimization. The law is used as a weapon against opponents and as a license for friends.

This has ramifications far beyond the administration of justice in criminal courts. Property rights and enforcement of contracts is the foundation of our civil law and prosperity. It's no accident most people in banana republics are destitute. Economic growth depends upon entrepreneurs being confident the fruits of their labor won't be confiscated and that agreements they've made will be enforced. When these guarantees are removed, the means of creating wealth are destroyed.

It seems like we're going backward in time. All the basic rules of civil society, even those transcending the Founding Fathers and the Constitution, seem to be breaking down. Among the allegations Jefferson made against King George III in the Declaration of Independence, was that he employed mercenaries against the colonists who waged war "with circumstances of cruelty and perfidy scarcely paralleled in the most barbarous ages." He refers to a time where the rules that make life freer and safer hadn't been established yet. I, for one, don't want to go back there.

It's easy to see why the Democrats and their Republican fellow travelers aren't as worried as I am: they are so intent on bringing down Donald Trump that they're willing to risk destroying civilized society to do it. You can bet the same biased perversion of our laws and constitutional principles will be applied to attacking the president between now and November 2020, whenever possible. It is imperative we fight to maintain the rule of law, regardless of what any one of us thinks about Donald Trump. We have far more to lose than an election.

CHAPTER SIX

The Democrat Clown Car

Outsider Donald Trump was elected president for a reason: Americans were tired of their interests not being protected. Donald Trump will win again in 2020 for the same reason. And it is one question—and one question only—that finished the entire Democrat field: "Raise your hand if your government plan would provide coverage for undocumented immigrants," requested moderator Savannah Guthrie during the second night of the first Democrat presidential primary debate.

Every candidate raised his or her hand.

The Democrat Clown Car, overloaded with mayors, governors, senators, socialists, and spiritual advisors, continued down its bumpy road to nowhere during the first presidential debate, held over two evenings so they could fit in all twenty clowns. 'Twas a sight to behold. Forget about everything you learned about the Constitution, law and order, "the rules," and playing fair. In their eyes, the world is an upside-down, backward, and inside-out place.

Biden was definitely in over his head and tripping over his clown shoes when he couldn't distinguish his approval of Obama's deportation of three million illegals and separation of children and families at the border—just as the Trump administration was legally required to do—except to say Obama did a "heck of a job." He's so unsure of himself that he only half raised his hand when eight other Demaclowns raised theirs, indicating they would like to decriminalize illegal immigration. Joe can't figure out what he stands for.

When Bernie Sanders was confronted with his own prior statement that states and not the federal government should make decisions on gun control, Sanders said—and this is an exact quote—his words were a "mischaracterization of his thinking." His own words are a mischaracterization of his thinking! What thinking? I guess he's saying his brain didn't engage with his mouth.

Elizabeth Warren wants to kick millions of Americans off private health insurance. She doesn't even bother to lie and say, "If you like your health plan, you can keep your health plan."

At one point, the debate became a contest about who could speak the best Spanish. Now, I believe in keeping your heritage alive, including my own Lebanese heritage. But I also believe this is an English-speaking nation, and the pandering to Spanish-speaking immigrants was over the top. Even Cory Booker was turned off by Beto O'Rourke's not-too-smooth attempt to pander to Hispanics. Booker's crazy stare rivaled Jack Nicholson's in *The Shining.* If Helen of Troy's beauty launched a thousand ships, then Booker's side-eyed stare launched a thousand internet memes.

Beto wants illegals to start voting right away. No surprise; he needs votes wherever he can find them. And speaking of Beto, I couldn't help but think of Richard Nixon. This guy needs a new makeup artist so he appears at least close to the living, rather than the walking dead.

Not to be outdone by his far-Left opponents, Julián Castro not only defended abortion rights for women; he said if he were elected he'd defend abortion rights for transgenders. Even liberal comedian Bill Maher recognized how ridiculous this was. "Julián Castro won the 'Woke Olympics' on the first night when he said, 'Trans females should have the right to an abortion.' I agree," said Maher. "Now if only they had a uterus."[1]

It got so ridiculous that even genius Alexandria Ocasio-Cortez said they all looked like high school students who didn't do their homework.[2] For once, I agree with her!

In the end, none of it matters. Just hold on to your pocketbooks, because these clowns want to put a lien on your money, your savings, and your retirement. Everything changed when the Democrats on that stage raised their hands saying all illegals should be given free health care. And by the way, it's not like they haven't already been getting free health care in our hospitals and emergency rooms.

Do you remember when Barack Obama said during his first address to a joint session of Congress in 2009, referring to Obamacare, "the reforms I'm proposing here would not apply to those who are here illegally"?[3] Republican Representative Joe Wilson yelled, "You lie!" He later apologized, only because it was the wrong time and place to say it, even if it was true.

Well, the Democrats aren't bothering to lie about this either, anymore. And the image of their raised hands indicating they would make American taxpayers pay for health care for illegal immigrants is the one that caused the Clown Car and everyone in it to veer off the road and lose the American people.

If anyone wants to "feel the pain" of the American people, the ones who elect a president and for whom a president actually works, they should feel this. Ordinary Americans are confronted at the end of their lives with no health insurance that covers long-term care. That means when they get out of the hospital, they have to pay for their own care. They are then left out in the cold, where they literally have nowhere to turn.

Middle-income Americans who every day choose between food and medications don't want to hear about people coming here illegally without a dime in their pockets being rewarded with health care they have not paid for. So, Americans have to pay for their own health care and then pay for the health care of illegals and in the end have absolutely no long-term care when they are incapable of caring for themselves? Maybe an illegal who got free health care paid for by that same American now in trouble will help.

I don't think so.

With all the crazy talk Sanders, Beto, Warren, and company were spouting, spiritual clown Marianne Williamson's New Age mumbo-jumbo sounded almost mainstream.

"So, Mr. President, if you're listening, I want you to hear me, please," said Williamson. "You have harnessed fear for political purposes, and only love can cast that out. So I, sir, I have a feeling you know what you're doing. I'm going to harness love for political purposes. I will meet you on that field. And sir, love will win."

Whoa.

Meanwhile, President Trump demonstrated clear leadership in his official kickoff announcement for a second term on June 18, 2019 in Orlando, Florida. If ever there was a week to see him turn the focus and the spotlight on himself—of which he is the master—that was it. People camped in chairs for several nights, many of them not even getting into the event.[4] The man can draw a crowd, create enthusiasm, and make people proud of America.

There were well over one hundred thousand requests to attend his 2020 campaign kickoff and over twenty thousand people seated inside the stadium.[5] This kind of enthusiasm has never been matched in American history. And I don't care what poll, what network, what statistical genius tells you who's ahead and who isn't. There is a chord Donald Trump strikes in the American heart: the American dream that the Left can't destroy, ravage and obliterate, no matter how hard they try.

The day after his rally, he raised nearly $25 million, the largest one-day haul by any candidate in presidential history.[6]

If ever there were a group of people not in tune with the values of most Americans, it's these twenty-four (so far) Democrats running for president. Their positions are so radical they're laughable. Their party has made so much noise about what they're against—namely Donald Trump, his family, his friends, and anything he proposes, no matter how good it is for the country—many people may not realize what these hysterical radicals are *for*.

However, as the subtitle of this book says, they are determined to remake America, whether it makes sense to you or not. And let's be honest, they've already made a lot of progress, progress that accelerated under Barack Obama. It's ironic in a way that they constantly screech about how terrible America is when these same progressives have largely had their way for the past century.

They wanted the New Deal and got it. They wanted the Great Society and got it. They wanted affirmative action and got it. They wanted God banished from the public square and got it. They wanted traditional mores about sex eliminated and they got that one, too.

They complain about income inequality, racism, patriarchy, and a whole host of other evils, but those problems still exist despite all their programs that were supposed to solve them. It never occurs to them that their economic policies may be causing extreme income inequality; that affirmative action may be doing more harm than good to minorities; or that perhaps people aren't better off by being forced to violate their deeply held religious beliefs in the name of "progress."

Progress toward what? Progress to where? What does progress mean to them anyway?

So, along comes Donald Trump, a man who not only rejects the progressive worldview but who—finally—wasn't afraid to call it what it is, frankly and without a lot of hemming and hawing or apologizing. He didn't meekly come to the podium and say, "I'm sorry, I don't mean to offend anyone," like so many terrified conservatives of the past. He came in and said, "It stops now. Today."

Donald Trump is the progressives' worst nightmare. He hasn't just dared to call the Left what it is, he's empowered millions of Americans to put aside their fear to do the same thing.

That alone is enough to earn the Left's hatred. When you add in black and Hispanic and Asian unemployment at record lows[7] and rising wages among the poorest Americans[8] as a result of tax cuts and deregulation, i.e., getting the government out of the way, the president becomes an existential threat to the Left, rather than to all of America as Joe Biden stupidly suggested.[9]

If Donald Trump succeeds in eliminating unemployment in the African American, Hispanic, and Asian communities, the Left can't co-opt them anymore by telling them only the Democrats "feel their pain."

The Progressive Nuclear Option

For these reasons, the Left has obviously decided they have no other choice but the nuclear option. With defeating Trump as their rallying cry, they have commenced an all-out assault on America, seeking to tear down everything that gives these United States any cohesive identity. For them, four more years of Donald Trump in the White House could break their hold on our body politic indefinitely. So, they've openly abandoned gradualism and committed themselves to radically changing America now. Consider that four years ago Bernie Sanders shocked everyone by running as a democratic socialist. Within three years, twenty candidates running for the Democrat nomination have bought into the socialist agenda.

No sooner had they been sworn into office after winning a majority in the House of Representatives in the 2018 midterm elections, than Democrat Steve Cohen proposed a constitutional amendment to abolish the Electoral College.[10] That's a radical, fundamental change to our Constitution, which establishes a *federal* republic for a reason. The Constitution identifies specific powers delegated to the federal government, all others are left to the states or the people, to prevent Washington, DC, from imposing the will of a few elites on every community in the country. Outside of national defense, interstate and international commerce, and a few other areas, the people of the states are supposed to be left to govern themselves.

The Electoral College goes hand in hand with this idea, as it ensures that the most populous states—the Democrat ones growing faster thanks to unchecked illegal immigration— cannot elect a president who pays no attention to the concerns of smaller states. The bill is going nowhere at the moment with a Republican Senate and Donald Trump in the White House— although one election could change that—so the Left is seeking to circumvent the Electoral College at the state level. As of this writing, fifteen states have passed bills to award all their electoral votes to the presidential candidate who wins the national popular vote, regardless of the results in their own state.[11]

Our current federal system allows deep blue states such as California or Massachusetts to be as progressive or socialist as they want, but that's not good enough for the Left. They can't stand for anyone who disagrees with them to run their communities as they wish. If California has transgender bathrooms, Arkansas must have them, Alabama must have them. Every state must have them as well. All must worship at the progressive altar, regardless of their political, moral, or religious beliefs.

The Democrat House is also intent upon erasing our borders to the extent we have them. Silly socialist Alexandria Ocasio-Cortez has called for abolishing the Immigration and Customs Enforcement (ICE) agency because "we are standing on Native land, and Latino people are descendants of Native people. And we cannot be told and criminalized simply for our identity and our status."[12]

Alexandria, not a single Latino has been prosecuted or detained because of his identity or status. Those who have been were prosecuted or detained *for breaking the law*. If identity had anything to do with it, the millions of Latino immigrants who came here legally and who contribute to our economy and society would be having the same problem. They're not. Stop making this about race or ethnicity and start keeping the oath you took to uphold the law.

Erasing our borders, nationalizing private industries such as health care and education, abolishing our federal republic and replacing it with a socialist pure democracy are just a few of the radical ways the Left wants to remake America. There seems no limit to the ridiculousness. Ideas we once could laugh about are being seriously proposed and backed by the speaker of the Democrat-controlled House.

One of these is reparations for slavery, a perennial Left-wing cause célèbre once relegated to the fringe. Now, there is a bill in Congress to create a commission to study this that has the backing of Speaker Nancy Pelosi, House Judiciary Committee Chairman Jerry Nadler, and at least sixty Democrats, as of this writing.[13]

I don't even know where to begin on this one. First, taking it as seriously as one can, it's another fundamental attack on the rule of law, particularly due process. No American alive has ever owned a slave. No American alive has ever been a slave. So, how can anyone justify punishing the former for something they've never done to reimburse the latter for an injury they've never suffered?

Don't forget that African Americans make up over 13 percent of the population,[14] so they'd be paying part of their own reparations. And what about the descendants of black slave owners? Yes, there were African American people who owned slaves in pre–Civil War America, from at least 1654.[15] Do they get reparations? What about descendants of black slave owners who were once slaves themselves, but purchased slaves after gaining their freedom? And no one seems to mention the fact that there was a civil war to make sure slavery ended. What about those brave men who gave their lives to make sure this horrible stain on America's history ended? Should they get reparations?

I could go on and on, but the point is made. This is an impossible idea to put into practice, even if it could be reconciled with any standard of justice. African Americans were treated abominably in this country for a long time, during and after slavery. I know. I grew up during the civil rights era, when Republicans led the way over the resistance and filibusters of Democrats to pass the Civil Rights Act of 1964. But the responsibility for those wrongs belongs to the people who perpetrated them, not to their innocent descendants.

I believe most Democrats know this. When you take away all the nonsensical hot air, this is just another attempt to divide and conquer, exploiting minority groups for votes and plundering everyone, majority and minority alike. The reparations idea is just an excuse for more socialist wealth redistribution, with an identity politics angle.

Socialists like Alexandria Ocasio-Cortez and Rashida Tlaib can win congressional districts while openly admitting they are socialists, even celebrating it. But winning a national election is a different story. While gaining in popularity, socialism is still looked upon unfavorably by most Americans—albeit far too slim a majority for me.[16]

At the same time, at least one survey showed up to 70 percent of Democrats supported some form of socialism.[17] So, any Democrat seeking the presidential nomination must walk a tightrope between appeasing the far-Left element in control of their party and avoiding alienating the independents and moderates they'll need to win the presidency.

New York City Mayor Bill de Blasio hasn't even been able to appease the far Left. This is in spite of his pledges to "introduce legislation to ban the glass and steel skyscrapers that have contributed so much to global warming"[18] and to reduce red meat consumption by 50 percent in public schools and other city facilities as part of a New York City Green New Deal.[19] One problem is Democrats just don't believe him.

"I think there's a lot of hypocrisy behind his actions and I think in a place like New York people see right through it," said Assemblyman Ron Kim, a Queens Democrat.[20] "Early on there was an imperiousness," added Neal Kwatra, a Democrat operative.[21]

I wish I could say his outlandish policies were the root of his problems, but de Blasio's presidential hopes were dead on arrival mostly because nobody seems to like the guy, now that they're really getting to know him. He doesn't even have the good sense to keep quiet about rooting for the Red Sox while he's mayor of New York City. So, his announcement for president back in May was met mostly with ridicule.

Even his hometown paper, the *New York Post*, reported his candidacy with a cover featuring the headline, "De Blasio Runs for President" superimposed over a picture of a crowd of people laughing hysterically.[22]

For most Democrats who have declared for president, though, appeasing the far Left is easy; they mostly agree with them. But they can't present themselves to the voting public at large as the radical socialists they are, so they try to obscure their radical positions any way they can. And it's already looking like any indication of moderation or centrism will be fatal to a Democrat's nomination hopes.

Front-runner Joe Biden is already learning this. With the first Democrat presidential debate just concluded, as of this writing, Biden is already showing signs of weakness. Self-described socialist Bernie Sanders remains in second place, with Fauxahontas Elizabeth Warren and small-town mayor Pete Buttigieg beginning to close the gap. The rest of the candidate Clown Car desperately struggles to attract attention with unintentionally funny attempts to appear to be the down-home, hardworking Americans they despise.

Elizabeth Warren was the first to go down this cringe-worthy road with her "get me a beer" video tweet back in January.[23] Warren seems obsessed with being somebody she's not. First, she wanted to be a Native American and now she wants to be a beer-drinking, blue collar American, despite her ill-gotten Harvard degree and finger-wagging, schoolmarm personality. Or maybe in this case Liz just doesn't want voters to know who she really is: a far-Left radical bent on fundamentally changing everything that makes America the greatest country in the world.

The rest of the Democlowns stuffed themselves into this perennially embarrassing car, except for Cory Booker, who at least had the dignity to admit he doesn't drink beer, despite his myriad other problems.[24] Kirsten Gillibrand was a little more honest. She posed dancing in a gay bar while sipping whiskey in a "Love Is Brave" T-shirt, yelling, "Gay rights!"[25] It didn't help. She's still a firmly entrenched member of the 1 percent—in the polls—and she's probably sitting in the trunk of the clown car.

It's far too early to even predict who the Democrat Party nominee might be. This year, the Democrats and their media allies don't seem to have decided in advance who is going to win, as they did in 2016. But you can bet that whoever it is, he or she will be far to the left even of Barack Obama. Many of the Democrat candidates are trying to differentiate themselves by claiming to oppose outright socialism, with some even maintaining they are "capitalists" out of one side of their mouths while supporting Medicare for All or the Green New Deal out of the other. But they all share one thing in common: they want to remake America into something other than what our founding documents say it is supposed to be.

Let's look at the front-runners as of this writing and some of their horrible highlights. This is by no means an exhaustive study, but rather a taste of what these radicals are selling. You might want to hold your nose and have some strong mouthwash handy, or a bottle of bourbon.

Creepy, Simple Joe

As Donald Trump stays strong and laser-focused on his strengths and the rocking economy with opportunity for all Americans to be part of the American dream, the Democrat Clown Car, overloaded with twenty-four candidates, bumbles down the path to nowhere. Like cannibals, their plan is not so much to promote themselves, as it is to eat each other alive.

Just look at how they've treated their current front-runner, Joe Biden, who has enough problems already. Past plagiarisms illustrate his lack of depth on important subjects. He earned his "Creepy" nickname from his penchant for sticking his nose in women's necks. I still haven't figured out what the man is sniffing for. Other than my dogs, I don't know any warm-blooded mammals who sniff like Creepy Joe.

But don't take it from me. You've heard what his own pals say about his flip-flopping on the Hyde Amendment.[26] One day the government should not pay for abortions; the next day, it should. Or consider the latest mess where his fellow Democrats savaged him on segregation.

Biden tried to use late senators James O. Eastland of Mississippi and Herman Talmadge of Georgia, both Democrats who were staunch opponents of desegregation, as examples of people he "didn't agree on much of anything" with, but with whom he was able to get things done in the Senate.[27] Prudent or not, Joe's point was obviously to say he can work with anyone. There was nothing complimentary about the senators' segregationist views in anything Biden said. But suddenly, he's a racist to his far-Left, eat-them-alive Democrat colleagues.

"But let's be very clear," said Kamala Harris. "The senators that he is speaking of with such adoration are individuals who made and built their reputations on segregation. The Ku Klux Klan celebrated the election of one of them. So, this is a very serious matter."

When Democrat senator and presidential primary rival Cory Booker suggested Biden should apologize for his remarks, Biden hit back, saying "Apologize for what? Cory [Booker] should apologize. He knows better."[28] To which Booker replied, "For his posture to be to me, 'I've done nothing wrong. You should apologize; I'm not a racist' is so insulting and so missing the larger point that he should have not have to have explained to him."[29]

On one hand, Creepy Joe is right. No matter how little one thinks of Joe's record, or lack thereof, his personal attributes, or the prospect of him being president, no reasonable person believes he is a racist. On the other, how many more decades in politics does Biden need to learn it's not a good idea to first proudly cite your record working with segregationists to make a point and then to demand an apology from an African American opponent when he calls you on it?

Let's be honest. Joe isn't the sharpest knife in the drawer. This is a guy who not only finished seventy-sixth in his law school class of eighty-five but wasn't smart enough to keep his mouth shut about it when he first ran for president thirty-two years ago. He claimed he finished in the top half of his class and then released the transcripts himself proving that this wasn't remotely true![30] Now, less than two months after announcing his bid for the presidency in 2020, he's already nullified the whole theme he launched his campaign on with this one gaffe, before even taking the stage for the first debate.

Of course I'm talking about the three-minute-thirty-second melodramatic plea to help save America from . . . a straw man.[31] That's right. With an opportunity to tell the whole country why he should be president, Creepy Joe rambled on about Donald Trump supposedly referring to white supremacists and neo-Nazis as "very fine people," something that is demonstrably untrue.

Basing his campaign solely on the *accusation* of hate against the president is a winner for a certain segment of the voters, who just can't articulate why they don't like President Trump. It's something they can grab on to. They can just say "This is why I hate him. He's a racist. That's the box I want to check." And that's a winner for a certain percentage of the electorate.

Now, when you press any of these people on the president's comments after the Charlottesville, Virginia, incident, they can't really back up their position. All they have is, "He thinks racists are fine people, because he said there were 'very fine people on both sides.'" Any honest person can listen to the president's comments themselves and hear him clearly say, "I'm not talking about the neo-Nazis and white nationalists because they should be condemned totally."[32]

Nevertheless, Biden hoped this was going to be the issue that would help him win, before he managed to get himself tangled up in his own unwarranted racism scandal. It's the position of a simpleton, taken by a simpleton, quite frankly.

Calling Donald Trump a racist didn't work in 2016 and it's not going to work in 2020, because it isn't true. This president has done more for the African American community, Hispanics, and Asians than any other president. He has appointed more women as top advisers than presidents Obama, Bush, or Clinton.[33]

The problem for Creepy, Simple Joe is that the racist card is the only one he has. He's not just holding a weak hand; he's holding an empty one. This is a man with no record of achievement but one who was part of the disastrous Obama-Biden economy. Remember those "shovel-ready jobs"?

Biden not only has major problems; he doesn't seem to be able to learn from his mistakes. He had a plagiarism scandal during his failed bid for the 1988 Democrat nomination and this year he seems to have plagiarized parts of his $1.7 trillion climate plan.[34] That helped distract from the specifics of the plan itself, which are terrible. Joe's pitching the same disastrous Democrat policies that gave us Solyndra and a decimated coal industry: subsidizing so-called green energy sources that don't produce enough energy at a price average people can afford, and attacking fossil fuels, which do.

Creepy Joe still hasn't learned the boundaries of personal space or personal contact when dealing with women, either. Even after the president and millions of others lampooned his infamous 2015 shoulder-grab-neck-nuzzle moment with then defense secretary Ashton Carter's wife, Stephanie,[35] and multiple women came forward to accuse him of inappropriate contact,[36] Creepy Joe just keeps on creeping. In yet another cringe-worthy moment at a campaign event in May, Biden called a ten-year-old girl "good-looking."[37]

All this tends to obscure how terrible Biden is on the issues. He wants to be a "centrist" who can win back the votes Donald Trump took from the Democrats in 2016. But Creepy Joe is only a centrist if Barack Obama—the most far-Left president since at least Lyndon Johnson, if not in all US history—was centrist. And now the Democrat Party has moved far to the left of Obama, making his former vice president seem almost moderate—until you look beyond his personal failings and examine his positions.

Just as Biden's climate plan only looks reasonable compared to AOC's Green New Deal, his health care position (remember "the big fucking deal"?) similarly departs from the virtually communist Medicare for All policy only by degree. Biden says he doesn't support Medicare for All, but does support a "public option," meaning the government would run a health insurance plan that would compete with private plans. "If the insurance company isn't doing the right thing by you, you should have another choice," according to Biden.[38]

This sounds very moderate and reasonable if you're Joe's target voter—virulently anti-Trump and not too bright. But it's not moderate or reasonable. It's a rather sinister plan to eventually destroy the private insurance market so the government can completely take over health care. There is no way private competition against a government program can ever be fair.

The government has the power to tax, which private companies don't. You can bet any public option program would end up being subsidized when it lost money, not to mention given regulatory advantages over its private competitors. Prices to the consumer would be set politically, rather than by the market, which means those using the program would pay a lower price and taxpayers who never agreed to join would pay the difference when the plan lost money.

The public option is based on a fantasy repeated often by the Left, including President Obama, that government-run enterprises can deliver products to consumers at a lower cost because they don't need to make a profit.[39] If that were true, the Soviet Union would still be around, Cubans wouldn't be driving cars made in the 1950s, and Venezuelans wouldn't be eating their pets and zoo animals.[40] It's the profit motive that fuels competition, lowers prices, and drives innovation. That's why virtually everything the market provides increases in quality and decreases in price, relative to inflation, while everything the government provides does exactly the opposite.

In another attempt to appear moderate, Biden has announced

that he supports the federal government guaranteeing two years of "free" community college, as opposed to candidates like Bernie Sanders who would make four-year colleges and universities free.[41] Joe seems to think offering only half the freebies Bernie offers makes him only half a socialist, but you can't be a little bit socialist any more than you can be a little bit pregnant. Once you've started handing out other people's money, you've surrendered 100 percent of the principle.

Free community college is just another Obama-era retread policy that will satisfy neither the radical Left nor the swing voters he is looking to lure back to his party's ticket. It's hard to make the case that the American people aren't educated enough when the American economy is leading the world, unemployment is at record lows, and wages are finally rising again.[42]

And what's with Joe's son? Now, I'm usually the first one to say that a family member's behavior is totally irrelevant to the candidate. But you just cannot here. Joe Biden admits that when his son Hunter was working for an energy company in Ukraine, he—Vice President Biden—threatened the president of Ukraine that he would withhold $1 billion in US aid if the prosecutor investigating the energy company where his son worked was not fired.[43] Biden is so stupid he proudly admits that after his threat the prosecutor was fired. It's shades of the Clinton Democrats, where foreign policy is shaped to benefit the family pocketbook. Curiously, his son had no background in energy and was making $50,000 a month from that company.[44]

Even Joe's best pal, Barack, is uncharacteristically silent these days. Joe once had to remind him that they are besties with a best friends forever bracelet.[45]

Joe, I wouldn't hold my breath waiting for your BFF,

Barack, to endorse you. Who knows? Maybe he's waiting for the perfect day when the sun, the moon, the stars, and all the planets are aligned to signal "Joe, you're the one." Regardless, Joe, you would probably make a pretty lousy president. So, stick to making your friendship bracelets and wishing and hoping.

America doesn't need a best friend. America doesn't need a sniffer or a plagiarist, or someone so dumb he admits threatening to withhold government money to end an investigation involving a company where a family member is working. So, I suspect the Clown Car will be dropping off Creepy Joe, as the other clowns continue to fight each other for the front seat.

Comrade Bernie

Bernie Sanders came out of the gate in the same place he left off in 2016—second—and I honestly think that's his ceiling. It's ironic that the party whose loudest voices regularly use the words *white guy* as a pejorative is being led by two "old white guys" who are also lifelong Washington, DC insiders. But Bernie is doing quite poorly considering his name recognition is almost as high as Biden's and most of his competition is completely unknown to large swaths of voters.[46]

Still, just as Creepy Joe has a pocket of low-information voters for whom calling the president a racist is enough to win their support, so, too, does Bernie have his core followers ready to follow him to the barricades when the "workers of the world unite." The problem for Bernie is he's no longer unique. When he ran in 2016, openly calling himself a socialist was exciting and new to the lunatic Left. In post-AOC 2019, with socialists winning elections in Congress and at the state level,[47] Bernie is yesterday's news. He's just another "old white guy" who is weak on guns—from the Left's perspective—and whose own ex-staffers say "struggles with women's issues."[48]

Whether he can break out above also-ran status to contend as he did in 2016 or not, Bernie is still talking loud and drawing a crowd. Just a glance at the "Issues" page on his campaign website tells you everything you need to know about this con man.[49] The first two links are titled, "Health Care for All" and "College for All and Cancel All Student Debt."

Bernie isn't talking about getting the government less involved or out of the way completely so the market can adjust prices to their natural, affordable level. He wants to make "public colleges, universities, and trade schools tuition-free" and establish a "Medicare-for-all, single-payer program" in place of private health insurance plans.

You don't need a PhD in economics to know there really is something quite insane about the idea that education and health care should be paid for by *everyone other* than the people consuming education and health care. This appeals not only to low-information voters but also to the worst aspects of human nature. "Consume all you want, and the government will force someone else to pick up the tab" fits my definition of *greed* better than anything I see the corporations who employ millions of people and give billions to charity doing.

Sanders wants to fundamentally change Social Security into a full-blown welfare program, with expanded benefits for Bernie's target voters. Right now, Americans only pay a percentage of income up to $132,900 toward Social Security. That's because it's not supposed to be a wealth-transfer program. You pay a tax up to a certain amount of income and you get a limited benefit that is supposed to supplement—not replace—your retirement savings.

Bernie's plan completely changes that. Instead of a supplement funded at least partially by one's own contributions, Bernie wants to make it a transfer program where "the rich" pay and Bernie's voters get higher benefits across the board, a higher minimum benefit, higher cost-of-living adjustments, and more disability benefits.

Bernie has a lot to say about the supposed greed of "the rich" and their supposed disregard for the environment, while owning three homes himself and spending almost $300,000 on airfare in October 2018 alone.[50] A large part of the $1 million-plus income he earned in 2017 came from a book pitching his horrible, un-American ideas, which I'd have no qualm with if Bernie would simply allow everyone else to keep the fruits of their labor as Bernie has. But like most self-described socialists, Bernie believes it's "capitalism for me, not for thee."

Outside of his and his wife's books over the past few years, virtually 100 percent of Bernie's wealth has come at taxpayer expense. As far as I know, he's never had a private sector job. This is a guy who was even kicked out of a hippie commune for laziness![51] That explains quite a bit about his economic ideas. He doesn't understand everyone can't live off someone else—someone out there has to be producing more than he or she consumes for every bum like Bernie consuming more than he produces.

Bernie became a rich man sponging off taxpayers and demagoguing socialist ideas. But you don't have to be nearly as rich as Bernie himself to be hit with a tax hike to pay for Bernie's giveaways. His plan would subject all income above $250,000 to the Social Security payroll tax.[52] That means it's no longer even ostensibly self-funded by the recipients. It's just more of what Bernie Sanders is quite honest about what he is selling: socialism.

Liz "Fauxahontas" Warren

If you think being a fake Native American pretending to enjoy drinking beer is the worst thing about Elizabeth Warren, think again. Beneath her facepalm-inspiring personal gaffes lurks a power-mad socialist.

That's not an exaggeration. Big Chief Liz doesn't just have one plan, she has a whole suitcase full of plans, about twenty as of this writing, that even the *New York Times* says would, "significantly remake the American economy, covering everything from tax policy to student debt relief."[53]

Of course, Warren is also on board with all or most of Comrade Bernie's giveaways. Under the somewhat deceptive title, "Rebuild the Middle Class," she casually mentions using her myriad new tax schemes to pay for a whole sleigh full of presents, including "universal childcare, student loan debt relief, and 'down payments' on a Green New Deal and Medicare for All."[54] But given the tens of trillions of dollars the Green New Deal or Medicare for All would cost—not to mention the rest of her gravy train—even her oppressive new tax regime doesn't seem to add up to nearly enough.

For example, Warren has proposed slapping a 7 percent tax on all profits over $100 million made by US corporations.[55] This tax would be in addition to anything they owed under the current tax code, after deductions for expenses and exemptions. Warren uses the much-demagogued example of Amazon making $10 billion in profits last year but paying no federal income taxes to triumphantly proclaim they would have paid $698 million under her plan. She leaves out that Amazon didn't pay any taxes in 2018 because the company reinvested their profits back into their business, taking advantage of a tax incentive that encourages innovation, expansion, and job creation.[56] Nevertheless, she says overall this plan would "bring in $1 trillion in revenue over the next ten years."

That might sound like a lot, but Medicare for All is estimated to cost $32 trillion over the first ten years.[57] That's assuming health care providers currently losing money on Medicare and Medicaid don't get a raise and nothing we can't foresee doesn't drive up the cost further. When Medicare was launched in 1965, the geniuses crunching numbers for the government estimated the program would cost about $12 billion by 1990. The actual cost that year was $90 billion. They thought Medicaid would cost $1 billion by 1992. It cost $17 billion that year.[58]

Last year, Medicare cost $582 billion and Medicaid $778 billion, counting the states' contributions.[59] So, I would be very skeptical about assuming these cost estimates are at all accurate.

Alexandria Ocasio-Cortez says her Green New Deal would cost about $10 trillion,[60] but a study coauthored by a former member of the Congressional Budget Office (CBO) says it would cost more like $93 trillion.[61] Giving Big Chief Liz the benefit of the doubt and assuming her own version of the Green New Deal would only cost $10 trillion, she's now up to $42 trillion with just two of her proposed spending programs and she's only collecting $1 trillion with her corporate tax.

Warren has another, even more destructive tax on the accumulated wealth of high-net-worth individuals that I'll talk more about in a later chapter. This one would raise an estimated \$2.75 trillion over ten years, not even enough to pay the \$3.2 trillion Warren would spend forgiving student loans, paying for universal child care, and raising teacher's wages,[62] much less the tens of trillions needed for Medicare for All or any Green New Deal.

When you do the math, "tax the rich" just isn't a realistic way to pay for anything Fauxahontas or any of her fellow radicals are promising. The so-called 1 percent may have a lot more money than you or me, but they don't have that much. So, where is the other 99 percent of the funds needed to pay for all this going to come from?

It's going to come from you, just like it does in any of the countries the Democlowns like to cite when pitching their socialist plans, something I'll also talk more about in a separate chapter. You're going to pay for their utopian schemes with higher taxes, a lower standard of living, and less opportunity to realize your dreams.

The Worst of the Rest

South Bend, Indiana, Mayor Pete Buttigieg and California Senator Kamala Harris are the last two candidates consistently polling in whole numbers as of this writing.[63] On the surface, both seem likable. But therein lies the rub. Once you get past the surface, what they have in mind for our country is as bad or worse than what the front-runners are saying.

Harris is noteworthy mainly for saying her administration would prosecute Donald Trump for obstruction of justice as a private citizen, after he's left the White House.[64] She may as well be telling the hysterical Left, "Elect me and I'll use the power of the presidency to persecute the man you hate for no reason." That's quite an inspiring message. Good luck with that, Kamala.

Buttigieg is especially disturbing given his clean-cut, reasonable-seeming persona. His campaign website says that America's values should "reflect a deep understanding of Americans' everyday lives and embody our country's highest values," the first one being freedom.[65]

That sounds great, until you read further. Freedom has nothing to do with the government forcing other people to pay one's medical bills, but Mayor Pete is on board with Medicare for All, albeit via a public option "along the way while allowing the economy to adjust."[66] He also promises college will be "completely free at lower incomes" and that "middle-income families at public colleges will pay zero tuition."

His website also says, "Freedom means building 21st century infrastructure, because you're not free to pursue happiness if you don't have access to safe roads or clean water," which is also wrong. We do need infrastructure improvements, but they have nothing to do with freedom. We'd have a bill passed, signed, and being executed if the Democrats would stop reinvestigating the Russia collusion delusion and do their jobs.

The rest of what Mayor Pete calls "freedom" is merely the usual litany of far-Left causes. He's on board with eliminating the Electoral College, paying reparations for slavery, the Equality Act, and the Green New Deal.[67] In other words, the young, boy-next-door Midwestern mayor is just as radically socialist as all the rest.

There are too many clowns in the car for me to talk about every one of them here. Like baggy-pants bozos, they continue to try to one-up each other with new, radical socialist gags that wouldn't be remotely funny if they managed to make them the law of the land. They'd like to drive their Clown Car over a cliff with all of America trapped in the backseat. Fortunately, Donald Trump is driving a Lamborghini and the Democrat Clown Car is in his rearview mirror.

CHAPTER SEVEN

Home Alone in the White House

It's Christmas 2018 and the leader of the free world is sitting alone in the West Wing. His family has already departed for the winter White House, Mar-a-Lago. He has stayed back because he is waiting for his invited guests to arrive, but much to his disappointment the Democrats never bother to show up. They're a little too busy to deal with urgent affairs of the nation, frolicking in places like Hawaii and Puerto Rico. The president has stayed back because he wants to make a deal. The issue to him and most Americans is much too serious to ignore. In fact, it is more than serious; it is a crisis.

Immigration is the single most controversial issue in America today. It is one that has resisted resolution for more than thirty years, since Ronald Reagan in 1986 granted what he thought was the last class of amnesty. He figured his action ended America's immigration problem and going forward the law would be followed. Reagan, however, had no idea the radicals of the twenty-first century would resist the law as written to get revenge for the election of Donald Trump.

They all talk about comprehensive immigration reform, but neither I nor most people have quite figured out what that oft-used phrase means. It's kind of like beauty: it's in the eyes of the beholder. To some it means ignore the law and let them all in; to others it means build a wall and keep them all out. I, for one, believe the law as written should be respected and followed.

It's really very simple. If you cross our border into our country, unless you do so at our invitation and with our approval, you are violating our law. But then again, I believe laws are meant to be followed and not ignored. The radical Left can't even be bothered to repeal the laws on the books. They don't even care to go through the process at all.

Politicians are elected to represent us. They are here to represent our interests over their political interests. Not only did the Democrats refuse to compromise, at first they refused to even show up when the president offered a working lunch. While the president spent the Christmas holiday in the White House, imploring legislators to put aside their political posturing and come back to the table for the sake of the people they represent, House speaker-designate Nancy Pelosi vacationed in Hawaii.[1] Apparently, that's how important Pelosi thought it was to fix immigration reform and end the partial government shutdown.

Refusal to work toward compromise is putting politics over people. President Trump was at the White House virtually every day trying to make a deal—bending, compromising, and offering solutions. The Democrats refused his every overture and dug in their heels, proving that politics are more important to them than putting people back to work. And they openly blamed Trump for the shutdown that they refused to try to end. While 800,000 federal employees faced the loss of a second paycheck in mid-January, the Democrats added to their distress by not even negotiating.

And that, my friends, is a problem.

They were willing to sacrifice the working class they claim to represent simply because they hate Donald Trump. They refused to negotiate for people who live paycheck to paycheck. They don't consider Americans whose lives, safety, economy, and social services are drained by these illegals. They turned their backs on average Americans, while President Trump worked through the holidays to try to reopen the government.

On January 19, the president offered yet another compromise to reopen the government. It included:

- $5.7 billion for a steel slat barrier fence, in lieu of a concrete wall, dropping the term *wall* altogether
- $805 million for drug-detection technology
- $800 million for humanitarian assistance
- 2,750 new border patrol agents
- 75 new immigration judges
- A 3-year extension for those with Temporary Protected Status (TPS) and Deferred Action for Childhood Arrivals (DACA)[2]
- Young people can seek asylum in their home country without having to resort to traveling with dangerous human traffickers and coyotes.

The president described in clear and direct language the humanitarian crises, including three hundred of our citizens dying every week from heroin overdoses, 90 percent of which comes through the porous Mexican border. The president also talked about what many of us in law enforcement already knew—that parents give their daughters birth control pills, because they know they will be raped along this dangerous journey.

The Democrats dismissed the proposal out of hand without taking any time to review it or negotiate with the president. The Democrats had their minds made up before even hearing the president's proposal. Nancy Pelosi called it unacceptable, saying, "What's original in his proposal is not good and what's good in his proposal is not original." Chuck Schumer called it "one-sided and ineffective."[3]

No surprise, the Democrats are dug into the theater of radicalism, resistance, and revenge, casting Donald Trump as evil while casting themselves as angels, supported by a mainstream media bent on publishing any anti-Trump story, no matter how absurd.

They went from political theater to theater of the absurd when Nancy Pelosi sent a letter to the president saying it was too dangerous for him to give the State of the Union speech. Hogwash: Pelosi never even spoke to security in charge of the event. There was never a single day when Congress was in session that it was shut down for lack of security.

Nancy concocted the security risk hoax in an obvious effort to keep the president from having the opportunity to speak directly to the American people. It was another new low for her and the Democrats. Never in the history of this great nation has a speaker refused the president the opportunity to give a State of the Union address. It may have been prescient on her part, given that the address he gave weeks later was universally applauded, with a CNN poll showing 76% of viewers approved of the speech.[4]

Of course, not one to be cowed, the president pulled Nancy and her pals off a government bus thirty minutes before a scheduled junket to Brussels, Egypt, and Afghanistan. The president reminded the Democrats of the priority to work on ending the government shutdown before taking a pleasure trip overseas.

Nancy, what the hell were you doing boarding a bus with your Democrat cronies on the way to Brussels to meet with NATO leaders? There's a partial government shutdown. We didn't need you in Brussels! How do you negotiate your way out of a stalemate at home while you're on a seven-day European excursion that we, the taxpayers, foot the bill for? You got some chutzpah, lady.

What were you going to do on this trip, anyway? Have another few parties on our dime? And bad-mouth the president to those who prefer that we foot their NATO bill, too? Then, you and your band of friendlies were going to Afghanistan, to find out what's going on from the troops on the ground. Really? You think some soldier is going to saunter up and whisper in your ear to tell you anything his bosses at the Pentagon wouldn't be happy to tell you in Washington? Or is it that you think the troops are dying to see you? Send them a video, Nancy, and thank them.

By the way, Nancy, is this how you reinforce your power base? By approving trips? Are you Speaker of the House or the official congressional junket organizer? But then again, you've never been one to sacrifice, have you? How about instead of the trips, you escrow that money for federal employees? You'd rather not? Is it because polling blames Trump for the shutdown and you're good with that?

I have news for you, Nancy: so is he. A leader takes the burden just to get it done. How about since you're in charge of all spending bills, Nancy, you forgo your check until this is over? Man up like the federal employees going through the shutdown? Donate congressional salaries to those who won't get theirs. After all, reports are you and your husband are worth over a hundred million dollars.

How did you make that money, Nancy? How long is it that you've been in Congress? President Trump hasn't even taken a paycheck. He's donated his salary since day one to several federal agencies.

Admit it, Nancy. Your big donors in California want people to pick grapes. You remember Cesar Chavez who fought tooth and nail to stop illegal immigrants, to protect legal immigrants and farmworkers. He's rolling over in his grave over how you and your rich liberal friends have sold out American labor.

The president, they say, is a fear monger. They say this is a manufactured crisis. Say that to the face of an Angel Mom whose child was murdered or massacred by illegal immigrants. And why did you approve securing the border in 2006 and 2013, but won't do so now? The obvious answer: because Donald Trump wants it.

You disrespect Americans and instead respect those who fight our laws while you and your ilk show pictures of furloughed federal employees while you won't meet with the Angel Moms who come to your office with pictures of American children killed by illegals.

So, let me see if I understand this: an American mother shows a picture of her child murdered by an illegal. And Chuck

Schumer and his gang, they come out and show pictures of federal employees. Is there a moral equivalency here? Are you folks schizo? Are you working for Americans or illegals? Or is it that you just don't give a damn? You vacation in Hawaii. Your buddies vacation with lobbyists in Puerto Rico during the shutdown. And you plan a jaunt to Europe while federal employees are trying to save every dollar to buy groceries. Admit it! You don't give a damn. Nancy, you're a hypocrite, a political operative. Your mantra? Destroy the president of the United States. To hell with the taxpaying, hardworking Americans. Let them eat cake. I've got a junket to go on, an ego to assuage, and an electorate to ignore.

Walls Work

The Democrats and their liberal media allies like to point out previous border security bills overwhelmingly supported by Democrats (including Chuck Schumer, Hillary Clinton, Barack Obama, and other prominent Democrats still infesting our Congress), referred to the barrier as a "fence" instead of a wall. "There is a difference between a fence and a wall," said Democrat Senator Jeff Merkley.[5] There is a difference, Jeff? What is the difference? Both are physical barriers the purpose of which is to prevent people from crossing the border other than through a legal point of entry. The only difference between a wall and a fence is a wall works better.

Crazy Nancy Pelosi went so far as to call the idea of a border wall "an immorality."[6] She doesn't explain how on God's earth a wall can be immoral. She immediately followed up her comment with, "It's the least effective way to protect the border, and the most costly. I can't think of any reason why any-one would think it's a good idea—unless this has something to do with something else." The "something else" is Pelosi's soph-omoric suggestion that the president views the wall as a sign of his manhood.[7] There seems no bottom to the depths to which the Democrats will sink in their desperate, unhinged plot to oppose President Trump.

Pelosi never got around to explaining why the wall is immoral. This won't be the Berlin Wall, which was designed to keep people inside an oppressive regime. On the contrary, it's designed merely to keep people from avoiding legal points of entry where they *will* be let into the country, provided they are not criminals or carrying dangerous diseases or drugs. What is immoral is putting children and other vulnerable people in harm's way by encouraging them to travel through deserts and other hostile environments so they can avoid legitimate immi-gration processes that are in place to protect the native popula-tion *and* legal immigrants.

Even if Pelosi were right about the wall being ineffective or costly, that has nothing to do with its supposed immorality. If merely being costly and ineffective were immoral, then every-thing the Democrats have ever done would be immoral. But one can be morally above reproach and still be wasteful and incom-petent. In the case of building a wall on the border, which even by the most inflated estimates would cost far less than one per-cent of the federal budget, there is no question of immorality, cost, or effectiveness. We have laws against illegal immigration. A physical barrier on the border would be a relatively inexpen-sive and highly effective way to enforce those laws. That's why the Democrats don't want it.

The truth is the Democrats oppose building the wall because it *would be* effective, and they know it. How could a thirty-foot-high wall not make it more difficult to cross a border than . . . nothing? If there were a thirty-foot wall around the building you work in, would it be harder for you to get to your desk? Of course, it would.

We don't have to rely on this intuitive argument. There are plenty of real-world examples of the effectiveness of border walls. Terrorist attacks on Israel dropped by 90 percent after it built a wall along the border with the Palestinian West Bank. Morocco put a stop to the insurgency and terrorist campaign waged against it with a 1,700-mile system of sand berms, fences, minefields, and ditches.[8] In fact, contrary to the counterintuitive mantra chanted ad nauseam by the Democrats and the media (but I repeat myself) that border walls are ineffective, the number of them built around the world has exploded in the post–World War II era. At the end of that war, there were seven border walls in the world. Today, there are seventy-seven.[9]

We even have proof border walls work right here in this country. I interviewed both current Acting Director of ICE, Mark Morgan, and his predecessor, Ron Vitiello, on my Fox News show, *Justice with Judge Jeanine*. They consider what is going on at the border both a humanitarian and a national security crisis, just as President Trump does. The sheer volume of people is overwhelming the ability of our law enforcement and social service agencies to find room to house them.

"Right now, we have the cartels that are helping smuggle children," said Morgan during his appearance on my show. "We actually have children being rented, coming across as fake families, then being recycled and re-rented coming across. It's outrageous. Congress should get together to fix this."

The Democrats will vote for border security measures as long as they don't work, which really isn't as crazy as it sounds. Nothing they vote for works. Just look at Obamacare. But as I said before, this is more than derangement—it's derangement by design. Approving border security measures that don't work allows them to appear as if they are truly interested in protecting our borders while continuing their agenda to fundamentally change the United States, demographically and politically.

The border wall isn't the only sensible border security measure the Democrats seek to shut down. The want to abolish ICE, the agency tasked with enforcing our immigration laws once people have either evaded CBP or overstayed their visas. This complements their resistance to a wall or any effective physical barrier perfectly. Make it as easy as possible for people to enter illegally and then eliminate the government's means to enforce immigration laws once they're here.

Trump Throws the Democrats a Rope

Contrary to the tortured visions of the ongoing liberal fever dream, President Trump's policies are not fascist or even "extreme right." As Bill Bennett astutely observed, the president's policies are "conservative, but mostly traditionally so with a good dash of moderation and compromise."[10] How else could one describe the president's willingness to accept a mere $5.7 billion in funding for a border wall, when building the wall he campaigned on would cost $20 to $30 billion? He's even compromised on building a wall, per se, opting to listen to border security professionals who told him a steel slat fence they could see through would be more effective.[11]

He's also made yet another offer on Deferred Action for Childhood Arrivals (DACA), in exchange for merely doing what the nonpartisan Border Patrol says would help them do their jobs better. As usual, when push comes to shove, the Democrats show how much they really care about the so-called DREAMers, who are people brought into this country illegally by their parents or others when they were still minors. Some of them were brought over our border as infants and have been here ever since.

Think about where we've been with this issue. President Trump inherited a mess, the result of President Obama's—or should I say "King Obama's"?—pen-and-phone decree, granting these people temporary amnesty based on his will alone, without legislative action by Congress. These people are still illegal aliens per the letter of the law, so Obama was literally abandoning his constitutional duty to faithfully execute the laws of this country.

President Trump rescinded Obama's unconstitutional executive action in September 2017 and called on Congress to do its job in addressing the situation through legislation.[12] One might think he would at least get a grudging nod from the liberal media for undoing this executive power grab and returning legislative power to Congress, where the Constitution clearly delegates it. But no, the deranged Left who call the president a "dictator" out of one side of their mouths accused the president of "punting" the issue to Congress.[13]

This is what we're dealing with, folks. We're through the looking glass where a president completely usurps the legislative power delegated to Congress and writes laws with his "pen and phone" to thunderous applause from the supposed champions of democracy. Then, when a subsequent president rescinds the unconstitutional executive power and returns it to Congress, he's called a dictator. Deranged, devious, or both? You tell me.

Did Congress do its job and pass a bill to address DACA? Of course not, because the Democrats don't want a deal on DACA. They want to use the DACA aliens for political purposes, keeping them perpetual victims of a president who has offered to sign deals offering relief to millions more DACA aliens than Obama ever did.

The president's first offer was to grant legal status to over 700,000 DACA aliens in exchange for funding for a border wall and other border security measures.[14] The Democrats rejected it. A few months later, the president offered the same type of deal for almost 2 million immigrants—not only the 700,000 who had applied for legal status under the program since 2012, but an additional 1.1 million who hadn't yet applied.[15] The Democrats rejected that, too.

Finally, this past January, with the government shut down and 800,000 federal workers not being paid, the president made a third version of the offer. Agree to a fraction of the funding needed for what is now proposed as a steel slat fence on the border—a mere $5.7 billion in a federal budget of over $4 trillion—and he would grant temporary relief to DACA aliens with an eye toward a permanent solution when the government reopened.

The Democrats rejected this offer before the president even made it, calling it a "nonstarter."[16] Senate Minority Leader Chuck Schumer went so far as to call it "more hostage taking." What more proof does anyone need that they will never agree to anything this president proposes, even when he is proposing something they say they want?

The government shutdown and the whole, far-Left Resistance is based on a Donald Trump that doesn't exist, one they made up in their minds during a postelection bout of derangement that still hasn't worn off. The president took a strong position on border security, but he's offered more than an olive branch in trying to reach a compromise. He's thrown the Democrats a rope with which they could have pulled themselves back up from the cliff they've jumped off. Instead, they used it to hang themselves.

You could say the president played them like a fiddle, but that's far too understated. It was more like a symphony. The Democrats were high-fiving each other over an apparent political victory with the shutdown, for which polls showed the president taking more blame from the public than the Democrats.[17] The Democrats had a full house, but the president had four aces. He knew that on the core issue of border security, the American public was with him. A Rasmussen poll in January showed two-thirds of Americans considered border security a serious issue and almost half thought the government wasn't doing enough about it, up from 43 percent just five months earlier.[18]

In other words, the shutdown was doing precisely what the president hoped it would: get Americans to take a hard look at border security and start thinking about whether more must be done. President Trump's core supporters have always known this is the crucial issue. During the shutdown, the rest of America started waking up to it, too.

Trump Turns the Tables

The Democrats started premature victory laps when President Trump signed a deal January 25 to reopen the government for three weeks without getting any new funding for a physical barrier on the southern border. The *New York Times* called it a "Surprise Retreat,"[19] while the *Washington Post* called it "a major victory for Speaker Nancy Pelosi."[20] But while liberals rejoiced over what they saw as a Trump defeat, Pelosi and New York Senator Chuck Schumer were reserved in their comments. They knew they had only won a round. The fight was far from over.

With the government reopened temporarily and the Democrats afforded another opportunity to put aside their petty resistance to anything the president suggests, the fight entered what they call in boxing "the championship rounds." You'll never guess who was ready with his best punches.

When Donald Trump stepped to the podium to deliver his State of the Union address on February 5, 2019, no one knew what to expect, at least in terms of public reaction. We knew what to expect from the Democrats in Congress: silence at best, overt contempt for the president at worst. We got some of the latter with Nancy Pelosi's sarcastic applause, if that was how it was intended.[21] The Left-wing media took it that way, with *Washington Post* columnist Monica Hesse atwitter over "the exquisite shade of Nancy Pelosi's applause at the State of the Union." Hesse even praised comedian Patton Oswalt's tweet congratulating Pelosi for "inventing the f*** you clap."[22]

The president is never one to shrink from a fight, but he wasn't going to let Pelosi drag him down to her petty level that night. Instead, he forced her to rise to her feet and applaud genuinely, simply by accurately stating his administration's results after two years:

No one has benefitted more from our thriving economy than women, who have filled 58 percent of the new jobs created in the last year. All Americans can be proud that we have more women in the workforce than ever before—and exactly one century after the Congress passed the Constitutional amendment giving women the right to vote, we also have more women serving in the Congress than ever before.[23]

A large group of female congresswomen on the Democrat side of the aisle, dressed in white to celebrate the hundredth anniversary year of the Nineteenth Amendment, were already on their feet cheering when the president reported on how well women were thriving in the job market under his administration. When he acknowledged the record number of women in Congress, even Nancy Pelosi had no choice but to stand and applaud. Soon, the entire hall erupted into chants of "USA! USA!" For a moment, there was unity and joy.

It wasn't the first time the president has acknowledged the accomplishments of people he vehemently disagrees with politically. For all their unhinged wailing about the president "preaching hate" or being "divisive," it is the Left who can't separate political disagreements from personal ones. When the Democrats won a majority in Congress and there were murmurs about Nancy Pelosi not being reelected Speaker of the House, the president spoke up for her. "I think she deserves it. She's fought long and hard, she's a very capable person, and you know, you have other people shooting at her trying to take over the speakership," the president said.[24]

He also had kind words for Bernie Sanders on the day Sanders announced he would again run for the Democrat Party nomination for president. "Personally, I think he missed his time," said the president. "But I like Bernie because he is one person that you know on trade, he sort of would agree on trade."[25]

Can you imagine anyone from the Democrat Party putting politics aside to say something nice about Donald Trump, or a Republican Speaker of the House? It just goes to show that even the Left's claims about the president's personality are fake news. This is a man who can separate politics from personal relationships and would like to get along with everyone. If you notice, he never hits first in a political fight. He just hits hardest.

He went on to hit hard for the rest of his historic address. He talked about an economy growing twice as fast as it was when he took office, with African American, Hispanic American, and Asian American unemployment all at the lowest point since they started measuring those groups. He talked about groundbreaking criminal justice reform and the first-ever progress in making our trade relationship with China fair to the American people. He spoke about the defeat of ISIS, which controlled over twenty thousand square miles of territory when he took office.

He told the truth about the crisis at our southern border and implored Congress to act, perhaps knowing they wouldn't. But he wasn't speaking just to Congress. He was speaking to an American public that knew it had been ignored on this issue and, deep down, knew the president was right.

In another defining moment of the speech, President Trump took direct aim at the far Left, which has become mainstream in the Democrat Party:

Here, in the United States, we are alarmed by new calls to adopt socialism in our country. America was founded on liberty and independence—not government coercion, domination, and control. We are born free, and we will stay free. Tonight, we renew our resolve that America will never be a socialist country.[26]

Again, the shouts of "USA! USA!" reverberated throughout the hall. Bernie Sanders scowled at the camera, but Chuck Schumer rose to his feet. Once again, Nancy Pelosi was forced to applaud.

A CNN poll immediately following the address showed it received an astounding 76 percent approval rating from the viewing audience.[27] I wasn't a bit surprised. Americans have an instinctual affinity for the truth, and the president spoke the truth with sincerity and conviction.

It's simple, folks. What do you want? Should America be a nation-state, should we be a country defined by borders, or should we simply be a repository for anyone who wants to come here? If we are a repository for anyone to come here, should we also have to pay for their education, health care, housing, food stamps, and yes, even Social Security? And should they get a free college education, while American kids must pay for theirs? And of course, should non-citizens get a driver's license and the right to vote? Does being an American citizen mean nothing anymore?

CHAPTER EIGHT

Invasion at the Border

I have only one question about the national security and humanitarian crises on our southern border: Why are we even having this conversation?

We are so past the talking stage, but as expected, Washington is mired down in politics and word games. Their reason is not only delusional, it's downright dangerous. They simply don't care about what's right for you and me and our families. Our pocketbooks, our health, our safety, our security. The Democrat bozos in Washington only care about winning, resisting, getting reelected, and getting revenge against Trump. It's all a game to them and you and I are pawns in the middle.

I have a message for these socialists in Democrat clothing: don't tell me that we need open borders or that walls or steel barriers, which we haven't even tried, don't work. I've got news for you: nothing that you've done so far has worked. And don't patronize me and tell me, "It's not who we are to turn people away." Really? Are we not a sovereign nation? Are we not entitled to reinforce our own borders? Or at least establish where the United States ends and the rest of the world begins? Why are we granting priority to those who want to sneak into our country illegally?

I'd ask Beto O'Rourke, but I'm not sure he'd answer in a language I understand after his cringeworthy first Democrat debate performance on June 26. Beto pandered to the Hispanic vote by answering in both English and Spanish, prompting Stephen Colbert—whom I rarely agree with—to quip, "He's either trying to lock up the Hispanic vote or he's running for embarrassing dad at a Mexican restaurant."[1]

What Beto, Elizabeth Warren, Julián Castro, and others were proposing is preposterous in any language: decriminalizing illegal immigration. These radical Democrats sit in the House of Representatives and promote lawlessness over the rule of law. If that's the case, we don't need them anymore. Their job is to pass laws. And if they violate the very laws they've actually passed and then refuse to pass laws to end this crisis, then, what the hell are we paying them for?

The whole system is absurd. It is falling apart from chain migration to the visa lottery to people who literally walk in illegally and are released into the population, because US Border Patrol is bound to do so by previous court decisions like the Flores Settlement. We simply need to stop the illegals, the drugs, and the sex trafficking. Why don't we just stop everyone, period? No one has a *right* to come to the United States of America without our approval. Coming here is a privilege we grant to those we deem acceptable. The influx of 144,000 in one month—May 2019—is overwhelming our overcrowded hospitals and classrooms, our communities and our social services, which simply cannot sustain this continuing and increasing financial burden.

At Nancy Pelosi's request, the president halted for two weeks major ICE raids that were scheduled across the country to start on June 23. These well-planned and orchestrated raids would have resulted in the deportation of illegals for whom a deportation order had been issued, where no further court action was required. There are over one million people against whom there is a formal order of removal[2] and another 850,000 waiting for a decision.[3] The raids were even planned in sanctuary cities where there was no concern for the locals suggesting that illegals were protected. By postponing these raids, the president exercised restraint and showed he was willing to work with the Democrats in the hopes of getting Congress to do what it has been unwilling to do since 1986.

The standoff was caused by Congress refusing to fund the Department of Health and Human Services, which is tasked with housing the children within seventy-two hours of detention of their parents or adult companions. "I can't put a kid in a bed that doesn't exist, and I can't make a bed that Congress doesn't fund," said Secretary of Health and Human Services Alex Azar.[4]

So, this was not about the standoff over funding the border wall, ICE, or even US Border Patrol. This was the Democrats withholding funding from a completely different agency whose only job regarding immigration is to take care of the children.

The Democrats had put themselves into such an impossible situation that Nancy Pelosi finally had to bring to a vote the $4.6 billion Senate bill appropriating $1 billion to shelter and feed migrants detained by US Border Patrol and almost $3 billion to care for unaccompanied migrant children who are turned over to the Department of Health and Human Services. The Democrats had been holding out for an alternative bill that would have put undue restrictions on how the Trump administration spent the money. God forbid it be spent on something that helps solve the immigration problem in the first place. Ocasio-Cortez, along with her pals Ilhan Omar and Rashida Tlaib opposed this humanitarian aid, voting no on the funding bill and instead called for the abolition of ICE.

Not only did she vote against the funding, Alexandria Ocasio-Cortez made the outrageous and deeply offensive statement comparing our overtaxed facilities at the border to concentration camps.[5] Ed Mosberg, one of the few living Holocaust survivors, thinks she should be removed from Congress, saying, "She's spreading anti-Semitism, hatred and stupidity. The people on the border aren't forced to be there—they go there on their own will. If someone doesn't know the difference, either they're playing stupid or they just don't care."[6]

"AOC—look at me," said Sami Steigmann. "I am a Holocaust survivor. I went through it . . . What you are doing is you are insulting every victim of the Holocaust. Shame on you!"[7]

This was a resounding victory for President Trump and a significant and well-deserved loss for Nancy Pelosi, who was not only forced to table her own bill due to a revolt by not only AOC and the progressives but eighteen centrist Democrats. She was left in a weakened position within her party when finally forced to move forward the Senate bill, which was eventually passed and signed by the president.

It's good Congress was finally able to pass a bill, but how

long will this money last? And am I the only one who finds it bizarre that the Democrats are willing to spend $4.6 billion to temporarily feed and house illegal immigrants but won't spend $5 billion for a wall that would solve the problem permanently?

Moving illegal aliens into the interior of the country, many of them in sanctuary cities, is a problem all its own. But we can certainly help things if we stop illegal crossings in the first place. Those coming in are not being deported. They're claiming asylum and are then released, pending return for their court hearing, generally scheduled a year or more later. Ninety percent of those who claim a need for asylum don't bother to return to have it officially reviewed by a judge. Do you think maybe they know their asylum claim is bogus?

These people are here to stay, especially if they come with children. And we are doing nothing more than building the next de facto amnesty class. This failure to protect our country and to burden our social services system is simply unsustainable.

The monthly influx of illegals is bigger than most towns in America. Think that one through. They are coming in numbers every month large enough to create their own towns. It has to stop. Words don't matter anymore. This is not time for talk, especially political hogwash.

No more talking about 90 percent of all heroin in the United States coming in through our southern border. It's killing our kids.

No more talking about kids being sex-trafficked and raped during the journey toward our border.

No more talking about transnational gangs bringing in 2,370 pounds of fentanyl through the border, enough to kill our entire country.[8]

No more talking about MS-13 gang members coming across the border, torturing and murdering innocent American citizens.

The truth is the Democrats want open borders to make sure they get more people here, on their side, to vote Democrat, so they never have to worry about getting reelected again. So that a Donald Trump can never happen again. Their revenge is so strong it's palpable.

Thirteen states have already legalized driver's licenses for illegals, including my home state of New York, which joined the others just as we are going to print. And in many states, most recently California, obtaining a driver's license automatically registers you to vote.[9] That's what I said—automatically registers you to vote. Why not give illegals pilot's licenses, too?

Do you get it now? Is their plot to remake America becoming clearer?

Don't worry about it, the lying liberals tell us. It's still technically illegal for noncitizens, including illegal aliens, to vote. Yeah, right. Just like it's illegal to present an unverified document to the FISA court. Who is going to stop them? The Left fights to make sure voter ID laws are burdensome and unconstitutional and many courts have agreed with them.

The Left doesn't want to enforce immigration laws. We know this because House Democrats told us so. House Republicans attempted to introduce a clause into HR 1, which read, "allowing illegal immigrants the right to vote devalues the franchise and diminishes the voting power of United States citizens." All but six House Democrats voted against adding that language.[10] You don't have to be a genius to figure this one out. They fight every day, in every venue, to make sure illegals have the right to vote.

It's not even about party anymore. They're all about ideology, not country. Their decisions are based upon ideology alone. They are bloated with political disregard for the American people. God help the United States of America.

The Can Stops Here

By May 2019, President Trump had had enough. The resist-at-all-cost Democrats and all-talk-no-action Republicans had exhausted his patience. So, he became the first president in modern history to actually *do something* about the crisis on our southern border. For thirty years, we'd listened to a lot of talk but seen zero action. Republican politicians raised plenty of money telling us they'd make this a priority and then kicked the can down the road once they got into office. Well, to paraphrase Harry Truman, President Trump decided the can stops here.

Finally, we have a president who is willing to put his political future and his legacy on the line to keep his promise to secure our borders. That's the difference between an outsider, owned by no one, who came to Washington to serve the public, and a politician only interested in getting reelected and serving himself.

The president had been asking Mexico to assist in holding back the influx. Mexico talked a good game, but did nothing. On May 30, President Trump released an official White House statement telling Mexico they were out of time. He basically told them to do something about the flood of immigrants using their country as a staging ground to invade ours or pay the consequences.[11]

He wrote, "As everyone knows, the United States of America has been invaded by hundreds of thousands of people coming through Mexico and entering our country illegally. This sustained influx of illegal aliens has profound consequences on every aspect of our national life—overwhelming our schools, overcrowding our hospitals, draining our welfare system, and causing untold amounts of crime."[12]

I couldn't have said it better myself.

The president told Mexico that if it did not take drastic steps to get their horrific immigration issues under control, there would be a series of tariffs implemented on "all goods imported from Mexico," and that these tariffs would only be lifted if "the illegal migration crisis is alleviated through effective actions taken by Mexico."[13] That night on Twitter, the president gave a hard deadline of Monday, June 10. If Mexico did not take appropriate action by that day, a 5 percent tariff would go into effect, rising an additional 5 percent for every month Mexico failed to take serious and effective action. Tariffs were scheduled to go up to 25 percent by October 1, 2019, if necessary. It was put-up-or-pay-up time for our southern neighbor.

As usual, the so-called Resistance went into overdrive. God forbid a president do something about immigration that actually works. The *New York Times* fired the first shot in a fake news broadside with an article that included a long quote from one of their loony Leftist staff economists calling the president's move "a colossal blunder."[14]

Really, *New York Times*? You mean like when you lined up a hundred experts who all told us that Hillary Clinton had the easiest path to the White House in decades?[15] Or when you ran with the Russia collusion delusion on the front page for months, despite knowing exactly how false the entire narrative was from the beginning? Or maybe when you were forced to retract your bombshell story condemning Brett Kavanaugh, a decent man and honorable judge whose only crime was being appointed by Donald J. Trump, because you didn't have your facts straight?[16]

That kind of blunder?

The Failing Gray Lady wasn't alone. Within hours, the *Wall Street Journal*, the *Washington Post*, and Politico had all published editorials denouncing the president's move. Not that I believe the president ever doubted he was doing the right thing, but there is no better indicator than the fake news brigade. How many times do these people have to commit 100 percent against the president and be proven 100 percent wrong before opening their mouths?

The fake news didn't get it, but Mexican President Andrés Manuel López Obrador did. Every year, Mexico relies on the money it makes from exports—a whopping 79 percent of which goes to consumers in the United States—for just over three-quarters of its GDP.[17] Almost every peso they make starts out as a dollar from the wallets of hardworking Americans in cities and towns all over the United States. The tariffs President Trump put on the negotiating table would have meant a big chunk of that money drying up overnight. This was not a hit Mexico could afford to take and President Trump knew it. So did President Obrador.

The message from President Trump to his Mexican counterpart was as clear as a shot of good tequila: either stop the flow of illegal immigrants, including those who are rapists, criminals, drug dealers, and their drugs, from coming across our borders, Señor Obrador, or *we* stop the flow of cash that you need to stay in office!

That, folks, is called pressure, and no one knows how to apply it better than Donald Trump, our dealmaker in chief.

He laid out the terms to Mexico in a way that was fair, even-handed, and just ruthless enough to let them know he meant business. There was no doubt in anyone's mind that if Mexico decided not to buckle down and get serious about their immigration crisis, President Trump would have let his tariffs go into effect and upped the pressure until they did. When you've got a man who's sharpened his skills in the brutal world of New York City real estate going up against a career bureaucrat from some proto-communist hellhole, it's barely a fair fight. And Mexico's president knew it.

Still, this move posed an enormous political risk to the president. Every day that his threat of tariffs went unaddressed by the Mexican government, another op-ed or speech came out denouncing his strategy. CNBC called it "dangerous" for the economy.[18] Former New York City mayor and failed presidential candidate Michael Bloomberg called it "dangerous and disturbing" in Bloomberg News.[19]

Some people can't accept or admit Donald Trump's policies are working. When will they see this president knows how to win? You don't need a PhD in economics to know one thing for sure: when a president's policies result in the lowest unemployment rate in the history of the United States, create over two million new jobs in three years, and send the stock market straight up while the Federal Reserve is *raising* interest rates, the guy deserves some room to maneuver.[20] If you don't understand what he's doing, keep your mouth shut and your eyes and ears open. You just might learn something.

No matter how many times the president's successes prove that good advice, nobody takes it, often not even members of his own party. For days after his Mexican tariff announcement, many Republicans—even those who had worked closely with him, some as advisers—warned against implementing tariffs. Even Steve Mnuchin and Robert Lighthizer expressed dissatisfaction with it.[21]

Rather than presenting a united front, skittish Republicans scattered like a bunch of frightened mice when the going got tough. Republican politicians were afraid of pushback from their constituents if President Trump had been forced to implement tariffs on Mexico. Sometimes, I think they'd be willing to welcome every convicted rapist and member of MS-13 from Central America into this country with open arms, and treat them to a free continental breakfast, rather than risk losing an election or their precious fund-raising opportunities.

For them, illegal immigration is a talking point, something they can exploit for money and votes during the next election cycle. For President Trump, it's about saving our country.

Why do you think he made illegal immigration such a major point of his announcement speech in 2015? The Left wants you to believe it's because he's a racist who hates anyone whose skin color is different from his. But anyone who knows him knows this is a lie. You need only spend five minutes with the man to know he doesn't have a racist bone in his body.

He told the truth about illegal immigration for the same reason he ran for president in the first place: because it was a serious threat to our country. Donald Trump watched presidents from both parties promise to get tough with Mexico and fix this calamity for decades, but no one stepped up. George H. W. Bush couldn't get it done. The immigration rate soared on his watch.[22] Clinton did nothing either; perhaps he was prescient and knew his wife would need their votes when she ran for president.

By the time Barack Obama took office, it was as if we had stopped trying altogether. Out of one side of his mouth he promised to secure the border and allowed his administration to deport close to three million people in reportedly inhumane ways, more than any president in the history of this country.[23] Out of the other, he told future illegals they had nothing to lose entering our country illegally by promoting radical legislation such as the DREAM Act, which gave amnesty to children whose parents had broken the law by entering the country illegally, without any corresponding legislation to secure the border and stop creating new DREAMers.[24]

From 2014 to 2015, America saw a huge influx of young males from Central America enter our country through Mexico at Obama's invitation, when he told them to come and apply for refugee status.[25] Throughout this period, members of violent street gangs and drug cartels streamed into this country. MS-13 gang members came over as unaccompanied minors and helped establish dangerous cells of that gang in our nation's neighborhoods.[26] They brought crime, drugs, and untold amounts of violence to the streets of our nation's once-safe suburbs.

Obama's party benefits from illegal immigration at the polls, both from the illegals themselves voting fraudulently and their children, granted citizenship automatically, even though their parents broke the law coming here. It's win-win for the Left.

Until Donald Trump upped the ante with the threat of tariffs, Mexico had no respect for Washington, DC. After all the empty threats during the Bush, Obama, and previous administrations, it's no wonder they believed Donald Trump was bluffing. But on the Friday before Trump's deadline, with the first 5 percent tariff just three days away and the president leaving for England for a state visit with the royal family, it finally dawned on Mexico that Trump wasn't bluffing.

In desperation, delegates from the Mexican government traveled to Washington and started working out the terms of an agreement. Cool as a cucumber, President Trump did not cancel or even delay his state visit to Europe for these negotiations. That told Mexico he wasn't desperate. Never let them see you sweat. As far as the president was concerned, the tariffs were fine with him.

Guess who blinked first.

Just before the president's deadline, the United States and Mexico came to an agreement. The United States agreed not to impose tariffs—yet—in exchange for Mexico doing the following:

- Send 6,000 Mexican National Guard troops up to the country's border with Guatemala, where they would patrol for people leaving the country illegally.
- Allow asylum seekers to wait in Mexico while their immigration claims were processed, instead of waiting in the United States.
- Expand the implementation of the Migrant Protection Protocol, also known as the "Remain in Mexico Plan," which provides incentives for migrants to stay in Mexico instead of crossing the border.[27]

Finally, Mexico had been forced to act. For years they had been ignoring the problem, counting the money they were raking in from exports to the United States, as well as money sent back home by illegals working here, and letting US law enforcement clean up their immigration mess. And why not? For them, it made perfect sense. Why send their military to the border when the United States was patrolling it with their own border agents, spending millions of dollars a year to make sure migrants who'd come through Mexico couldn't get across? Why waste any resources at all with the United States footing the bill? Like so many of our so-called allies, Mexico had been taking advantage of the United States for too long. President Trump made it as clear to the Mexicans as he made it to our NATO allies: those days are over.

The Do-Nothing Congress—Fire Them All

You may be wondering why I made no mention of the role played by the fine men and women in Congress in this stunning foreign policy achievement. It's simple. They had no role. Throughout the entire negotiation, only a few Republicans in Congress lifted a finger to support their president. They were happy to let Trump go into the fight alone, then jump on board the ship of success or castigate him if he failed.

Do nothings and cowards all. I ask again, what are we paying these people for?

Well, I shouldn't say they did *nothing*. While the president was negotiating with Mexico, the Democrat House voted on two bills they thought were important. There was even one about illegal immigration.

On June 4, 2019, they voted on a bill that would allow full amnesty to about 2.5 million DREAMers, after rejecting a similar offer from President Trump just a few months earlier.[28] They passed the bill days before the deadline to undercut the president. Congress knew damn well what they were doing. While President Trump was telling Mexico that we would no longer be pushed around, Congress sent an invitation to push us around even more—and even harder.

Oh, and they moved forward with one more piece of legislation that day: one that would give them—get this—a pay raise![29]

Can you believe the gall of these people? It's one thing to throw your constituents under the bus and do nothing about illegal immigration—or anything else for that matter—purely because you hate the president. It's quite another to ask for a *raise* for doing nothing! Have they no shame at all?

If anything, these people should get a pay cut. Or, maybe we should pay them by the hour, based on the hours they actually spend working instead of promoting hoaxes, going on junkets, and trying to destroy the president. I'd say someone should pass a bill that pays them based on how many bills they pass, but they probably couldn't get *that* passed either!

The far-Left House will pass anything they think will expand their power, no matter what it does to the country. It doesn't matter if it's sanctuary cities, prison voting, or a bill to confiscate every gun in the United States. But when it comes to supporting anything the president does, no matter how much *good* it will do for the country, forget it.

When Nancy Pelosi was asked about President Trump's successful border agreement with Mexico on immigration, she brushed it off as nothing, parroting her pals in the liberal media by calling President Trump "reckless."[30]

Nancy, I've got news for you. You and your Democrat gang are the reckless ones. Taking a vacation to Hawaii during the longest partial government shutdown in American history?

That's reckless. Opening the door for gang members and drug dealers to come in and declare open season on American citizens? *That,* Madam Speaker, is reckless. What President Trump did was bold and good for America.

President Trump built a multibillion-dollar business largely because of his negotiating skills. He literally wrote the book on negotiation. It was a number-one *New York Times* best-seller called *The Art of the Deal.* When he brings pressure in a negotiation, it's not reckless. Unlike Congress with its 20 percent approval rating,[31] he knows what he is doing.

Think of it in terms of sports, Nancy. If you or I were to suit up during a playoff game and go running across Giants Stadium with a football under our arms, that would be reckless. We aren't professional football players. We don't know how to protect the ball or outrun defenders. Like almost anything your party is doing now, it would end badly.

But when Saquon Barkley tucks the ball and runs, it's not reckless. It's just the opposite. It's a skilled professional doing what he's supposed to do. Is there some risk? Sure. But his team usually wins when he takes risks, just as America does when Donald Trump takes them.

So, the next time you're sitting with your feet up in Hawaii watching your president make "reckless" moves on television, maybe stop and think about it before you open your mouth. President Trump has been making deals since before you started running unopposed for the safest Democrat seat in the country. He knows what to offer, what to threaten, what to give up, and when. You, as I'm sure you've realized by now, do not. So, either get on board and help President Trump fix the country, if only for the sake of your own constituents, or get out of the people's

House and make your schoolyard taunts from the sidewalks of that liberal hellhole you represent. Just watch out for the human feces and used needles.

Either put up or shut up, Nancy. We're all getting tired of listening to you.

If you ask me, we should fire the whole lot of these lazy, entitled blowhards and see how they hack it in the real world, where results matter and "resistance" gets you nowhere. I don't imagine they would last very long.

A Tale of Two Immigrants

I'm going to tell you about two immigrants who came to live in the United States. You tell me which one you think Nancy Pelosi, Chuck Schumer, and the rest of the radical liberals in Congress care more about.

The first one, Immigrant A, is an aspiring doctor from El Salvador. From the time he was old enough to work, he saved his money. Eventually, he applied for a student visa and used it to attend college in the United States. He did well in school, applied for and received an extension on his visa to go to an American medical school. After graduating, he got his dream job at an American hospital, which sponsored his application for a green card. Immigrant A hired a lawyer at his own expense, learned the English language and our nation's history, and filled out every form required of him by our government agencies. He took the citizenship test and agreed to pay taxes to our government. It took almost a decade, but in the end, Immigrant A became a US citizen at a swearing-in ceremony in front of a judge. He now contributes enormously to America, economically and otherwise.

Both when I was district attorney in Westchester, New York, and as Westchester County court judge, I had the privilege of watching hundreds, if not thousands of hardworking men and women like Immigrant A stand up and take their oaths of citizenship. It was a great honor to watch people, some with tears in their eyes and lumps in their throats, recite the Pledge of Allegiance for the first time as US citizens.

I always knew that they appreciated the awesome responsibilities that come with being a citizen of the United States. If they hadn't understood those responsibilities, they wouldn't have been there to be naturalized. When I hear the word *immigrant*, these are the people I think of. The hard workers, the strivers, the people who pay their own way, respect our flag, and follow the law to achieve the American dream.

Now let me tell you about Immigrant B. He grew up a few streets away from Immigrant A. Back in El Salvador, while A is studying and saving his money, B is hanging out in the streets and selling drugs. He joins a gang called MS-13 and is regularly involved in violent confrontations. One day, when he's about fourteen years old, Immigrant B is smuggled into the United States in a trailer. When he gets to a small community in Long Island called Brentwood, he doesn't attempt to learn English or the norms of behavior in the United States. He simply shows up at the local high school in town, which is legally required to register him and place him in classes. They provide teachers who speak to him in Spanish.

He's one of many undocumented immigrants at the school and starts making trouble. He and his buddies from MS-13 start terrorizing innocent people. Sometime in the spring of 2017, he gets into an argument with four guys he mistakenly believes are part of a rival gang. A few weeks later, he plots to kill all four of those young men. He and three friends lure them into the forest and cut them with machetes. No one discovers the bodies until months later, when police find them in the woods outside an abandoned psychiatric hospital—a place locals have nicknamed "the killing fields" because of all the bodies of MS-13 victims that are found there.

Sadly, that second story is not a hypothetical. It really happened. It's the story of Josue Portillo, an eighteen-year-old undocumented immigrant who came to the United States from El Salvador as a child, and then enrolled in Brentwood High School on Long Island.[32] Too often, these savage gang members are enrolled in school with our children and commit horrible acts of violence like this. In 2016 and 2017 alone, MS-13 was responsible for twenty-eight murders, mostly of young people. It was only when President Trump got tough on the gang at the end of 2017 that the violence declined. In 2018 and 2019, the number of murders linked to MS-13 on Long Island fell almost to zero.[33]

And yet these are the very people our Congress voted to protect on June 4, 2019. They think it's more important to extend protections to people whose very first act on American soil was a violation of our laws than it is to make it easier for people who come to this country legally, who want to work and do things the right way. Right now, when Immigrant B enters this country illegally, everything is provided for him. If he doesn't have a place to stay, we give him one. If he doesn't have food, we give him that, too. We provide shelter and transportation and lawyers and free health care because we feel it's our "duty" as Americans.

Why do we have a duty to Immigrant B that we don't have to Immigrant A? They both came from the same circumstances, yet we roll out the red carpet for violent, law-breaking Immigrant B, while law-abiding, productive Immigrant A has to work for everything, just like the rest of us.

Am I missing something?

When Congress allows a doctor or a lawyer to work at the border helping illegals, the money to pay that person isn't coming out of *their* pockets. It's coming out of yours and mine—the pockets of Americans—natural born and legal immigrants—who go to work and pay their taxes and follow the law. It's not Washington elites who are hurt by illegal immigration. The only times *they* interact with illegals are when they tip their maids and limo drivers at Christmas.

The people hurt by illegal immigration are those who have their children in schools with the children of illegals, who get half the education they would otherwise because the teacher has to slow down and teach every lesson in English and Spanish. They must pay double the taxes for half the benefit because illegals are sucking resources from our already strained welfare system, while paying *nothing* into it. And they are the ones whose children will be hurt when we allow violent gangs to walk off the streets of their violent home countries and straight into once safe suburban neighborhoods. Do you think the parents of Nisa Mickens and Kayla Cuevas, who were both murdered by MS-13,[34] give a damn about making sure illegal aliens are treated with respect at the border after breaking our laws? Or do you think they'd rather have their daughters back?

The same goes for the families of Paige Gomer, Jessica Wilson, Pierce Corcoran, and countless others.[35] Although the rest of the world, especially Washington, DC, seems to have forgotten their names, I certainly haven't. I've actually prosecuted homicides committed by MS-13 when I was the sitting District Attorney in Westchester County. Let me be clear about how I feel about them. They are animals, pure and simple. The president was right. These are people who have to murder someone in order to become a member of MS-13. They murder them in front of other members to make sure they can become part of the brotherhood. These are not the kinds of people we want in the United States. It is a guarantee that they will kill someone. And in sentencing these violent criminals, I've called them animals, for which I was made accountable as a sitting judge. I don't much care. That's what they are. They don't deserve to be here. *They're* the ones who deserve to be locked up in cages where they belong.

The memories of Nisa Mickens, Kayla Cuevas, Paige Gomert, Jessica Wilson, Pierce Corcoran, and countless others should be a reminder to everyone about the true costs of illegal immigration, and what happens when we put politics and optics above national security and justice. It's no wonder that when the Angel Moms went to Capitol Hill hoping for a meeting with Nancy Pelosi and the Democrats, they were turned away and made to sit in the halls in silence.[36]

If I were Nancy Pelosi, I wouldn't be able to look them in the eye, either.

Let me be clear. I am not suggesting that all or even most illegals are criminals. In truth, many of them come to work and enjoy the American dream. Many of them are educated here and go on to be successful members of society. What I am saying is that until we vet the people coming in or at the very least prevent them from being released into the interior of this nation until we do so, we will continue to read about cases like Immigrant B.

In addition, I am not suggesting everyone coming across the border is necessarily from Central America or Mexico. In a two-week period, more than 740 individuals from African nations were apprehended in the Del Rio, Texas, section alone.[37] Families from Brazil, Nicaragua, Ecuador, Peru, Romania, and Vietnam are taking the same pathways as migrants from Central America and taking advantage of legal loopholes in our system.

Fake News Sleight of Hand

Just like the magician who waves his left hand dramatically in the air to distract you from seeing the coin or red rubber ball he's deftly hiding in his right, the Democrats use outrage over nonissues to distract us from the realities of illegal immigration. It's not the mothers of people killed by illegal immigrants the Democrats and the media want you to focus on. After all, if we *did* focus on those people, and the real human toll that illegal immigration takes on our country, we'd throw every Democrat in Congress out on the street the next day.

Instead, the Democrats cook up fake scandals and distort the truth to keep people's attention focused on the empty hand, while they hide destruction of our communities up their sleeves. The Trump administration "keeping kids in cages" and "separating families at the border" is a perfect example. The fact that Obama did the same thing does not affect them in the slightest.

Separating immigrant children from the adults they are traveling with if the adults are detained is required by law. The

1997 Flores Settlement, the resolution of the *Flores v. Reno* case, requires children be placed in a different facility when the adults they are with are apprehended crossing the border. Within twenty days of apprehension, the children must be moved to a nonsecure, licensed facility. The intent of the law is to release the children from immigration detention without unnecessary delay. But the settlement has created a myriad of problems by forcing the government to separate children from their parents.

The president tried to get out from under that decree, issuing an executive order that would have allowed children to remain with their parents indefinitely. Los Angeles–based US District Court Judge Dolly Gee rejected the White House's request to alter the agreement.[38] So, the administration was forced to return to the Flores requirement.

All these are complicated issues that will continue to create chaos and havoc at the border as our agents are overwhelmed with the influx of children and minors. Until Congress is willing to do something—anything—to resolve this, everyone loses.

If an unaccompanied minor or a family with minor children is caught coming into the country illegally it is inevitable that they will be released. Under our law they cannot be housed long enough to wait for an immigration judge to determine if their refugee or asylum claim is legitimate. That could take as long as two years. So, they are boarded on vans and buses, as I'm sure you've seen on television.

Where are they going? They're headed to the interior of the United States, to a town, village, or city near you. They are not tracked; they are not monitored; they're simply politely asked to return for their court hearing. Do they? Not most of them. Ninety percent don't bother to return.[39] As a result, deportation orders are issued for their removal from the United States.

So, while the Left bemoans illegals hiding in the shadows, one need only ask who, if anyone, forced them there. The answer is obvious.

The agency charged with the job of removing those against whom an order of deportation has been lodged is Immigration and Customs Enforcement (ICE). The Left has recently been promoting the abolition of this agency. Many running for president, including Kirsten Gillibrand and Kamala Harris, as well as several in Congress, including Alexandria Ocasio-Cortez (she's running for House idiot), want this agency eliminated. But why are so many hell-bent on abolishing ICE while no one talks about abolishing US Border Patrol, USBP? Part of it is the different roles each agency plays in immigration enforcement. USBP is supposed to be charged with apprehending illegal aliens while they are attempting to enter the country. In reality, they're relegated to catching, counting, accommodating, and then releasing them into the interior. Fifty percent of USBP personnel are routinely pulled from their duties to perform babysitting and social service duties for illegals, and then they must release them into the interior. The Left isn't worried about USBP being stuck changing diapers.

ICE, on the other hand, is charged with enforcing our customs and immigration laws in the interior of the country. ICE arrests those against whom deportation orders are issued and literally deports them. That's why radicals in Congress want to defund ICE. They want those illegals here to vote and remake America, without gerrymandering, without redistricting, and without changing any laws. Just let them in and they'll vote Democrat.

Major ICE raids were scheduled to take place across the country, commencing on June 23 of this year under Acting Director Mark Morgan, a former chief of the El Paso FBI Office, USBP chief, and marine. A last-minute halt was put on these raids hours before they were scheduled to begin because Nancy Pelosi asked the president for a two-week delay, ostensibly to get Congress to do in that time what it hasn't been able to do since 1986.[40]

Do I have any hope that Nancy Pelosi will really try to get Congress to actually work on a bill that will resolve the immigration problem? No. Less than two weeks earlier, Pelosi said she wanted to see the president in prison. The Democrats have no plan to stop the immigration flow into the country. Their mantra: Trump is a racist for not letting everyone in.

But the president did the right thing by agreeing to a delay and giving them the opportunity to try to work something out. It was a gracious move that showed he's willing to give Congress a chance to do their job. In the end it will be the president who will resolve the border problem, just as he leveraged Mexico with tariffs.

CHAPTER NINE

The Radicals' Revenge
Now They're Getting Downright Nasty

The Democrats came into 2019 with Nancy Pelosi swinging her gavel like an executioner's hatchet, looking to decapitate the First Amendment with the inaugural bill introduced during her historic second speakership. The Democrats introduced articles of impeachment against President Trump based on . . . well, I suppose Nancy would say we have to impeach the president to find out why we did it. Representatives Brad Sherman, Al Green, and Steve Cohen actually introduced three different resolutions containing articles of impeachment. And one congresswoman, apparently with nothing else to contribute, simply provided foul language.

Newly elected congresswoman Rashida Tlaib, who just hours after the honor of being sworn into the United States

Congress, had this to spew: "And when your son looks at you and says, 'Mama look, you won. Bullies don't win,' and I said, 'Baby, they don't,' because we're gonna go in there and we're going to impeach the motherf****r."[1]

So, our country gives her parents the opportunity to start a new life in America with all its advantages, protections, and privileges, unlike anything they experienced in Palestine. And her first act after running for US Congress and winning a seat in that hallowed chamber, the people's House, is to curse out the president of the United States in words too foul to print but apparently okay for her to say in front of her nine-year-old son, promising the president's impeachment with absolutely no facts to support the charge?

So much for the Constitution she'd just sworn to uphold. I'd like Rashida to show me where in the Constitution it says you can impeach a president just because you hate him. Apparently, Rashida believes reducing unemployment to its lowest level in almost fifty years[2] is a "high crime" and signing historic tax reform a "misdemeanor."

The greatest nation on earth, through its largesse, opened its doors and laid out the welcome mat for her mother and father, who I'm sure thanked God when they got here, and she gets to the national stage and calls the president a motherf****r in a public forum, demanding impeachment? Who is this person?

Nevertheless, she has promised to vote against all US military aid to America's close ally Israel, because they "discriminate" against Palestinians. Discriminate? Is she kidding? Defending themselves against missiles launched into their cities is not "discrimination."

If the congresswoman doesn't like Israel, I have a suggestion for her. When the Palestinians and the PLO cease their attacks on Israel, then we won't need to send Israel money. And in case she has forgotten, Hamas is a designated terrorist organization that was birthed in Palestine. Is she really against racism or just Israel? Like her friend Linda Sarsour, does she want Israel eliminated from the river to the sea?

Although Rashida is ethnically Palestinian, and they may have been cheering her and waving flags for her in the Palestinian territories,[3] she is an American citizen elected to the US Congress. Her job, instead of cursing out the president of the United States and threatening to impeach him on day one, is to represent Americans, not Palestinians.

A primer for Congresswoman Tlaib: do what you were elected to do; stand up for your country and your constituents, Americans. Americans want a strong economy, so they can get jobs, put food on their tables, and pay their rent or mortgages. They want safety and security for their families. They want the law to be applied equally with no one above it and no one below it. Your constituents want legislators who will work toward these goals and not waste time or taxpayer dollars engaging in personal vendettas against the president.

But the hypocrisy is not just yours, Congresswoman. It's your party's new MO! They talked a good game while campaigning: civility, working together for the American people. They said they wouldn't focus on hate. Yet, what was their first order of business on their inaugural day as the majority party in the House? Reintroduce articles of impeachment, previously introduced during President Trump's first year in office.

Democrat Congressman Brad Sherman of California wasted no time introducing articles of impeachment against the president,[4] at the same time we got the best jobs report this country has seen in nearly a decade.[5]

Rashida, you call him a "motherf****r" because you don't like the way he talks? Yet, you don't have the guts to follow through with your claim. When you're confronted by the press, you whimper and run away from the media. The president is improving the economy, making us safer and, yes, building a wall. And you want to impeach him. Is this what we can look forward to for the next two years?

Representative Tlaib avoided reporters after her crude outburst. Did incoming Speaker of the House Nancy Pelosi rein her in? Pelosi's response, "I'm not in the censorship business," leads me to believe the civility promise was dead on arrival.[6]

Nancy, are you kidding? Bill number one on your agenda as speaker is your party's so-called For the People Act, which not only includes support for a constitutional amendment to overturn the historic Citizens United Supreme Court decision, but also funnels taxpayer money to your preferred candidates.[7] The Citizens United decision was not about empowering corporations, it was about protecting free speech. As Justice Anthony Kennedy wrote in the majority opinion of that decision, "If the First Amendment has any force, it prohibits Congress from fining or jailing citizens, or associations of citizens, for simply engaging in political speech."[8]

So, you're not in the censorship business when it comes to liberals, but for conservatives it's a different story, right? Nancy is willing to abolish the First Amendment if it might benefit Republicans or conservatives.

It's not even as if corporate money always goes to Republicans. In 2016, six times more corporate money went to Hillary Clinton than to Donald Trump.[9] The Democrats just don't want any donations going to Republicans at all. They'd make the whole country a one-party state like California, if they could get away with it.

Pelosi has been agitating for a constitutional amendment to overturn Citizens United since 2012.[10] In other words, she wants to abolish the First Amendment. The free speech clause was written specifically to empower political speech. Campaign contributions are political speech, as is refusing to contribute to political campaigns and refusing to vote. The Democrats want to bring the heavy hand of government upon all of the above.

The bill would not only make the First Amendment a dead letter, it would attack states' prerogatives under our federal system by taking away their districting power and hand it to "independent commissions." In other words, liberal bureaucracies. It would also intrude heavily into the business processes of social media companies such as Facebook and Google, under the pretense of preventing the insignificant political ad purchases by foreign governments the Democrats and their Deep State friends have exaggerated into the Russia collusion hoax.[11]

The First Amendment isn't the only part of the Constitution in the Democrats' crosshairs. Pelosi's fellow Democrat, Steve Cohen of Tennessee, has already introduced a constitutional amendment to eliminate the Electoral College.[12] His bill also contains a provision prohibiting the president from pardoning himself. Both are radical changes to the structure of our Constitution, the framework that has sustained America for 230 years. Of course, some Democrats don't just want to change the Constitution; they're thinking about getting rid of it. In an interview with the *Washington Post*, Beto O'Rourke had this to say:

> Can an empire like ours with military presence in over 170 countries around the globe, with trading relationships . . . and security agreements in every continent, can it still be managed by the same principles that were set down 230-plus years ago?[13]

Under the guise of innocuous-sounding words like *campaign finance reform* and *fighting corruption*, the Democrats are willing to neuter the First Amendment; fundamentally change our federal system by eliminating the Electoral College and taking away powers reserved for the states; alter the balance of power between branches of government as delegated in the Constitution; and further invade the realm of private business. All to see that neither Donald Trump nor anyone like him ever gets elected again. They just can't bear the thought of anyone opposing their rule, least of all President Trump or his "deplorable" supporters.

Off with Their Heads!

Appearing on CNN January 2, 2019, Nancy Pelosi's daughter, filmmaker Alexandra Pelosi, was asked to comment on her mother's second stint as speaker of the House.[14] "How does she approach meetings with President Trump, A," asked host John Berman, "and B, just what are your feelings about this person, whom you know quite well, becoming Speaker of the House for a second time?"

Alexandra answered, "She'll cut your head off and you won't even know you're bleeding. That's all you need to know about her. No one ever won betting against Nancy Pelosi."

I'm not sure if the decapitation reference was in answer to the A or B part of the question, or both, but it got my attention. I don't want to make too much of this passing comment, which seemed lighthearted enough in the context of the whole interview. Yet, I can't help noticing the connection to comedian Kathy Griffin's infamous photo showing her holding the bloody, severed head of Donald Trump.[15]

Although she apologized for her actions, once it became apparent to Griffin that her "sincere" apology wasn't going to save her job at CNN or her career in general, she rescinded her apology, while throwing f-bombs at not only the president, but also his whole family.[16] So, she's standing by the original message she sent, something even the women on *The View* recognized could prompt a second Secret Service investigation.

It started almost immediately after President Trump was sworn in. During the summer of 2017, Johnny Depp joked about assassinating the president on foreign soil, during an appearance in Glastonbury, United Kingdom. He was there to introduce a screening of his 2004 movie, *The Libertine*, but couldn't resist hauling forth with opinions on President Trump. "When was the last time an actor assassinated a president?" Depp asked a cheering crowd. He went on to add, "I want to clarify, I am not an actor. I lie for a living. However, it has been a while and maybe it is time."[17] It's become downright fashionable among prominent liberals to muse aloud about assassinating the president, with nary a peep from the Left-wing media.

The Public Theater in New York City got into the assassination meme act that same summer, putting on a Shakespeare in the Park performance of *Julius Caesar* in which the titular character is redone as Donald Trump, while Caesar's wife Calpurnia is played as Melania.[18] The play ends as Shakespeare wrote it, of course, only this time the audience is treated to seeing a man who looks like and is dressed like the president brutally murdered by his senators.

I did a "Street Justice" segment in Central Park, questioning people about the blatant depiction of Donald Trump being assassinated. Like the "Street Justice" segment near NYU campus, asking students about conservativism, we were made to feel extremely uncomfortable and people were very reluctant to talk to us.

The Public Theater is an organization that has received over $30 million in taxpayer funds since 2009, including federal money.[19] That means that even if you don't live in New York City or New York State, your tax dollars were used to fund this shameful display.

Last September, as ninety-five-year-old actress Carole Cook was leaving a restaurant in West Hollywood, California, she was asked her thoughts about an audience member holding up a "Trump 2020" sign during a performance of *Frozen*. Her reply? "Where's John Wilkes Booth when you need him?"[20]

A month later, actress Ellen Barkin replied to a tweet showing the president interacting with a hostile reporter, saying, "This man should be removed . . . and not just from office."[21] Apparently, the president's assassination wouldn't satisfy this disturbed person's thirst for blood. On New Year's Eve, Barkin added that she hoped comedian Louis C.K. got raped and shot,[22] presumably as vigilante justice for the sexual misconduct the comedian admitted to in 2017.

Can you imagine what would happen to a conservative talking like this about Barack Obama? About anyone? No, you can't. Conservatives don't talk this way. Sure, there are a few yahoos in every movement, including the conservative movement. But I'm not talking about a few loser keyboard warriors on the Internet peddling shock. I'm talking for the most part about well-known celebrities and persons who have a national or global platform. People who are listened to and whom we all used to think had a responsibility not to abuse that platform.

It isn't just liberals in the entertainment industry, either. Former prosecutor, US senator and 2020 presidential candidate Kamala Harris made a joke about killing either President Trump, Vice President Mike Pence, or Attorney General Jeff Sessions, while appearing on *The Ellen DeGeneres Show*. Asked by DeGeneres, "If you had to be stuck in an elevator with either President Trump, Mike Pence, or Jeff Sessions, who would it be?" Harris replied, "Does one of us have to come out alive?" Which is nonsense when you think about it. Harris punctuated her morbid musing with an evil cackle worthy of Hillary Clinton.[23] DeGeneres and the crowd gleefully joined in.

Democrat state senator Maria Chappelle-Nadal joined the violent chorus and she wasn't even joking. Chappelle-Nadal responded to a post on her Facebook page suggesting Vice President Mike Pence would try to oust Trump from office with "I hope Trump is assassinated!"[24]

Leftists don't limit "assassination humor" to the president. They also directed this vile form of intimidation at Representative Steve Scalise during a debate the congressman was having with newly elected congresswoman Alexandria Ocasio-Cortez. The two legislators were having an honest discussion about taxes, when some of Ocasio-Cortez's followers began making light of Scalise's brush with death at the hands of unhinged gunman James Hodgkinson, who opened fire on the Republican Congressional baseball team. "Snipe his a—," tweeted one Ocasio-Cortez supporter, while another responded, "She's got better aim than James Hodgkinson, that's for sure." A third added, "Kick his cane."[25]

Many opposed Barack Obama's presidency, as did I, but it never even entered my mind to joke about assassinating him. Nor did I ever hear anyone else joke about assassinating him. Who are these people? These radicals like to repeat the vapid phrase, "We oppose hate," but their whole philosophy is built upon it. They seethe with anger at everyone they imagine is oppressing them and revel in thoughts of murder, mayhem, and destruction.

This underlying rage permeates their movement and inspires real violence. Hate is hate. Hate leads to violence. Violence leads to retaliation, which ultimately leads to community unrest. And that, my friends, is the radical Left's playbook to remake America.

I'm not talking about lone wolf, mentally ill gunmen such as James Hodgkinson, who opened fire on the Republican congressional baseball team back in 2017 after asking a bystander if they were Democrats or Republicans. There are people like that from all parts of the political spectrum. I'm talking about organized movements, like Antifa, whose stated raison d'être is to commit violence against anyone they deem a "fascist." I'm talking about well-educated Democrat politicians who rationalize violent action and rhetoric when they know better. But, in their minds, the ends justify the means.

I'm talking about a corrupt national media who ignore or rationalize intimidating tactics like these, while twisting the often innocuous words of conservatives into weeklong outrage fests.

There is no conservative equivalent of Antifa, just as you've never seen a mob of conservative college students storm into a lecture hall and shout down or chase out a liberal speaker or attempt to burn down the building, for that matter. You didn't hear prominent conservatives joking about assassinating Barack Obama and you don't see mobs of conservative activists storming buildings, blocking highways, or "occupying" private property.

This contempt for the fundamentals of civilized society— property rights, the rule of law, nonaggression—is written into the Left's DNA. And if you thought what you saw after Donald Trump's election or during the run up to the 2018 midterm elections was bad, just wait until election season 2020.

More Than Words

I know it might be tempting to write off some of this as hyperbole. Certainly, Johnny Depp wouldn't scare anyone who has dealt with some of the rough customers I've sent to the slammer. But the haters are not all pretty-boy actors and pampered limousine liberals. There is a violent element among the far Left that hasn't been afraid to put the violent rhetoric into action.

I'm sure you remember the street violence perpetrated against Trump supporters during the 2016 campaign. As just one example of many, "protestors" at a Trump campaign rally in San Jose, California, jumped on cars, threw eggs and water balloons at Trump supporters, stole their signs and "Make America Great Again" (MAGA) hats, and even physically assaulted some of them. Many of these so-called protestors were carrying the flags of other countries.[26] When the violence is perpetrated against Trump supporters, the perpetrators are called "protestors."

Well, three years later, nothing has changed. A man simply standing in his yard watching fireworks on the Fourth of July was assaulted by a man driving down the street who took issue with the Trump flag the man had on his lawn. The driver ordered the man to take down the flag. When the man refused, the driver punched him. The victim hit back in self-defense and the driver sped off with the victim's arm inside the car, dragging him over thirty feet.[27]

A few months later, a Washington State Trump supporter's truck was vandalized with spray paint and then firebombed while parked outside a bar, apparently because it was adorned with Trump 2020 bumper stickers. The man had had a few drinks and did the responsible thing by taking an Uber home. He'd left his truck under a streetlamp, thinking it would be safe there overnight. When he returned the next morning, his truck was nothing more than a burned-out shell with "Trump" spray-painted in white letters across the driver's side. A neighbor who lives near the bar heard and felt the explosion.[28]

Even Left-wing women are feeling empowered to imitate the behavior of violent activists. Earlier this year, Rosiane Santos was caught on video swatting the MAGA hat off a male patron in a Massachusetts diner, right in front of four police officers. The allegedly intoxicated woman was not only arrested, but it turned out Santos, originally from Brazil, was living in the US "without documentation." Now, she's facing deportation. Rosi, what makes you think you can menace a patron in a diner in front of four cops when you're illegal and not expect to be deported?[29]

As bad as these violent attacks by individuals may be, the organized violence that pervades the twenty-first century Left is even more disturbing. As far back as Obama's second term, we've increasingly seen what the liberal media call "protests" erupt into full-scale riots, sometimes leaving whole sections of towns in ashes.

The Democrats are determined to erase this country's borders, eager to welcome millions of illegal immigrants they hope will someday show up in the voting booths, voting Democrat as most immigrants do. To that end, they've been campaigning on abolishing Immigration and Customs Enforcement (ICE), the federal agency charged with enforcing our immigration laws regarding people already in the United States (the US Border Patrol is a separate entity, charged with patrolling the borders by Customs and Border Protection). They've gone so far as to compare ICE to the Ku Klux Klan, an outrageous charge that US Senator Kamala Harris of California nevertheless repeated during a confirmation hearing held by the Senate Homeland Security and Governmental Affairs Committee.[30]

Harris dignifying that slander in the hallowed halls of the US Senate was bad enough, but the far-Left terrorist group Antifa took it up several more levels. First, a prominent member of the group "doxed" 1,600 ICE employees, which means he published personal, identifying information about the employees, in this case their home addresses.[31] In case you're wondering what kind of person would do something like this, which has the potential for untold acts of violence against people he never met, let me fill you in. Antifa got the database, compiled from the employees' LinkedIn accounts, from a New York University professor named Sam Lavigne, a far-Left artist and game designer.[32]

As I said before, this is not some mentally ill loner taking psychotropic drugs. This is a person who teaches students at a prestigious university. This is what is deemed an acceptable political tactic by the Left, all the while implying it is Trump supporters who are violent, in the absence of any evidence whatsoever.

Professors like him have certainly done a good job indoctrinating students with their poisonous ideas. Not only did a Texas student group called Autonomous Student Network—Austin (ASN) tweet out ICE employees' personal information, they walked the line between protected political speech and incitement to violence with statements like, "Beware of these scum & encourage them to get out of the city & quiet [sic] their jobs if you see them."[33] I'm sure they're hoping for their followers to "encourage" their targets with lively debate. And if you believe that . . .

These lovely youngsters also regularly encourage their followers to "spread anarchy" and "live communism!" I don't know if they've studied the history of communism and are consciously emulating their heroes or if they are just demonstrating the violence that naturally springs from this horrible ideology. Either way, it seems the Left's legacy of violence is secured for at least one more generation.

Usually, Antifa's violent nature is not so subtle. It was on display again last December when a gang of approximately twelve men and women assaulted two marines whom they mistakenly thought had participated in a "We the People" rally in Old City, Philadelphia.[34] Two of the thugs asked the marines if they were "Proud Boys," one of the groups that organized the rally. The Proud Boys are a right-wing organization founded by Gavin McInnes whom the Left considers neo-fascist, a hate group, etc., although the group disputes those characterizations. When one of the marines replied that he didn't know what the name meant, the whole gang jumped them, kicking them, punching them, and spraying them with mace.

Oh, they also hurled racial slurs at the two marines, who are both Hispanic. I suppose when you wear a marine uniform, racism against you is okay.

There is no end of rationalizing, apologizing, and outright misreporting Left-wing mob violence as "peaceful protests." Marching through the streets of Portland last summer to protest ICE, chanting, "Whose streets? Our streets!" Antifa protestors broke the law with impunity, pounding on passing cars, blocking traffic, and harassing bystanders. They were protected by the local police, despite chanting, "A-C-A-B! All cops are bastards!"[35]

All this happened in a midterm election year. It was just a warm-up for what we're going to see going into the 2020 presidential election. The grassroots Left will continue to show its true, violent colors while its leaders and the media rationalize the violence away.

Chapter Ten

Resisting Reality
Media Madness

The Left-wing media is by no means immune to the rest of their movement's incivility. We've grown accustomed to the news being fake in the Age of Trump, but as 2019 began, they added a new wrinkle: downright maliciousness. An example of this was the way a group of teenagers from Covington Catholic High School were treated.

Because there are no consequences to journalistic untruths, the media simply goes from one fake news story to the next. Before getting to the Covington media farce, it should be noted that it happened only one day after another media farce so outrageous that even Bob Mueller issued a statement to correct it. Mueller made a rare statement to the media refuting the fake news story by that paragon of journalism, BuzzFeed.[1]

Following up on their disgraceful publication of the infamous, fake Trump "dossier," BuzzFeed ran a story on January 17 claiming federal officials had told them the president's former personal attorney, Michael Cohen, had informed the special counsel that the president had directed him to lie to Congress.[2] Here was yet another "smoking gun" that would finally validate the Left's insane Russian collusion delusion and end the presidency that has unhinged so many millions of Leftists.

The Left-wing media joyously jumped on the so-called breaking news. MSNBC's Ali Velshi immediately brought one of the reporters who wrote it on the air, calling the story "strong reporting."[3] Chuck Todd told NBC's *Today*, "You can't overstate how significant this development is, with the caveat 'if true.'" CNN's John Berman said the news was so big he almost spilled his coffee.[4]

You could almost hear the impeachment parties being planned in newsrooms, Hollywood dressing rooms, and university professors' lounges all over America.

There was only one problem; it wasn't true. For Robert Mueller to feel compelled to make a statement correcting the report tells you how far from the truth the report was, which was confirmed later when Cohen himself testified to Congress that Trump never instructed him to lie to them.

Now, one would think having a story they just ran with reckless abandon blow up in their faces would inject a little humility into even the arrogant finger-waggers who inhabit national newsrooms. One might assume that if another negative story about Trump or his supporters started circulating the very next day, which fit the media's own anti-Trump narrative just a little too perfectly not to invite suspicion, that they may have taken a breath before running with another fake report.

Nope. Not even twenty-fours hours after Mueller killed the BuzzFeed story, the media were at it again, breathlessly reporting a completely false story about some Catholic high school boys who attended a pro-life rally in Washington, DC.

Media Child Abuse

Let me start with what was initially reported. Carefully edited videos showed an elderly Native American man beating on a drum in front of a smiling teenage boy, surrounded by other boys who appeared to be about his age. One of the boys begins clapping along with the drumbeat. Several others eventually begin singing along. Most of the initial videos were thirty seconds to a minute long and none showed how the Native American man came to be among the crowd of teenage boys.

It appeared that a lone, elderly Native American was being surrounded by mostly white teenagers having a good old time while wearing red "Make America Great Again" hats, which completely short-circuited the truth and whatever journalistic integrity the liberal media had left. Without stopping to check any facts and apparently not at all curious about how the elderly Native American man came to be beating a drum a few inches from a teenage boy's face, they unleashed a venomous fake news tsunami against the boys. According to the media, the boys— since they were wearing MAGA hats—epitomized the racism, insensitivity, and hatred of all things right and good harbored by anyone who supports President Trump.

Why check the story when you can just make one up?

The fake news media set out to do precisely that after that video went viral. Early reports portrayed the event as if the elderly Native American, Nathan Phillips, was marching in an indigenous people's march toward the Lincoln Memorial when the boys, who had participated in a March for Life event earlier that day, "swarmed" around him and began taunting him. Immediately, the image of Phillips heroically playing his drum while a "smirking," MAGA hat-wearing Nicholas Sandmann stares him down became ubiquitous.

The reaction from the Left on social media was swift, hateful, and often violent. Trevor Noah said, "Everyone that sees that smug look wants to punch that kid."[5] CNN's Bakari Sellers also mused that, "Some ppl can also be punched in the face," in a since-deleted tweet.[6] Reza Aslan, whose Trump Derangement Syndrome was too severe even for CNN,[7] tweeted rhetorically, "Honest question. Have you ever seen a more punchable face than this kid's?"[8] As of this writing, that tweet still hasn't been deleted nor has Aslan's account been suspended.

It didn't take long for the fake news to reach the boys' high school and Catholic diocese. Even they issued a joint statement condemning the boys' actions, apologizing to Phillips, and promising an investigation and appropriate action "up to and including expulsion."[9] The *Chicago Tribune* gleefully reported that sad real news along with plenty of fake news, including that the boys "surrounded" Nathan Phillips and his associates, "laughing and jeering." It uncritically repeated Phillips's claim the boys were chanting, "Build that wall, build that wall," which video evidence showed they never chanted once.[10]

In addition to referring to the boys as "jeering and disrespectful" and repeating the false claims the boys chanted, "Build that wall," the *Washington Post* repeated Phillips's further false claim that the boys had blocked his path to the Lincoln Memorial. Phillips, who in later videos was seen walking a clear path up the center of the stairs to the memorial and into the group of boys waiting for their bus, went on to say, "He just blocked my way and wouldn't allow me to retreat."[11]

The *Post* printed this claim, apparently without even bothering to check it. They've since updated that story online to include an editor's note amounting to a complete retraction, linking to several subsequent articles that grudgingly report at least some of the truth of what happened. I say "grudgingly" because even after extensive video of what really happened that day was available to everyone, the *Post* still headlined their supposed mea culpa, "Viral Standoff Between a Tribal Elder and a High Schooler Is More Complicated Than It First Seemed."[12]

It's not complicated. It's quite simple. The original story wasn't just inaccurate; it was the opposite of what really happened. It was the boys who were subjected to racially motivated taunts. It was political activist Nathan Phillips, who I'll get to in a minute, who initiated the incident. It was the Covington Catholic School boys who tried to defuse the situation. At least 99 percent of everything reported, tweeted, and otherwise disseminated on January 19 was false. It was politically motivated fake news, the result of devious dishonesty by some, and rats-in-the-attic derangement by others. And it brutally victimized innocent teenage boys who emerged as the real heroes of this story.

So, what really happened? It wasn't the boys or Nathan Phillips, but a hateful group of political/religious activists called the Black Hebrew Israelites. They didn't just taunt the students; they launched invective at the Native Americans as well. Apparently, one of the beliefs this group holds is that both they and the Native Americans are descendants of the ancient Israelites, the latter having turned away from worshipping

Yahweh. They jeered the Native Americans for "worshipping totem poles" and shouted that God had taken away their land here in America as punishment.

They then turned their attention toward the Covington boys and became even more abusive. They called the boys crackers, pedophiles, and "incest kids." At one point, one of them derisively shouted, "you give faggots rights," prompting a loud chorus of boos from the boys.[13] These Black Hebrew Israelites were adult men not only shouting obscenities and other ugly epithets at teenage boys, but clearly trying to instigate a physical confrontation with them.

The boys, according to Nicholas Sandmann's statement, then obtained permission from their adult chaperone to engage in "school spirit chants to counter the hateful things that were being shouted at our group."[14] They didn't chant "Build the wall" as Nathan Phillips would later claim. In fact, they chanted no political statements whatsoever. Their chants were the garden variety school spirit cheers you'd hear at any high school basketball game.

Gee, I wonder why the Catholic diocese didn't at least talk to the chaperone and get their facts straight before they issued their "politically correct" apology.

Do you remember any condemnation by the media of this racist, homophobic, potentially violent hate group the Black Hebrew Israelites? Neither do I. To this day, the media are still trying to assign some culpability *to the victims* of this vile harassment, rather than the perpetrators. The video clearly shows the boys booing the Black Hebrew Israelites' homophobic epithets, yet it is the boys who are still considered bigots by the devious and the deranged.

Let's turn our attention now to Nathan Phillips, the central figure in this liberal media propaganda effort. On the day of the incident, Phillips was portrayed as a hero by virtually every so-called journalist who reported on this story. He was incorrectly called a Vietnam veteran, based on his statement, "You know, I'm from Vietnam times. I'm what they call a recon ranger." But Phillips was never actually deployed to Vietnam.[15] I'm not sure if Phillips was being intentionally misleading on this point, but that's only the tip of the iceberg.

Phillips originally claimed he was trying to get to the Lincoln Memorial when he was "swarmed" by the Covington boys. He said Sandmann blocked his path and he was unable to either continue to the memorial or retreat. "He just blocked my way and wouldn't allow me to retreat," said Phillips.[16] Those were both outright lies. The boys didn't swarm Phillips; he marched into them and up to Sandmann, who never made a single move toward him. Neither did anyone prevent Phillips from leaving.

When video evidence clearly exposed his lie, he changed his story. Story number two was that he was intervening between the Covington boys and the Black Hebrew Israelites—to protect the Black Hebrew Israelites! He actually had the gall to claim the teenage boys, who were waiting for their bus, were attacking the grown men who were hurling vile, racist, homophobic, and threatening insults at them. "These young men were beastly and these old black individuals was their prey, and I stood in between them and so they needed their pounds of flesh and they were looking at me for that," Phillips said.[17]

Now, as a prosecutor hypothetically interviewing Phillips for possible action in this case, red flags would have been waving everywhere the minute Phillips changed his story in such a substantive way. First, he says he was trying to get to the Lincoln Memorial and was stopped by boys who swarmed him and prevented him from either continuing or leaving. Then, when video evidence showed that wasn't remotely true, he claims he approached the boys to protect another group from them. I would immediately start challenging Phillips at that point.

Real journalists would have done the same thing. They're supposed to dispassionately seek the truth, not promote political narratives that fly in its face. Yet, for days after Phillips blatantly changed a crucial part of his story, the media went right on uncritically portraying him as a stoic hero who faced down Trump-supporting, privileged, white racists.

Not only did Nathan Phillips lie repeatedly about what happened, he refused to call off his cynical attack on the boys even when confronted with his lies. When Nicholas Sandmann put out his statement on the incident—a statement his Catholic diocese finally concluded was "consistent with videos," prompting their apology to Sandmann and his fellow students for their initial reaction[18]—Phillips had the temerity to double down and call for the students' expulsion from school. "For the students, I was against any expulsions, but now I have to revisit that," he said.[19]

Four days after the incident, when anyone interested could have seen extensive video that clearly shows the students' story is true and Phillips' story is false, the producers of NBC's *Today* just couldn't bring themselves to let go of the false narrative. Even while showing clips of the Black Hebrew Israelites hurling hateful invective at the boys and Nathan Phillips clearly going out of his way to approach the boys, contrary to his initial story, *Today*'s Savannah Guthrie still questioned Sandmann as if he were the defendant in a criminal trial.

"Do you feel, from this experience, that you owe anybody an apology? Do you see your own fault in any way?" she asked.[20] When Sandmann said he didn't, Guthrie went on to question him on whether he thought it was a bad idea for the boys to "chant back," which is a misleading characterization of their response. She asked Sandmann if he heard any of his fellow schoolmates yell, "Build the wall," even though her own voice-over reporting said NBC had reviewed all available video and could not find any evidence anyone yelled that "hot button phrase."

One might be inclined to defend Guthrie as simply doing hard-nosed reporting, even given she was questioning a sixteen-year-old kid like he was on the stand for murder. But that goes out the window when one watches her subsequent interview with Phillips the next day. Gone is the ominous lighting and the grave tone of voice. Guthrie opens the interview with a smile on her face, as if greeting a friend who just got out of the hospital:

> First of all, first question, how are you doing? This has been a whirlwind few days for you. You find yourself on the front page of every newspaper. How are you doing and how are you feeling?[21]

Guthrie went on to ask Phillips how he felt about Sandmann's statement, whether he thought Sandmann should apologize, and allowed him to clarify his military service record. At no time did she challenge either of Phillips's two self-contradictory accounts of what happened. Never did she intimate that Sandmann's account of the incident matched the videos, while neither Phillips's first story nor his second did so.

What happened to the hard-nosed reporter?

Even assuming the worst of the liberal media, it's hard to come up with an explanation for how this story has been treated. It would seem against their own interests, no matter how much they might hate President Trump and his supporters, to go on clinging to a narrative that is so flatly contradicted by extensive video evidence. Let's not forget that it is swing voters, those not deeply committed to either side, who decide elections. Aren't they worried they will turn off potential anti-Trump voters by so persuasively confirming the president's claims that the news is fake?

It may be that they just can't help themselves. The Left is so deeply rooted in identity politics that even incontrovertible evidence they see with their own eyes has no effect. Unable to even think about Sandmann, Phillips, or the Black Hebrew Israelites as individuals, but only as members of privileged or victimized groups, respectively, they can't bring themselves to even consider that Phillips might be a liar, the Black Hebrew Israelites might be racists, or Sandmann might be completely blameless in this affair. Those results just won't compute for them, no matter how many hours of video they watch, no matter how much evidence is presented.

Sandmann has filed lawsuits against CNN, the *Washington Post*, and NBC/MSNBC. The lawsuit against CNN claims the network "aired four defamatory" broadcasts and nine online articles falsely accusing Sandmann, 16, and his classmates of "engaging in racist conduct."[22] That's legalese for running fake news stories that may have permanently damaged the reputation of a sixteen-year-old kid. His suits against the other networks claim similar torts.

I do a lot of traveling, speaking before large groups on a variety of issues, talking about my books and making on-location appearances for my television show, *Justice with Judge Jeanine*. No matter where I go, there is always somebody accusing President Trump and even his supporters of racism. It is insulting to all of us.

The word *racism* has a definition. According to Merriam-Webster, it is "a belief that race is the primary determinant of human traits and capacities and that racial differences produce an inherent superiority of a particular race."[23] You may also hear talking heads say it is "judging people solely by their immutable characteristics," which means basically the same thing.

Newsflash: the way the mainstream media and political Left reacted to the Lincoln Memorial incident was racist in the true sense of the word. They assumed the boys were guilty and the Black Hebrew Israelites and Nathan Phillips were innocent based solely on their respective races, and many continued to do so even when presented with incontrovertible video evidence that they had the story wrong.

Compare their behavior to any of the statements President Trump has made, going all the way back to his famous announcement in 2015, after riding down the escalator in Trump Tower. What did he say? "They're not sending their best."[24] That statement explicitly acknowledges that not all people from Latin America in general or Mexico in particular are the same. In fact, he wasn't even talking about all Mexicans or even all Mexican immigrants. He was talking about the subset of Mexican immigrants who choose to enter the country illegally. And even among that small subgroup, he said he assumed some were good people.

Calling those statements racist is akin to George Orwell's famous "War Is Peace, Freedom Is Slavery, Ignorance Is Strength," statements written on the Ministry of Truth in *1984*. It is not hyperbole to say that's what the Left-wing media have become in this country, a Ministry of Truth, whose purpose is to distort and destroy the truth to further a political agenda.

The Fake "Lynching"

Well, at least after running wild with two straight fake news stories in the same week, the media showed some restraint in taking a story that fit their anti-Trump narrative too perfectly at face value, right? Certainly, even dishonest but self-interested Leftist news reporters would have enough sense to not put themselves in the same position of having to retract demonstrably inaccurate reporting for a third time in the same month, would they?

Never say never. Just eleven days after publicly botching the Covington High School story and less than two weeks after running with the fake Cohen story, the media and Left-wing allies did it again. Jussie Smollett made his now infamous call to the police and the media swallowed his story hook, line, and sinker. Not only did they again wrongly assume white Trump supporters had victimized a member of a minority group, they doubled down. They didn't just call it an assault, or a possible hate crime, but a "lynching."

A *USA Today* headline proclaimed, "Assault on 'Empire' Actor Jussie Smollett Serves as Reminder—Lynching, Noose Symbolism Still Prevalent."[25] Really? Prevalent? The story says that doing a web search on the word *noose* returned—gasp!—18 results. Now, of course if any of those were genuine incidents in which a noose was used to intimidate or threaten a black person —or anyone, for that matter—I condemn it with all my heart. In fact, as a prosecutor, hate crimes specifically infuriated me. As District Attorney, I not only prosecuted them with a vengeance, I fought for a hate crimes law in New York and was present with the governor when he actually signed the law. I also testified before Congress on the ripple effect that hate crimes have throughout a community. As we now know, Smollett's allegations turned out to be a hoax and, unfortunately, hate crime hoaxes have become a cottage industry in the Age of Trump. The Daily Caller compiled a list of almost two dozen of them since 2016.[26]

More important, this particular hoax should have sent up red flags immediately to any competent journalist, regardless of his or her political beliefs. First, you have an attack that occurs in the wee hours of the morning when temperatures were well below zero. Even given that Smollett had reported receiving a threatening letter prior to the attack, is it plausible that his supposed attackers would be waiting outside his apartment in subzero weather just in case he decided to get a sandwich at 2 a.m.?

Not only were these supposed "rednecks" impervious to extreme cold, they had no sense of subtlety whatsoever. They were reported to have yelled "This is MAGA country" while assaulting Smollett. That was very convenient, as was his being on his cell phone to his manager just as the attack occurred, allowing his manager to hear the damning words identifying the assailants as the evil, racist, homophobic deplorables the Left considers all Trump supporters to be.

I don't necessarily blame CNN for its initial reporting on the day after Smollett made his report. They were basically relaying what police were saying about the incident, including that it was being investigated as a possible hate crime. But even that first report contained some red flags. Even though the area around Smollett's apartment had "a very high density of city and private surveillance cameras," according to Chicago police spokesman Anthony Guglielmi, and the police had, by the time CNN reported the story, "canvassed and reviewed hundreds of hours of video" and no evidence of Smollett's assailants had been found.

They initially didn't even find any evidence of Smollett himself, other than an image of him standing alone inside a Subway restaurant nearby. Later, they were able to find video of most of Smollett's trip to and from the Subway, which cast even more doubt on his story. How likely is it that with a plethora of cameras in the neighborhood, which captured him going to and from the sub shop, that he would be attacked during the brief moments he was not recorded on surveillance cameras?

Apparently, this did not give anyone in the media pause. I would have been intensely questioning Smollett about those details even if I were intending to prosecute on his behalf. Why don't security cameras show any evidence of the attack, Jussie? How do you explain your invisible attackers? These are the kinds of questions I'd expect from defense counsel for anyone accused of perpetrating this assault. They're also the kinds of questions real journalists ask when they haven't made up their minds about what happened before they start investigating.

Instead, the American public was treated to actress Ellen Page's melodramatic diatribe on *The Late Show with Stephen Colbert*, during which she blamed—surprise, surprise—President Trump, although she also "connected the dots" to

Vice President Mike Pence, presumably because of his previous opposition to gay marriage.[27] Page failed to assign any responsibility to Barack Obama or Hillary Clinton, both of whom opposed gay marriage just two elections ago in 2008.[28]

Meanwhile, back here in that rapidly vanishing space we call "reality," some of us had our doubts about the whole thing right from the start. Just two days after the initial reports of the assault, I could already read between the lines of the police statements on the investigation. "We don't have anything that we've actually been able to view....He's a victim right now, and we'll treat him like a victim. He's been very cooperative, and we have no reason, at this point, to think that he's not being genuine with us," said Chicago Police Superintendent Eddie Johnson.[29]

That's a strange statement for a police superintendent to make. How did the idea Smollett *wasn't* being genuine get introduced? My prosecutor's instincts told me the police already had their doubts about Smollett's story, as any competent law enforcement officer would, but were probably too afraid to articulate them about a gay black man. That they possibly went on investigating a crime they believed never happened is a concern in and of itself. What if they had mistakenly arrested an innocent person?

A day earlier, Smollett had refused to hand his cell phone over to police, who were interested in establishing the precise time of the assault. Since Smollett claimed he was on the phone with his manager at the time he was attacked and his manager supposedly heard the attackers yelling racial and homophobic slurs, in addition to saying, "This is MAGA country," the contents of his phone constituted material evidence.

That would raise any law enforcement officer's or prosecutor's suspicions. Why would the victim of such a hateful crime want to withhold evidence that could help police find the perpetrators?

Smollett eventually gave the Chicago police "limited and redacted" phone records that were insufficient to verify he was talking to his manager at the time of the alleged attack.[30] We now know why he was so reluctant to hand over the records. The entire attack was a hoax, supposedly perpetrated by Smollett to leverage a higher salary from Fox for his job on the television show *Empire*.[31] But anyone who has watched the video of Smollett and Abel and Ola Osundairo, the two men he hired to help perpetrate the fake attack, can see at least part of the motivation was to smear Trump supporters.

While rehearsing the attack, Abel and Ola begin by rehearsing their lines without attempting to alter their Nigerian accents. Smollett scolds them, saying, "Guys, c'mon! The accent! More white, more racist, hillbilly." The brothers then repeat their lines in surprisingly convincing southern drawls, yelling racist and homophobic epithets and being sure to get in, "This is MAGA country."

At the time of this writing, the video of Smollet and the two brothers rehearsing the fake attack was widely available on independent YouTube channels, but no mainstream media outlet hosted it. That alone is a sad statement on the media. Hopefully, those interested in verifying my own reporting here on this incident won't find the videos of Smollett's rehearsal "disappeared" from the Internet, as so many conservative voices have been.

Of course, we all know the punch line to this very unamusing joke. After first charging Smollett with sixteen felony counts related to making a false report, the Cook County state's attorney's office eventually dropped all the charges against Smollett.[32] This was such a miscarriage of justice that even Rahm Emanuel was upset about it. The city of Chicago's law department has filed suit against Smollett demanding Smollett repay the city for the costs of investigating his phony crime.[33]

Interestingly, even State's Attorney for Cook County Kim Foxx, who recused herself from the case before charges were filed against Smollett, admits that dropping the charges did not amount to an exoneration of Smollett. "He has not been exonerated; he has not been found innocent," wrote Foxx in an op-ed attempting to justify her office's bizarre decision.[34] Foxx goes on to argue her office dropped the charges by measuring the seriousness of the crime against the likelihood of a conviction. Since when is a crime not serious when there is $130,000 of taxpayer dollars in overtime? It could have been worked on. How can you possibly say there is no likelihood of conviction when all evidence points to the suspect's guilt?

This trend of prosecutors deciding they won't charge someone with a crime but publicly commenting on the wrongdoing committed by the target is its own category of fake news. There is no "we will not indict, but . . ." You either have the evidence to charge someone or you don't. If you don't, you keep your mouth shut. The target is then put in the impossible position of fending off the public accusations of a prosecutor without the opportunity to present his case. This limbo was never anticipated by the framers of the Constitution.

I would like to point out the irony here in terms of how a liberal state's attorney's office in ultra-liberal Chicago treats an ultra-liberal celebrity suspect, whom we must legally presume innocent until proven guilty, but against whom there is ubiquitous video evidence of his obvious guilt all over the Internet, compared to how the president of the United States is being treated. Both men were investigated. In Smollett's case, the evidence of his guilt was overwhelming. Indictments on sixteen felonies were sought and obtained. Yet, he walks free and the national media is virtually silent, after having taken a tremendous interest in Smollett's case before they knew it was a hoax. In one of the few articles outside Chicago reporting on the charges being dropped, the *New York Times* ran an uncritical piece titled, "Jussie Smollett Charges Were Dropped Because Conviction Was Uncertain, Prosecutor Says."[35]

To be fair, this was a rather dry piece of news reporting, devoid of opinion one way or the other. That may be a first for the Failing Gray Lady since Trump was elected. Outside of this, there is nothing but crickets as far as commentary on Smollett's case. No outrage over video evidence of Smollett rehearsing his fake attack or over Smollett continuing to maintain his innocence!

There is still a chance justice will prevail in this case. Just before this book went to print, the *Times* again reported without fanfare that Judge Michael P. Toomin of the Circuit Court of Cook County ordered a special prosecutor be appointed to investigate the decision to drop the charges against Smollett, writing that it was something Foxx's office should have done before making that decision. The judge said Foxx created a "fic-

titious office" with "no legal existence" when she recused herself from the case and appointed her deputy, Joseph Magats, as
"acting state's attorney." [36]

Contrast that with the reaction to the Mueller report,
which found no evidence of the crime the special counsel was
created to investigate. After the report was made public and
the two-year long Russiagate collusion delusion was exposed,
the *New York Times* ran an article titled, "The Danger in Not
Impeaching Trump"[37] while *The Atlantic* mused in print, "To
impeach or not to impeach?"[38] Impeach for what?

Post–No Collusion Self-Delusion

It's one thing when politically motivated, compromised journalists lie to the public. We've had plenty of that in the Age
of Trump. But far worse is when the media lie to themselves
and may actually start believing their own hogwash. Given
the power media exercise over public opinion, that prospect is
downright terrifying.

One would think that after Mueller's report was publicly
known and Russiagate was exposed for the sham it was, the
media would have the good sense, even if purely self-interested,
to keep their mouths shut on the two years of lying they had
done to the American public. Their reaction was quite the opposite. Many of them are trying to argue the Mueller report shows
the reporting over the past two years has been mostly accurate!

"While there are a few exceptions, Mueller's investigation
repeatedly supports news reporting that was done on the Russia
probe over the last two years and details several instances where
the president and his team sought to mislead the public," writes

David Bauder of the Associated Press.[39] "The media looks a lot stronger today than it did before the release of this report," added Kyle Pope, editor of the *Columbia Journalism Review*.[40]

My favorite has to be the statement made by the commander in chief of fake news, Jake Tapper, on CNN's *State of the Union* show shortly after the report was made public. While engaging White House Chief of Staff Mick Mulvaney, Tapper had the gall to say, "I'm not sure what you're saying the media got wrong. The media reported the investigation was going on. Other than the people in the media on the Left, not on this network, I don't know anybody that got anything wrong."[41]

Jake, do you believe we're all that stupid or are you completely delusional? Your own network was peddling the collusion delusion practically to the day Mueller turned in his report. On January 8 of this year, CNN reporter Marshall Cohen claimed Paul Manafort's lawyers, "accidentally revealed on Tuesday the clearest public evidence of coordination between the campaign and Russians, adding new details to the murky mosaic of potential collusion in 2016—including sharing polling data with an alleged Russian operative."[42] The *Washington Post* claimed "The collusion case against Trump just got a lot stronger" the next day.[43]

A month earlier, CNN ran the story, "Trump Tries to Change the Story, but Russia Cloud Darkens," in which another CNN fake news specialist claimed routine investigative filings by the special counsel "increased the President's vulnerability and raised new questions about whether his campaign cooperated with a Russian election meddling effort."[44]

I could go on and on, but all of America knows the media overwhelmingly promoted the theory that President Trump or his campaign colluded, coordinated, or otherwise partic-ipated with the Russians in interfering in the 2016 election, a theory unambiguously discredited by the Mueller report. To now say the media didn't get anything wrong is worthy of sat-ire. If the potential consequences weren't so grave, it would be hilarious.

Believe it or not, there are a few voices on the Left who rec-ognize just how badly the media performed over the past few years. Glenn Greenwald, no fan of the president but intellectu-ally honest and a lawyer himself, had this to say:

> The two-pronged conspiracy theory that has domi-nated U.S. political discourse for almost three years—that (1) Trump, his family and his campaign conspired or coordinated with Russia to interfere in the 2016 elec-tion, and (2) Trump is beholden to Russian President Vladimir Putin—was not merely rejected today by the final report of Special Counsel Robert Mueller. It was obliterated: in an undeniable and definitive manner.[45]

Matt Taibbi at *Rolling Stone* has a similar observation in his piece titled, "The Press Will Learn Nothing from the Russiagate Fiasco." He writes,

> He didn't just "fail to establish" evidence of crime. His report is full of incredibly damning passages, like one about Russian officialdom's efforts to reach the Trump campaign after the election: "They appeared not to have preexisting contacts and struggled to connect with senior officials around the President-Elect."

Not only was there no "collusion," the two camps didn't even have each others' phone numbers![46]

Glenn and Matt, my hat is off to you both. We don't agree on much politically, but at least you have the integrity to acknowledge there is a problem in your own ranks. I wish I could say the same for the rest of the media, who continue to double down on disparaging the president and his supporters, no matter how badly their lies blow up in their faces.

If we can't get honesty from the media, is it too much to ask that they at least develop a healthy sense of shame?

CHAPTER ELEVEN

The Radicals' Attack on Life Itself

If you don't think they're trying to remake the America where the Founding Fathers declared everyone is entitled to life, liberty, and the pursuit of happiness (the operative word being *life*) then consider this: it is life that is at the center of the worst cultural shift our country has ever witnessed.

I'm talking about the legalization of infanticide—or, to put it in simpler terms—the intentional killing of full-term babies on demand, babies born alive who are then murdered or allowed to die on the mother's say-so. This means that the mother has the power to give a thumbs-up or thumbs-down, like an emperor in the Roman Coliseum, in deciding whether her baby lives or dies.

A Virginia bill, ultimately defeated in a House subcommittee 5-3, with all five Republicans voting to table it and all three Democrats voting against,[1] would have repealed most of that state's legal restrictions on abortions, allowing a woman to abort her baby right up to and including the time she goes into labor.[2] Aborting a pregnancy while a woman is in labor means the baby is going to be alive outside the womb before it is killed or allowed to die. The procedure was described by Virginia Governor Ralph Northam, a pediatric neurologist no less, who coldly detailed and defended the killing of babies after they're born. He said,

> If a mother's in labor, I can tell you exactly what would happen. The infant would be delivered, the infant would be kept comfortable, the infant would be resuscitated if that's what the mother and the family desired. And then a discussion would ensue between the physician and the mother.[3]

Now, he didn't say "how" but the meaning is clear. If the mother wants the baby dead and gone, the baby dies. By way of motivation, consider this: Governor Northam received nearly $2 million from Planned Parenthood.[4] He has since become involved in a blackface scandal for which he later apologized, but then took back his apology when he said it wasn't really him. He remains in the governor's mansion today.

I'm sure you remember those undercover films where the sale of baby parts is discussed by this same organization. Planned Parenthood denied it profited from such sales and a Texas federal court ruled in its favor, saying the state could not defund Planned Parenthood in its Medicaid program, based on the organization's claim the videos were deceptively edited or otherwise misleading. That ruling was trumpeted by the liberal media as a vindication of Planned Parenthood. The *Washington Post* declared there wasn't "a scintilla of evidence" of wrongdoing by Planned Parenthood while reporting on a federal judge blocking a Texas defunding effort.[5] "Judge Blocks Medicaid Cuts to Planned Parenthood in Texas," the *New York Times* gleefully reported.[6]

Well, this past January, the tables were turned. The Fifth Circuit Court of Appeals overturned that decision.[7] Among the bases for the court's ruling, it unambiguously stated, "the video was authentic and not deceptively edited."

Translation: it means what we saw on those videos was an accurate depiction of what was going on inside Planned Parenthood. The ruling also mentions parts of the video where officials at Planned Parenthood admitted to violating federal laws by altering the abortion procedure to allow for the harvesting of babies' organs to be sold for profit.[8]

The liberal media has such a resistance to the truth that they reported this with somewhat less fanfare and editorializing than they did the 2017 ruling. The case is being sent back to the district court to proceed based on the circuit court's ruling that the videos were accurate.

New York Joins the Seven Deadly States

Virginia isn't alone in seeking abortion up to the moment of birth and after. You can add New York to the list of states seeking to legalize infanticide. Its Reproductive Health Act (RHA), passed by the New York legislature and signed by Governor Andrew Cuomo on January 22, 2019, allows third-term abortions where a baby can be delivered full-term, born alive, and then allowed to die or worse.[9] There is a requirement, based on *Roe v. Wade*, that the woman's "health" be endangered for the abortion to be legal. And a subsequent SCOTUS decision (*Doe v. Bolton*) established "that the medical judgment may be exercised in the light of all factors—physical, emotional, psychological, familial, and the woman's age—relevant to the well-being of the patient. All these factors may relate to health. This allows the attending physician the room he needs to make his best medical judgment."[10]

In other words, a physician can decide an abortion meets *Roe v. Wade*'s standards for virtually any reason whatsoever, including "emotional factors." Think about how cheaply human life is valued when it can be snuffed out due to how a baby's life might make the mother feel. And let's be honest; this has nothing to do with women's health and everything to do with killing babies on demand. What ever happened to "safe, legal and *rare?*" The bill also makes it legal for nondoctors to perform abortions.

Governor Andrew Cuomo openly celebrated this government-sanctioned infanticide by lighting up New York's World Trade Center in pink.[11] Now, I've run for elected office five times and the one election I lost was against Andrew Cuomo. I've avoided criticizing him until now. But I can't remain silent about this. What he and those of his ilk were really celebrating are barbaric homicides where an entire class of helpless human beings, born alive, are not only denied equal protection under the law, but denied the even more basic, natural rights to life, liberty, and the pursuit of happiness. They celebrated killing innocent, helpless babies who enjoy less protection by the lawless Left than endangered species of turtles and caterpillars.

Anyone who can celebrate lethal violence against an innocent baby after it is born is a savage.

Governor Cuomo, what would your father, Governor Mario Cuomo, who was a godly man and whose political career was deeply informed by his Catholic faith, say if he were alive? And don't give me this hogwash or this endless list of possibilities that maybe the baby is deformed. There are so many tests—sonograms, amniocentesis, and much more—long before the thirty-eighth week. But you would celebrate the ideological justification to take the lives of innocent human beings with no requirement other than the "health" of the mother, which is defined so broadly that even emotional factors are relevant. They, too, are amorphously defined.

Sadly, seven other states and the District of Columbia already allowed these barbaric procedures before New York joined them this past January. For the unborn, these are the Seven Deadly States, where babies aren't safe even after they've left their mothers' bodies. New York is now the eighth and the governor of Rhode Island would like to see her state become the ninth. Rhode Island has a bill called the Reproductive Health Care Act that is substantially the same as New York's.[12]

Rhode Island's law is especially disheartening for two reasons. One, it has the full-throated support of Democrat Governor Gina Raimondo, nominally a Catholic, who not only supported the bill in her 2019 State of the State address, but doubled down on support on Twitter, writing, "I believe that no one should get in the middle of a decision between a woman and her doctor and that no woman should have to choose between health care and making ends meet. #RHCA."[13] This is the same governor who sends out cards to Rhode Island parents of newborn children calling each one "a special gift" that will fill the parents' home with joy. The card says "how concerned the governor is about the health" of each baby.[14]

Gina, are you kidding? You're concerned about the health of

newborn babies in your state, but you're trying to legalize killing them after they're born? How are they going to live healthy lives if they never make it out of the delivery room? You're either a hypocrite or deranged. Maybe you're both.

Rhode Island's bill also removes language from the state law that says, "human life commences at the instant of conception and that said human life at said instant of conception is a person within the language and meaning of the Fourteenth Amendment of the Constitution of the United States." That may seem moot since abortions are already legal in Rhode Island but remember that is only because their legality is imposed upon the state by *Roe v. Wade*. Removing this language paves the way for legalizing infanticide, even if *Roe v. Wade* is overturned.

I've prosecuted infanticide cases in my home state of New York where infants are killed intentionally. It's a homicide, folks, not an abortion. It's about the child's death and not the mother's reproductive health. If the mother is concerned about reproductive health, she should start with contraception and certainly not wait until the baby is born.

I wonder if Governor Cuomo is concerned that the homicide statute remains on the books in New York State. Article 125 of New York State's Penal Law defines a "person" as a human being who has been born and is alive.[15] It does not mention the word *person* in its definition of abortion or "abortional acts." The law considers an abortion "committed upon or with respect to a female . . . with intent to cause a miscarriage of such female."[16]

In other words, by adopting Article 125's definition of *person*, in the legal sense,[17] New York's RHA maintains it is illegal to kill a living baby outside the womb, even though it repeals the sections of Article 125, which previously criminalized abortion after the twenty-fourth week of pregnancy. So, a New York State physician who acts in the manner Virginia Governor Northam described regarding a baby born alive would be exposed to prosecution for killing a person, even though he had performed what the law now considers a legal abortion.

I don't think Governor Cuomo and his Left-loving cronies thought that one through. Ironically, we have "no-kill" cities, where animals will not be euthanized even if they're not adopted, and yet this horrifying trend concerning human babies continues. And don't bother calling me an animal hater—I've prosecuted animal cruelty cases in which animals were intentionally killed. Perpetrators can get a maximum of two years in jail! But it's not criminal to kill babies carried in the mother's womb for nine months or even born alive?

The Suddenly Silent Pope

Where is the Catholic Church on this? Certainly, the laity has responded as one would expect. Some are demanding Cuomo be excommunicated for his brazen assault on what they consider the sacred gift of life.[18] I remember when that wouldn't have been a debatable issue within the church, but New York's bishops are suddenly hesitant to stand up for this long-held church position where a liberal politician is concerned. Albany Bishop Edward Scharfenberger wrote an open letter to Governor Cuomo appealing to him as a Catholic who claimed to "stand with Pope Francis" not to support the RHA.[19] After Cuomo signed and celebrated the bill, Scharfenberger called excommunicating the governor a "last resort."[20]

With all due respect, Bishop Scharfenberger, a last resort after what? If gleefully ordering the World Trade Center and other public structures to be lit pink in celebration of killing babies is not egregious enough to warrant excommunication, what is? Will the governor have to publicly pledge his allegiance to Satan?

New York City Archbishop, Cardinal Timothy Dolan, was similarly reluctant. While joining Bishop Scharfenberger in condemning the law and its celebration by the governor, he called excommunicating Cuomo "counterproductive."[21] Cardinal Dolan argues Cuomo uses his dissent from Catholic Church teaching on issues like abortion as "applause lines."

Perhaps New York bishops are hesitant to take a stronger stand against the governor because of what Pope Francis has said about this law: nothing. We've got a Pope who's more worried about climate change and equal pay for women than attending to his own flock in the Middle East, where genocide against Christians occurs, or providing guidance to his bishops on an important issue like this one, even though he has been a vocal critic of abortion in the past.

As recently as June 2018, the Pope compared abortion to Nazi eugenics efforts, saying, "We do the same as the Nazis to maintain the purity of the race, but with white gloves on."[22] A few months later, he compared abortion to "hiring a hitman to resolve a problem."[23]

But when a popular and powerful Democrat politician not only signs, but celebrates a law allowing babies to be killed outside the womb, we hear nothing. This is a Pope who has had plenty to say in the past about political matters, including in this country. He's never missed an opportunity to promote socialism and attack capitalism, even authoring an apostolic exhortation on the subject. On President Trump's efforts to secure funding for a border wall, the Pope said earlier this year, "It is the fear that makes us crazy," the fear being of immigration.[24] Like all opponents of border security, the Pope did not distinguish between legal and illegal immigration.

Ironically, the same Pope called on followers just a few weeks later to pray to Saint Josephine Bakhita for an end to human trafficking.[25] I share his desire to see this horrible practice eliminated, which is why I support President Trump's border wall. Human trafficking is currently rampant across our southern border. I encourage prayer, but God helps those who help themselves. I have to think St. Josephine follows suit.

Capitalism, climate change, border security, the women's pay gap—Pope Francis has had plenty to say about American political issues throughout his tenure. But suddenly, when it comes to what has been arguably the most important political issue for the Church over the past several decades—an issue, unlike economics or climate science, which he is qualified to lead on—he is silent. And why? Could it be that it would require him to criticize a liberal Democrat, instead of a Republican politician?

The Catholic Church has lost enough credibility in the last few years for them to not step up in every pulpit and every church in this nation and implore their congregants to recognize the evil being committed. If they don't do this, then they are part of the problem. If you're Catholic, listen closely to what your priest says. Hopefully, he will talk about the evil that is occurring under the law across this country.

The Left's Changing Story

Twenty-three years ago, Bill Clinton said abortion should be "safe, legal, and rare."[26] His party agreed with him then, stating in the 1996 Democrat Party platform that its goal was to "make abortion less necessary and more rare, not more difficult and more dangerous." The platform went on to note the abortion rate was dropping at the time, that efforts to reduce unwanted pregnancies should be supported, and even called on Americans to "take personal responsibility to meet this important goal."[27]

There were Republicans who agreed with that concept of abortion. There were Republicans who were pro-choice, but it was rare to find a Republican who supported third-term abortions. In fact, 87 percent of Americans are against third-term abortions. The radicals are pushing past third-term abortion to out-and-out infanticide.

Today, there is a website called Shout Your Abortion.[28] Leftists today would probably consider the 1996 Democrat Party platform "hate speech" for suggesting an abortion might not be something to be shouted or celebrated. I'm not exaggerating; at a recent Shout Your Abortion event, actress Martha Plimpton told the audience she had her first abortion at the Seattle Planned Parenthood, punctuating her announcement by raising her arm and yelling, "Yaaaaay!" The audience cheered. Plimpton went on to say, "Notice I said first. And I don't want you guys to feel insecure. It was my best one. Heads and tails above the rest. If I could 'Yelp' review it I totally would."[29]

One might assume Democrat Party presidential hopefuls are taking a more moderate stance than Plimpton or governors Northam, Cuomo, and Raimondo. That would be assuming too much. For the most part, they've avoided commenting on the bill, even when asked directly. When Democrat presidential candidate and New York senator Kirsten Gillibrand was asked by the *Washington Post* if there should be any restrictions on late-term abortions, she replied, "There is zero place for politicians to be involved in these very complicated medical decisions, and they should only be made between a woman and her doctor—period, full stop."[30] Translation: She's not able to answer whether or not she believes a mother should be able to take a child's life. And she does a political two-step in talking about a doctor and a patient, when in truth it's about the law and the right to live pursuant to the Declaration of Independence. Zero place for politicians to be involved? Defending the right to life is the primary duty of politicians. And these are not complicated medical decisions. The decision to kill is not complicated.

That's about as much as anyone has been able to get out of the far-Left Democrats who have announced for president, which isn't surprising. Only 13 percent of Americans support abortion in the third trimester.[31] The Democrats are hoping they can avoid taking a position on this subject, leaving them free to support what New York is doing on a national level. They are devious in their derangement, aren't they?

In stark contrast, President Trump took an unambiguous stand against this horror in his State of the Union address earlier this year:

> There could be no greater contrast to the beautiful image of a mother holding her infant child than the chilling displays our nation saw in recent days. Lawmakers in New York cheered with delight upon the passage of legislation that would allow a baby to be ripped from

the mother's womb moments before birth. These are living, feeling, beautiful babies who will never get the chance to share their love and dreams with the world. And then, we had the case of the governor of Virginia where he basically stated he would execute a baby after birth.

To defend the dignity of every person, I am asking the Congress to pass legislation to prohibit the late-term abortion of children who can feel pain in the mother's womb.

Let us work together to build a culture that cherishes innocent life. And let us reaffirm a fundamental truth: all children—born and unborn—are made in the holy image of God.[32]

The president's thunderous statement begins very similarly to those cards Governor Raimondo of Rhode Island is sending to newborn mothers—but in the president's case, his actions match his words. As our founding document says, we are endowed by our Creator with an inalienable right to life, which governments are instituted to secure. The president is promising to do so; his opponents respond with eerie silence.

It's hard not to dismiss this insanity as fringe extremism that would never win elections, but it isn't. Like their calls to abolish ICE, eradicate the health insurance industry and replace it with "single payer," get rid of air travel as part of their Green New Deal, and a host of other anti-American positions, the Left has made celebrating abortion mainstream. The radicals continue to resist everything that has made America what it is in order to remake America into what they want. They've made abortion up to and including the moment of birth the law in eight states and they will make it the supreme law of the land if they get the White House and Congress together. That this could be our future is both heartbreaking and terrifying.

CHAPTER TWELVE

The Democrats' Siren Song of Socialism

We're reaching a turning point that will forever determine our future—how we live our lives and how our children will live theirs. The gap between the Left and the Right has never been wider. And yet, amazingly, it continues to widen. Every time we turn on the TV, open a laptop, or listen to the radio, another bizarre, offbeat, outlandish idea is being pushed by the Left to destroy capitalism and bring us closer to socialism.

You have a decision to make. Do you want to live in a country where no matter how hard you work, what you do, or how much you succeed, you simply won't improve your lot? Do you want to benefit from your own success or would you prefer the government take over and use your hard work to benefit everyone else?

Unfortunately, it's hard for many people to resist the siren song of socialism. I call it that because the Sirens in ancient Greek myth were female creatures who stood on the shore of their island and sang beautiful songs that sailors couldn't resist. But they only sang to lure sailors to doom on their rocky coast.

Socialism is like that beautiful song. As Dennis Prager, conservative radio talk show host, writer, and founder of PragerU, said on my show, "Socialism appeals to human nature. And the reason is this, and this is critical. Liberty is not what people most yearn for. People most yearn to be taken care of." The problem is, it doesn't work.

As Prager also observed, "There is only one economic system that has lifted humanity—and I mean the bulk of humanity—from poverty." And that is capitalism. Socialism creates no wealth. Only capitalism has created wealth. Poverty is the human norm. So, the only question intelligent people should ask is, "How has wealth ever been created? Not, "Why is there poverty?" Poverty is like air. It is there. The question is, "How do we create wealth?" Capitalism is the only answer, but who learns that? Who is going to teach that in schools today, given the indoctrination that has supplanted education in our schooling?

As part of their subversive "resistance" to President Trump, many on the lunatic Left have removed their moderate masks to show their true socialist colors. Whether they call themselves socialists or not, every one of the Democrat 2020 presidential candidates supports the Green New Deal proposed by a freshman congresswoman so knowledgeable about Washington that she thinks she went there to sign bills![1] Alexandria Ocasio-Cortez's (aka AOC) Green New Deal will literally pull planes out of the sky.

I suppose that's just fine with the Left, since they're happy with the influx coming in on foot through our southern border. No air travel required for them!

Green New Deal

This Green New Deal requires every building in America to be retrofitted for environmental reasons and high-speed rail developed to make air travel supposedly unnecessary.

My favorite part is where they seek a "net zero greenhouse gas" in ten years. Now, why net zero as opposed to just plain zero? The reason—and no, I'm not kidding—is they're not sure they'll be able to get rid of bovine flatulence. Yes, you understood correctly, they're worried about cows farting. These "emissions" from cows are a grave concern to the Left because they have an environmental impact. The methane gas produced by bovine flatulence is a greenhouse gas. I thought it was a farmhouse gas, but what do I know? Apparently, ol' Bessie's indigestion contributes to global warming.

Need I say more?

Modern Monetary Madness

Proponents of the Green New Deal and Medicare for All consider exploding deficits no big deal because—according to AOC—we can just print more money.[2] Yes, in addition to her other departures from reality, AOC subscribes to Modern Monetary Theory (MMT), a particularly bizarre corollary to the "deficits don't matter" fallacy used by politicians to rationalize their profligate spending.

According to this theory—or at least AOC's understanding of it, which may not be any better than her understanding of anything else—worrying about deficits is unnecessary. Because the government prints its own money, it should simply print enough to cover all the Democrats' programs. And if this causes inflation? Just raise taxes to "remove excess money" from the economy! Brilliant!

You know what, Congresswoman? You should have left your Monopoly game home when you came to Washington.

Look, I'm not an economist, but you don't have to be to know this theory is nonsense. No matter how they try to confuse you with this sort of mumbo-jumbo, the government can't legislate scarcity out of existence. Money is only a medium of exchange. No matter how the monetary system is configured, the amount of goods and services being produced is finite. Life in the real world means trade-offs.

Nothing the Democrats propose acknowledges this inescapable reality. Even under MMT, with the government printing the money instead of taxing or borrowing it, real resources are consumed, whether it's steel for a bridge to nowhere, food, clothing, and healthcare for illegal aliens, or construction labor and equipment to retrofit every building in the country, once those real resources are consumed, they are no longer available for someone else to use. All MMT does is obscure what is really going on: the government is deciding how scarce resources are to be exchanged and consumed, just like in the old Soviet Union or in Venezuela today. MMT attempts to obscure that reality with pseudo-economic sleight of hand.

Like all socialists, the Democrats promise you the world and tell you it won't cost you anything. That is why they're always talking about taxing the rich, even for amounts well in excess of 100 percent of their income. "I'm tired of freeloading billionaires," said Elizabeth Warren. Who are they freeloading from? The top one percent of income earners pay more than the bottom ninety percent combined. Who's freeloading from whom?[3]

Demagogues like Warren are always talking about the rich not paying their fair share to give their voters an excuse to loot them. They know there is a percentage of the population greedy enough not to care about the moral implications of using the government to steal for them and stupid enough to believe there is no downside.

Now, realistic people know that every dollar you take away from a rich job creator is a dollar they can't use to create a job. The Green New Deal promises to create government jobs, but those are jobs that don't provide more benefits to people than they cost. If they did, they would have been created in the private sector for profit. Besides, whenever the government does undertake to build something or "fix" something, it costs more and is far less efficient than when the private sector does it.

This is why we have a booming economy under Donald Trump, while we were supposed to be happy with 1 percent GDP growth under Obama. Even President Trump's infrastructure plan gets the private sector involved in rebuilding America. Only $200 billion of the estimated $2 trillion comes from the federal government.[4]

This is a plan that would actually work, as opposed to the Obama "stimulus" that built almost nothing with over $800 billion. Biden had the gall to brag about this "shovel-ready" disaster—and we know what they ended up shoveling—before joining his Democrat colleagues in calling the president names.

Besides childish name calling, the Democrats offer nothing but more cartoonish fantasy. When I say "cartoonish," I mean it literally. They construct a dreamworld for the slow-witted in which rich people "hoard" their wealth, like a wealthy person in a cartoon who has a room full of money and just rolls around in it all day. According to this childish fantasy, there is enough cash just sitting in the bank accounts of Jeff Bezos, Bill Gates, Warren Buffet, and other superrich businesspeople to pay for everything they propose, as if the rest of us should be their problem.

I have news for anyone who believes this nonsense. Jeff Bezos doesn't have $150 billion in cash in his bank account. Like most people who become rich by founding successful companies, his fortune is comprised mostly of stock in the company he created. It's the same for Bill Gates, Mark Zuckerberg, Larry Ellison, and the rest of those among the richest people in the world.

Their wealth is part of the market capitalization of companies that employ hundreds of thousands of people and provide valuable products to hundreds of millions. Now, you can try to tax those assets, as Elizabeth Warren has suggested, but there is a cost and not just to Bezos, Gates, and Ellison. If they must liquidate stock in the companies they created, not once but every year, it will shrink the market cap of those companies over time. That means that Amazon, Microsoft, and Oracle will not be worth as much, will not have as much capital to get loans, create jobs, and further innovate. That means fewer jobs for new people entering the workforce. This scheme will backfire on the people the Democrats say they want to help.

For economically ignorant leftists like Warren, this probably sounds like a value-added benefit to her confiscation scheme, because it will make big corporations smaller, thus moving toward more "equality." Warren claims to be a "capitalist to her bones,"[5] and, in her mind, making big corporations smaller probably promotes competition or "gives smaller firms a fair shot."

I have news for you, Liz, that isn't capitalism; it's socialism. I don't care what you think is in your bones, Native American or otherwise, artificially shrinking a company's size through confiscatory taxes has nothing to do with capitalism or competition. Increased competition is achieved by what Donald Trump has been doing: getting rid of outdated or otherwise useless regulations that create barriers to entry into the market for new businesses that can compete with the established giants. Those regulations create compliance costs that big, established companies can afford but new startups often can't.

A House Built on Lies

One of the more alarming developments in American politics over the past several years has been the rise in popularity of socialism with American voters, especially among young people. As recently as 2010, 68 percent of Americans aged eighteen to twenty-nine favored capitalism, while 51 percent said they approved of socialism. In a poll last summer, that same age group preferred socialism to capitalism by 51 percent to 45 percent.[6]

The same poll showed 57 percent of Democrats overall said they approved of socialism, while just 47 percent said they approved of capitalism. I hope President Trump was right when he said, "America will never be a socialist country," during his 2019 State of the Union speech. But one thing seems blatantly obvious: the Democrat Party has become a socialist party, whether their politicians admit it or not.

Of course, some of them do, notably Bernie Sanders, Alexandria Ocasio-Cortez, and Rashida Tlaib. However, most of the Democrats seeking the presidential nomination have tried to distance themselves from the socialist label. Like Elizabeth Warren, almost all the other candidates who have announced have proclaimed themselves capitalists.

"The people of New Hampshire will tell me what's required to compete in New Hampshire, but I will tell you I am not a democratic socialist," said Kamala Harris in February.[7] "I'm a capitalist," said Beto O'Rourke ten days later. "I don't see how we're able to meet any of the fundamental challenges that we have as a country without, in part, harnessing the power of the market. Climate change is the most immediate example of that."[8] Cory Booker says, "I am not for socialism. I am for capitalism,"[9] while Amy Klobuchar adds, "Put me down as a capitalist."

Elizabeth Warren, Kamala Harris, Beto O'Rourke, and the rest all say they're not socialists like Bernie, but most are on board with Medicare for All, free college, a Green New Deal, and the rest of Bernie's socialist policies. It's like someone saying I'm not an alcoholic but drinking a fifth of bourbon with every meal.

It's relatively easy to see through the Democrats when they say they're not socialists, but the lies don't end there. Literally everything they tell you about capitalism and socialism, who will pay for the programs they are running on and even the supposed distinction between "democratic socialism" and plain old socialism is a lie. Just as the architects of Obamacare lied to the American people, whom they considered "too stupid" to make an informed decision, the socialists, overt and covert, pushing this economic transformation are lying about what they're proposing.

Democratic Socialism

Bernie Sanders admits he's a socialist, although he pivoted away from answering Savannah Guthrie during the first Democrat debate when asked, "What is your response to those who say nominating a socialist would reelect Donald Trump?" Bernie also resorted to name-calling. One might think admitting he's a socialist makes him seem more honest, but he isn't. He tries to distinguish his brand of socialism from the one that killed hundreds of millions in the last century by calling it "democratic socialism." Bernie leads his deluded supporters to believe there were not elections in the Soviet Union, China under Mao, Cambodia under Pol Pot, or any of the other socialist nightmares of the twentieth century. There were. That was the whole problem.

Democracy in and of itself is no guarantee of freedom or justice. That's why our founders didn't construct "a democracy." They gave us a republic whose Constitution includes democratic and antidemocratic elements. You heard that right. Our Constitution has antidemocratic elements. Why do you suppose there is a veto power? So, the president can protect us from laws passed by the democratically elected Congress. Why are there two houses of Congress? So, the more deliberative Senate—originally elected by state legislatures to represent the state governments—can protect us from unwise legislation passed by the democratically elected House.

The entire Bill of Rights is composed of amendments to the Constitution designed to make it even more antidemocratic. Just think about the very first words of the very first amendment: "Congress shall make no law . . ."

Which Congress? The democratically elected Congress.

The founders understood that, left free to pursue their own individual happiness, the common people were capable of virtue and greatness, but were also capable of being just as tyrannical as a monarchy, if what Madison called, "the passions of the multitude," or "mob rule" were left unchecked. So, they built a system within which representatives were democratically elected, but the power those leaders had was carefully limited.

This is why I lose it every time I hear many Republicans referring to the United States as a "democracy." It's not. It's a republic. You'd think members of the Republican Party of all people would emphasize that! If nothing else, it would be good branding.

Let me be clear. Belief in the *principle* of democracy or recognizing the Deep State Russia collusion delusion, or the Resistance in general, as a threat to democratic elections is not the same thing as referring to the United States of America as "a democracy." Democracy is a component of our system, but there are other components, most of which exist to check it.

All socialism is "democratic." Socialism represents the worst aspect of democracy: the propensity for the majority to vote themselves the property of the minority. When Bernie promises "free college" or "free health care," every thinking person knows it won't really be free. He admitted as much on his Fox News town hall: "So, if you're asking me—if your question is a fair question—are people going to pay more in taxes? Yes," Sanders finally admitted when pressed.[10]

So, if it's not going to be free, who is going to pay for it? Bernie's first answer is always "the rich." Without suggesting I agree with taxing one person for the express purpose of providing material benefits to another, Bernie is lying about this, too. The so-called rich, the one percent or whatever name you want to give to this demonized group, don't have enough money to pay for everything the Left says it will give you for free.

The truthful answer is you're going to pay for it, just like you pay for all the social programs the Left sold you in the past. Most Americans don't know this, but the income tax was originally sold to the public as a tax mostly on the very wealthy. Under the Revenue Act of 1913, which established the first income tax after the Sixteenth Amendment was ratified, incomes up to the equivalent of over $77,000 today weren't taxed at all and, after that, average Americans only paid one percent until they got to the equivalent of $500,000 per year. The top rate of seven percent wouldn't apply until one had earnings that would equate to over $7.5 million today.[11]

So, they got the income tax established by telling the public only the rich would pay it, and even they would pay very little. Then, they pulled the old bait and switch and, today, middle-class families pay a lot more than one percent. Why anyone would believe it's going to be different this time around is beyond me.

Whenever Bernie is confronted with the horrors socialism produced in the former Soviet Union, communist China, or modern Venezuela, he says he doesn't want a system like they had.[12] He wants something like what they have in Scandinavia. But first, it's important to realize Bernie is lying about this, too.

He says now that he doesn't want the Soviet or Venezuelan

form of socialism because they've already failed. But he sure sang a different tune before they failed. Back in the 1980s, after visiting the Soviet Union, Sanders had nothing but praise for the communist country. He extolled its public transportation system, its "palaces of culture," and even its breadlines, which Sanders said were a good thing!

"You know, sometimes American journalists talk about how bad a country is because people are lining up for food. That's a good thing. In other countries, people don't line up for food. The rich get the food and the poor starve to death," said Comrade Bernie at the time.[13] Bernie, are you stoopid?

Can you believe that? I wouldn't have believed it myself if I didn't watch video of Sanders speaking those words. This was in the 1980s, after tens of millions had already starved in the Soviet Union and communist China.[14] Meanwhile, the poor in the United States face a much different problem—obesity![15]

Bernie is lying about Venezuela, too. Today, he says the Venezuelan version of socialism isn't the one he's promoting, but that's not what he said in 2011. An op-ed Sanders posted on his official US Senate website, said, "These days, the American dream is more apt to be realized in South America, in places such as Ecuador, Venezuela and Argentina, where incomes are actually more equal today than they are in the land of Horatio Alger. Who's the banana republic now?"[16]

As of this writing, that op-ed is still available on Bernie's official US Senate website, although when I followed the link to the *Valley News* article, it appears that newspaper has since had the good sense to take it down. But to answer the question it posed, Venezuela is the banana republic now, a previously rich country led into chaos by two democratically elected socialists just like Bernie, making all the same false promises Bernie is making today.

Scandinavian "Socialism"

When invited to observe the real-time results of so-called democratic socialism in Venezuela, Bernie and his fellow socialists in the Democrat Party respond with yet another lie. This one has two parts. Part one is that Venezuela is, of course, "not real socialism" or at least not real democratic socialism, despite both the late president Hugo Chávez and current president Nicolás Maduro having been elected in landslides—although Maduro's reelection in 2018 has been disputed.[17]

When the economic results are disastrous, the Left claims it wasn't "real" socialism and when the election looks rigged, even by the DNC's standards, they say it isn't "real" democracy. It never occurs to them that perhaps poverty, authoritarianism, and rigged elections are the hallmarks of socialist countries, rather than coincidental misfortunes.

Part two of the big lie is that, while socialism has been a disaster in every country that comes to mind when you think of socialism—Venezuela, the Soviet Union, China, Cambodia, Vietnam, North Korea, Cuba, a dozen countries in Africa, etcetera—it has worked in the supposedly idyllic utopias of Scandinavia. There, so the Left's fairy tale goes, democratic socialism works, the rich pay their "fair share," health care and college are free, and every child gallops through meadows chasing rainbows on his or her own pony.

Okay, that last part was an exaggeration. But only slightly.

Like everything else the Left tells you, the truth about Scandinavia is almost completely the opposite. First and foremost, Scandinavia is not socialist. We know this because they've said so, sometimes rather emphatically. When Comrade Bernie was on the campaign trail peddling his nonsense about Scandinavian socialism in 2015, Danish Prime Minister Lars Løkke Rasmussen offered a sharp rebuke:

> I know that some people in the US associate the Nordic model with some sort of socialism. Therefore, I would like to make one thing clear. Denmark is far from a socialist planned economy. Denmark is a market economy. The Nordic model is an expanded welfare state, which provides a high level of security to its citizens, but it is also a successful market economy with much freedom to pursue your dreams and live your life as you wish.[18]

Now, one might say the prime minister is as deluded or dishonest as the Democrats who say they're capitalists but support some version of all of Bernie's giveaways. Not true. There is real substance to Prime Minister Rasmussen's statement about Denmark having a market economy. In fact, outside of the more generous welfare programs, it has in many ways a much freer market than the United States.

For example, here's one thing you didn't hear from overtly socialist Bernie or any of his closet socialist comrades: Denmark has no national minimum wage. That's right, the American Left is trying to double the national minimum wage to fifteen dollars an hour, but supposedly socialist Denmark gets along just fine without one at all. And you'll never guess what other countries don't have national minimum wage laws: Sweden, Iceland, Norway, and Switzerland.[19]

That seems like a rather important detail our Democrat politicians are leaving out, doesn't it?

It doesn't end there. The Heritage Foundation publishes an annual report called the "Index of Economic Freedom," which I'm sure the Left would have you believe shows the United States at the top of the list. Hardly. Even with all the work President Trump has done in signing individual and corporate tax cuts and reducing the regulatory burden on American businesses, the United States still only ranks number twelve on the list.[20]

Now, it's true the Scandinavian countries are scored lower overall than the United States because of their low scores in the Government Spending and Tax Burden categories. However, they score higher than the United States in several other key categories:

	Property Rights	Business Freedom	Investment Freedom
United States	79.3	83.8	85.0
Denmark	86.2	90.7	90.0
Sweden	89.5	88.0	85.0
Norway	86.1	89.4	75.0

So, one reason Scandinavia can support more generous welfare states is that they have much freer markets in other respects, especially in the regulatory and property rights areas, allowing their economies to be more productive and efficient. That means they produce more stuff per capita and spend less money complying with regulations.

Even after Donald Trump supposedly "gutted" the American regulatory structure, we're still far more regulated than

Denmark, Sweden, or Norway, as the Business Freedom scores clearly show. Studies put the cost of regulation on the U.S. economy at almost $2 trillion per year. President Trump actually cut the annual cost of regulations by $23 billion during his first two years, where Obama raised them $245 billion during the same period.[21] But, contrary to what the hysterical Left would have you believe, we need far more deregulation, not a return to no-growth Obama policies.

What about the corporate tax cuts, supposedly a "giveaway to the rich," according to virtually every Democrat alive? Surely, Scandinavia must tax their corporations at a higher rate so the rich will pay their "fair share" of all this welfare, right? Wrong. When President Trump signed his historic tax cuts in 2017, it merely brought the United States in line with the Scandinavian countries, whose corporate tax rates are all between 20 percent and 22 percent.[22]

At no time in this century have Scandinavian corporate tax rates been anywhere near the 39 percent corporate tax rate imposed by Obama and the Democrats, which was the third highest in the world in 2015.[23]

Are you beginning to feel like you've been lied to by the Democrats? God forbid. But wait until you hear the punch line.

Every far-Left Democrat pushing Medicare for All, free college, and other giveaways has told you they will tax the rich to pay for the programs, hoping Americans will completely abandon their common sense and start believing there really is a free lunch. But, of course, there isn't; not here in America and not in Scandinavia, either. The truth is the United States already has the most progressive income tax system in the world, with the top 10 percent of income earners paying over 45 percent of all income taxes. In Sweden, the top 10 percent pay only 26.6 percent.[24]

So, if Scandinavian corporations don't pay more and the top 10 percent of income earners in Scandinavian countries are paying a *lower* share of the tax burden, who is paying the additional taxes needed for these generous welfare benefits?

Answer: the Scandinavian middle class pays for it, just as the American middle class will if Comrade Bernie or anyone of his ilk gets their way. This isn't a theory; it's a fact. In Denmark, you must only earn $77,730 per year to be liable for the top tax rate of 55.8 percent, while you don't pay the top rate of 37 percent in this country until you're making over $500,000 per year. That's not to mention Denmark and most European countries having a value added tax (VAT) on top of their income tax to collect enough revenue to pay for all that welfare.[25]

The VAT paid by Europeans, including Scandinavians, is one of the more convenient things American liberals forget to tell you about. The VAT raises the price of every good and service it's levied on, raising the prices of those products by 21.3 percent on average across Europe. Sweden, Norway, and Denmark have 25 percent VAT rates, second only to Hungary as the highest in Europe.[26]

These taxes are not just paid by the rich and middle class; they're paid by everyone, including the poorest Scandinavians, who can afford it the least. Talk about breaking your leg and handing you a crutch. They raise the price of everything their poor people need to survive and then promise them free stuff to make up for it. Wouldn't any sane person prefer freedom?

The welfare state doesn't just compromise the freedom of Scandinavians; it makes them materially poorer than they would be without being required to pay the taxes that support it. And I'm not just talking about the rich. As I've just shown, everyone pays substantially higher taxes than they would without these government benefits. That means they give the government money they could otherwise spend on something else.

That's fine for those who value the security they believe the programs give them in return. For those who don't? Too bad, they must pay regardless. And that's what we're really talking about when we talk about making health care or education "free." It means forcing people to buy the government's program whether they want to or not. It means not having the choice to buy any of the things you might have spent that money on instead.

The economist Thomas Sowell once wrote, "The first lesson of economics is scarcity: There is never enough of anything to satisfy all those who want it. The first lesson of politics is to disregard the first lesson of economics."[27] Never was this truer than it is today, where far-Left American Democrats are ignoring the costs of Scandinavian welfare and the trade-offs that go with it.

It would be one thing if they were seeking an honest conversation with American voters, asking if Americans were willing to trade some freedom of choice for security, but they're not. They're lying to Americans, telling them they can deliver all these wonderful benefits without Americans giving up anything to get them.

Neither are the Democrats ready to take the economy in a direction in any way resembling the relatively freer markets of Scandinavia. Have you heard a Democrat calling for an abolition of the minimum wage or radical deregulation of the business environment? No, they're calling for precisely the opposite, even though those are two reasons Scandinavia has been productive enough to have such a large welfare state in the first place.

How Capitalism Saved Scandinavia—Twice

Even representing the Scandinavian countries as some sort of successful balance of capitalism and socialism—as if the large welfare states contribute to their prosperity—is misleading. Scandinavia prospers to the extent it does despite, rather than because of, its welfare state. In fact, the trend in the Nordic countries over the past several decades has been to move away from the more socialist model they adopted briefly in the 1970s and toward the more capitalist model they have now.

In the late nineteenth century, Sweden was a relatively poor country. But by 1968, it was the third richest country in the world.[28] This was not the result of its large welfare state, which it hadn't yet constructed. Rather, Sweden became rich with low taxes, free markets, and a relatively small welfare state. It was not until the 1970s and 1980s that Sweden adopted the kind of economy Bernie Sanders and the rest are suggesting for America.

It was a disaster. In less than two decades, Sweden went from being the third richest to the seventeenth richest country in the world, culminating in a financial and real estate crisis in 1991.[29] Since that crisis, Sweden has actually been reforming its economy to be more capitalist and its welfare state to be less generous. Sweden's economic disaster was caused by implementing the kinds of taxes the Democrats are selling today. Their taxes[30] and government spending have decreased substantially since their peak in 1993.[31] They're still higher than in the United States, but the trend in Sweden is downward, while in the United States it has been upward. The story in Denmark is basically the same.[32]

The real story of Scandinavia, the one the lunatic Left doesn't want you to hear, is that capitalism saved it from poverty not once, but twice. The Scandinavian countries became rich in the twentieth century on a limited-government, free-market model that they abandoned to their detriment in the 1970s and '80s. They have since rebounded by reforming their welfare programs, curbing government spending, cutting corporate tax rates, and freeing their markets with less regulation.

The move away from socialism hasn't ended. Just as they are all over the world, conservative political parties are gaining traction in Scandinavia. This is both a recognition that even their reformed welfare states will eventually bankrupt them and a rejection of the open border policies that have brought Sweden soaring crime rates and overburdened public services.[33] The Swedes, like the rest of Scandinavia, have learned from their mistakes and are reversing course.

All Socialism Is Eventually Authoritarian

"I'm the boss," said Alexandria Ocasio-Cortez when confronted with criticism of her Green New Deal.[34] And when you hear the Democrats standing on the debate stage spewing their socialist agenda, they're saying the exact same thing. They want to be your boss. They're talking about government control, the antithesis of our most important value: freedom. We cannot let this happen.

Socialism can't be maintained without authoritarianism because it defies human nature. It is in everyone's nature to pursue his or her individual economic interests, to pursue his or her own dreams. This is so basic a right it's in our Declaration of Independence. The pursuit of happiness is an individual right, not a collective one, and our Founding Fathers believed it is inalienable. That means it can't be taken away, not even by majority vote. The Declaration of Independence says the whole purpose of government is to secure this right and if it doesn't, the people are justified in getting rid of the government, not the right.

A socialist system can get along all right temporarily, depending upon how rich the country was before it was instituted. The people don't notice their rights being infringed because there is lots of free stuff being handed out. But as soon as the country's wealth is depleted, and the capitalist means aren't there to produce new wealth, the authoritarianism becomes necessary to prevent people from doing what they naturally do in tough circumstances—work hard and attempt to keep the fruits of their own labor.

This is why Venezuela is an authoritarian nightmare today. Scandinavia would likely have been the same if it didn't turn away from socialism and make their markets even freer than ours outside of their welfare states. Bernie says, "I believe that health care is a human right, not a privilege. And I believe that there is something embarrassingly wrong when the United States of America is the only major country not to guarantee health care to all people."[35]

But he doesn't tell you the countries that have government-provided health care are in other respects freer economically than the United States, although they'd be better off freer and *without* the welfare programs. It is their capitalism that pays for the folly of their socialism, not the other way around.

Even within these mixed-economy systems, it is the socialist parts that are in crisis. The British system has been in place for seventy years, but just as Prime Minister Margaret Thatcher warned, they have run out of other people's money.[36] Emergency room doctors in the UK told CNN people are dying in hospital hallways waiting for a room to become available.[37] Canada's system is right behind it, with government spending growing at "unsustainable rates," according to the Canadian Fraser Institute.[38] That's not to mention the long waiting times, care rationing, and other issues that go along with letting the government run health care.

As attractive as free health care or free college might sound, there is no such thing. Should America listen to the Democrats' siren song of socialism, our ship of state will end up wrecked on the rocky shore of bankruptcy and debt.

CHAPTER THIRTEEN

Ghosting Conservatives

No plan to remake America would be complete without an attack on the very first freedom protected in our Bill of Rights: free speech. In Europe hate speech is prosecuted on a regular basis. The Left would very much like to bring that thinking as well as that ability to prosecute to America.

The purported reason for prosecution of hate speech is that it combats discrimination, intimidation, bullying, and violence. But in reality, these laws are often used to silence voices and to erase certain views from public consciousness.

I've been saying for years that hate speech, protected by the First Amendment as the United States Supreme Court has repeatedly ruled, is a term that is being used to thwart free speech that the Left does not want heard. We don't have hate speech laws in the United States, at least not until the Left succeeds in radically amending this fundamental right.

Free speech is one of those truisms, a fundamental right that for the most part is inviolate, or at least assumed to be. Not only does the First Amendment to the United States Constitution say so, but the United States Supreme Court has affirmed this concept throughout American history. There are of course a few exceptions: the classic shouting "fire" in a crowded theater; obscenity; or call to imminent attack, such as inciting or producing lawless action—like Antifa.

The Supreme Court has repeatedly ruled that hate speech is specifically protected free speech. After all, why even have the First Amendment if unpopular speech can be squelched? The Court has even addressed the issue of hate, saying there is no First Amendment exception that punishes hate speech. In fact, it is broadly protected.

Those on the Left prefer to limit our free speech if someone is offended or triggered, using their own subjective definition of hate speech. The Supreme Court disagrees, ruling specifically that provocative and offensive speech—by anyone's definition—is protected.

In Europe, however, hate speech is prosecuted on a regular basis. I interviewed Professor Elisabeth Sabaditsch-Wolff who was prosecuted for "offending" Muslims by talking about Muhammad. Her conviction was affirmed by the European Court of Human Rights. The opinion stated Elisabeth's "freedom of expression" infringed upon "the right of others to have their religious feelings protected."[1] So, in short, the right not to be offended when it comes to your religion trumps another person's free speech.

I don't really give a damn about how you *feel* about what I'm saying. I have a right to say it! But apparently the European court disagrees.

As this concept moves across the pond, we're hearing from the Left that speech needs to be prohibited here if it offends others. They insist that free speech not always be protected.

You may recall on September 25, 2012, two weeks after Benghazi, President Barack Obama stood before members of the United Nations and said "the future cannot belong to those who slander the prophet of Islam." I remember thinking to myself back then: What does slander have to do with the killing of four Americans? But, it was a prescient statement about where the Left, starting with Obama, wants to take the United States.

The Left's mantra is that our free speech is the enemy of their political correctness. In other words if what we say does not jive with their view of the world, it must be suppressed and punished. But never in the history of this country has there been a balancing test weighing free speech against how others feel about that speech. There is no measuring of the harm to someone's psyche or feelings when weighing the legality of someone's speech. This is not only unconstitutional, it's crazy. It is how the Left is trying to change the way we think. If people are shamed or outright prosecuted, as they are in Europe, for speech the Left feels is contrary to their worldview, then free speech is a right of the past.

Tech Giants Censor Conservatives

We haven't gone as far as Europe in prosecuting free speech. Instead, the Left's agenda to eliminate conservative speech has been taken up by social media giants. Near monopolies like Google, Facebook, Twitter, and other web search and social media companies have twisted their own terms of service agreements in knots to find ways to either limit the exposure conservatives get on their platforms or ban them altogether.

Technically, this is not a First Amendment issue, as the Bill of Rights only protects us from infringement of our rights by the government. But there are still legal questions to be answered regarding this behavior. Regardless, this trend represents not only a danger to our free society, but a glimpse of what the Left would like the government to do in terms of limiting conservative speech.

In the beginning, the Left went after obvious targets—people everyone could get behind hating. They took down the conservative provocateurs and conspiracy theorists who spread outrageous ideas that not only misinformed the public, but also were in fact unnecessarily offensive to many people.

These fringe figures were banned because they had engaged in what people at Twitter consider "harassment," although they did not physically hurt anyone or attempt to incite violence. I don't think anyone was too upset to see them go. They were the kind of people who are always the first to be singled out when freedom is being assaulted—people whom no one will miss.

So said German pastor Martin Niemöller, who gave lectures in the years before World War II. This was when the Nazis were just beginning to burn books, destroy works of art, and decide who in Germany had the right to free speech and who did not.

"First they came for the socialists," Niemöller said, "and I did not speak out—because I was not a socialist. Then they came for the trade unionists, and I did not speak out—because I was not a trade unionist. Then they came for the Jews, and I did not speak out—because I was not a Jew. Then they came for me—and there was no one left to speak for me."[2]

If Niemöller were here in the United States today, he might say, "First, they came for the extremists." The pattern is eerily familiar. Already, the Left has moved from banning fringe figures to people who articulate mainstream, previously uncontroversial conservative positions.

In other words, they are coming for anyone who opposes their radical plan to remake America, and they are doing it out in the open.

They came for YouTube commentator Steven Crowder, whose show *Louder with Crowder* goes out live on YouTube to about three million people. In May 2019, Crowder got into an online argument with Carlos Maza, a commentator for far-Left Vox. Crowder used a few words he probably shouldn't have and Maza fired right back. At one point in the exchange, while on a kind of comedic run, Crowder called Maza, who is gay, a "lispy queer."

Should he have said that? Probably not, and had he said it in my presence I would have let him know it. But did it violate YouTube's terms of service? According to YouTube, no, it did not.

Right after the incident, the company released a statement saying that it would not suspend Crowder's account because he hadn't encouraged anyone to harass or commit acts of violence against Maza or anyone else. But being the crazed Leftist he is, Maza refused to accept the company's judgment about what it does and does not allow on its platform.

Within a few days, he and his followers on Twitter had organized a boycott against YouTube and posted a message online to the company's mostly liberal employees. The message read, in part, "YouTube has decided to side with the people who made our lives miserable in high school. It's decided to use the platform you've helped create in order to arm bigots and bullies with massive megaphones. Why do you stick around? What are you going to do about it?" [3]

In that situation, only one person was acting like a bully, and it wasn't Steven Crowder. It was the lunatic liberal journalist who thinks he can silence people just because they're mean to him. Maza had every right to disagree with Crowder, to tell Crowder his comments were homophobic or at least in poor taste, if meant as humor. He had every right to refuse to associate with Crowder. But he didn't have the right to silence him, which is what he tried to do.

As is usually the case, YouTube caved to the pressure and "demonetized" Steven Crowder's account. This means that although he would still be allowed to broadcast his show, he wouldn't make any money from it. This was a clear-cut case of the liberal mob getting its way, bullying a company into submission with the kind of tactics we haven't seen in this country since the Salem Witch Trials.

First, they came for the conspiracy theorists, then they came for the off-color, somewhat offensive commentators like Crowder. Did it stop there? Of course not.

When Laura Loomer, a conservative activist who broadcasts her views primarily through Twitter, criticized Representative Ilhan Omar for being "anti-Jewish," she was banned from Twitter for hate speech. Loomer is an extremely bright, quick-witted millennial, who tears into anything she sees as un-American or anti-Semitic, consequences be damned. Having been banned from social media, she is suing Twitter, Facebook, and Google. There is talk of her running for Congress in 2020.

Another one banned was actor James Woods. In May 2019, Woods was locked out of his Twitter account for posting this message after the release of the Mueller report: "If you try to kill the king, you best not miss #HangThemAll." According to Twitter, the tweet constituted "harassment."

Seriously? Harassment against whom? All Democrats? Did anyone at Twitter sincerely believe James Woods literally wanted to hang Jim Comey, Andrew McCabe, John Brennan, or Peter Strzok? Of course not. They saw that they had a clear and plausible shot against a conservative (one of the few in Hollywood), and they took it. Clearly, this is not about protecting anyone or creating a safe environment for sharing ideas. It's about making sure conservatives have no right to free speech or expression in the digital sphere and remaking social media the same way they remade old media in a distinctly liberal direction.

By the way, Woods is a phenomenal actor, but when was the last time you saw him in a movie? Need I say any more about the Left's censorship or Hollywood's hypocrisy?

Just before this book went to print, they came for someone not even the furthest-Left loony could claim was publishing hateful, offensive, or intimidating content, unless you consider traditional American values like due process, freedom of speech, and free enterprise intimidating. I'm talking about Dennis Prager, a well-educated, well-spoken, and thoughtful conservative I've had on my show, *Justice*, several times.

Mr. Prager is the founder of Prager University (PragerU), an organization that publishes short videos online, lending conservative perspectives on a range of topics. Unable to find a pretense under which to completely ban PragerU from their platforms, Google and Twitter have instead found ways to limit its reach. YouTube, which is owned by Google, has either restricted or demonetized over fifty of PragerU's videos. Google/YouTube claims these videos, including two titled, "Ten Commandments: Do Not Murder" and "The World's Most Persecuted Minority: Christians," respectively,[4] are "inappropriate for younger audiences."

You heard that right. The Ten Commandments are now inappropriate for younger audiences. Of course they are! They're part of the foundation of Western civilization, which the Left despises and wants to destroy. This is such baloney. The most popular movies, video games, and songs today are laced with hate, violence, and profanity. And the Left wants to censor the Bible? The truth? Our history? How dare they?

"We're living in America through the greatest assault on free speech in American history," said Prager. "If it is pro-America, if it's pro-Israel, if it is pro-religion, it is likely to be censored by Google or YouTube."[5] PragerU has filed a lawsuit against Google/YouTube for "continuing to unlawfully restrict and restrain speech and expression," which is still pending as of this writing.[6]

From fringe conspiracy theories to off-color humor to legitimate accusations against anti-Semitism to the Ten Commandments, the types of things conservatives are not allowed to say online have become less and less controversial. What will be next? God forbid that Donald Trump doesn't win in 2020. This will be the new reality, where we may not be able to quote our own founding documents, not even to articulate our inalienable rights to life, liberty, and the pursuit of happiness.

Once we are no longer allowed to talk about them, they literally cease to exist.

The New Public Square

The First Amendment provides the strongest protection of free speech anywhere in the world. Not even relatively free societies like the United Kingdom and France go as far as we do in guaranteeing this right. With few limitations, we are essentially free to say whatever we want, whenever we want.

Our founders believed liberty could not be preserved unless everyone, regardless of their political views, was allowed to express those views freely and without fear of government reprisal. Once those views were out in the open, previously literally and now figuratively in "the public square," they would compete with conflicting views, the best ideas prevailing and becoming public policy. Legal scholars call this the "marketplace of ideas" theory, and it depends on having an inalienable right to free speech.[7] Without that right, it would be impossible to discover the truth regarding important political matters. Truth itself dies when people are denied the right to express it.

For most of our nation's history, political ideas have been disseminated through the media. First it was broadsides, newspapers, and pamphlets, then newspapers and magazines, then newspapers and cable television. Even in the early days of the Internet, you simply couldn't stay informed if you didn't read a newspaper or watch a nightly news broadcast.

Although often accused of a liberal bias, perhaps not without justification, twentieth-century newspapers and major television news organizations at least made an effort to deliver the news of the day objectively, without inserting their political biases. Believe it or not, it wasn't that long ago that it was difficult to know for sure what political beliefs news reporters held, even if you suspected they were liberal.

But somewhere along the line, the leaders of these news organizations—from the *New York Times* and the *Washington Post* to CNN and MSNBC—abdicated their roles as seekers of truth and chose instead to use the influence of their platforms to push liberal agendas. Major news organizations became nothing more than liberal echo chambers. Over time, reporters at the *New York Times* started selecting their story assignments based on politics, letting their points of view seep into what was supposed to be "unbiased" news stories. The same thing happened at places like the *Washington Post* and CNN. Before we knew it, the mainstream media in this country had become nothing more than a propaganda arm for the Democrat party. I talked about reporters literally running stories by the DNC during the 2016 elections in my last book, *Liars, Leakers, and Liberals*. *New York Times* senior home page editor and self-described "curator of the front page" Des Shoe admitted in 2017 her paper had been extremely biased against Trump. "Our main stories are supposed to be objective. It's very difficult in this day and age to do that," said Shoe, adding, "the last couple years it's changed for the bad."[8]

Shoe said the *Times*' business model was built on delivering news the subscribers want to hear and that the subscribers were liberal. She called the spike in subscriptions due to people seeking to hear negative news on Donald Trump after his election the "Trump bump."

And if you don't believe me, just look at the numbers.

Trump put the liberal media on full tilt, but their bias

certainly didn't start with his candidacy or presidency. In a study conducted in 2013 by two professors from Indiana University, only 7 percent of journalists in the United States identified as Republican.[9] Of the other 93 percent, about a third self-identified as liberal, while 50 percent of respondents identified as independent.

Considering that the split in the country at large usually runs about fifty-fifty (that's why we don't have any huge land-slide elections) this number is absurd. It's the kind of bias that should make any news organization want to go out and hire a staff that bears at least some glancing resemblance to the country they're writing about. And if you think for a second that the 50 percent of journalists who responded independent aren't just as liberal as the ones who admitted their bias outright, think again. There are numbers on that, too, and numbers do not lie.

After the 2008 election, the *Washington Examiner,* one of the few right-leaning newspapers in the country, kept track of how much money was leaving the pockets of top journalists and going to Democrat candidates. The results were shocking—but only if you hadn't been paying attention. Of the roughly $1.2 million that was donated by journalists and TV executives during that election cycle, about 88 percent of it went to Barack Obama and other Democrats.[10] Donations to Democrats from television journalists came to just over a million dollars that year, while the Republican total was just under $150,000. With numbers like that, I find it very hard to believe—in fact, *impossible* to believe—that there isn't a liberal bias in the mainstream media.

It's not a coincidence that the American public's trust in the media plummeted to all-time lows during this period. In a survey taken in 2018, the Knight Foundation reported that 69 percent of all adults (95 percent of Republicans) in the United States had lost some trust in news media over the preceding decade.[11] That's not quite as bad as their loss of trust in Congress.

Clearly, there was a problem. The organizations that once served as our public square—the place where we air our ideas and share our thoughts on issues—had become so corrupted by one side of the aisle that it simply wasn't a fair fight anymore. They lied about Republicans and conservatives, demonizing half the country.

The Internet and the rise of social media disrupted this. It broke the stranglehold the traditional, liberal media had over the flow of ideas. It had certainly helped Barack Obama get elected, but it also helped fuel the rise of the Tea Party (which, last I heard, hadn't beaten anybody up) and the Republican takeover of Congress. The Internet didn't just bypass the information gatekeepers, it trampled the fences.

Nobody exploited social media better than Donald Trump. Over the two-year period spanning 2015 and 2016, using nothing but the Twitter app on his Samsung Galaxy smartphone, Trump rewrote the rules for running a presidential campaign. He perfected the art of bypassing the liberal-controlled media and talked directly to the voters. By the time the 2016 campaign really got going, the future president had already amassed nearly seven million followers on Twitter.[12] That's more than double the online readership of the *New York Times*![13] It was the kind of audience anyone with an opinion column or a television show (including yours truly) would kill to have.

Donald Trump's interaction with his audience demonstrated not only the true power of social media but the Trump marketing genius for the first time. Trump bypassed the mainstream media's lies and distortions by talking directly to his followers. It was the next best thing to being in the room with the man. You didn't have to turn on a television, buy a newspaper, or sit and wonder whether the "objective" journalist who was reporting on the story was giving you the *real* story.

No wonder the media hate him so much. He not only tells the unvarnished truth about progressive policies, destroying political correctness in the process, he all but renders the legacy media (newspapers, radio, television, etc.) obsolete. Not since President Roosevelt began having his "fireside chats" with the nation via radio had a politician been so able to manipulate a new medium to his own ends.

Instead of trying to beat the media at its own game, Donald Trump created a brand-new game. By the end of the 2016 election cycle, we had a new public square called Twitter, and it operated according to the rules of the free market. Everyone in the world had an equal opportunity to express their ideas freely, and there was virtually nothing standing between candidates and voters.

The Left's Revenge

From the Left's perspective, something obviously had to be done. Allowing this free market of ideas to continue would be fatal to the progressive agenda. Why? Simple. Conservative ideas are better. They work. The failures of progressivism and the monumental success of Donald Trump's policies provide a pretty stark contrast when the public is allowed to examine them in the light of day. Somehow, the Left had to find a way to reimpose its liberal filter over social media the way it had over the legacy media.

Fortunately for the Left and unfortunately for America, the management of the Silicon Valley tech companies who control Google, Facebook, Twitter and other dominant web search and social media platforms are dyed-in-the-wool, far-Left Democrats. They found a way to leverage their market dominance to once again tilt the playing field heavily in the Left's favor.

When you sign up for an account on Twitter, Facebook, or YouTube (which is owned by Google), you agree to about 4,900 words of legal jargon. When you accept the terms of these agreements, you're accepting that Twitter, Facebook, and YouTube have the right to kick you, or anyone else, off their platform whenever they see fit. This means that if you post something that the people working at either of these companies deem "offensive," they can remove your posts, suspend your account, or even delete your online profile permanently.

Because these two companies have a virtual monopoly on social media throughout the world, once you're banned, there's nowhere else to turn. It's not like you can go sign up for Twitter's main competitor in the marketplace, because there isn't one. When it comes to the digital public square, Facebook, Twitter, and Google are the only games in town.

We have antitrust laws in the United States that govern every other type of corporation. When the phone company AT&T got so big that it eliminated competition in the marketplace, the government broke it up into smaller phone companies. The same thing happened to U.S. Steel at the beginning of the twentieth century. But so far, antitrust laws have not been applied to Google, Facebook, or Twitter, even though some

Democrats are calling for them to be broken up. In June 2019, House Democrats initiated a review of Facebook, Google, and Twitter to, according to the *Washington Post*, "determine if they've become so large and powerful that they stifled competition and harm consumers."[14]

Regardless of what you think about the antitrust side of this case, one thing is certain. In our current political climate, when so many important interactions happen via Twitter, Facebook, and YouTube, a ban from just one of these platforms is the digital equivalent of a life sentence in Siberia. They are such a part of daily life that some legal theorists have even attempted to classify them as "public utilities," the way we do with things like electricity and water. I'm not so sure about that, but I get the point.

There is a case to be made that when you remove a person from one of these platforms, you are damaging our republican form of government. Think about it. Some of the most vital announcements and conversations occurring in our country today are happening on social media platforms like Twitter and Facebook. There are so many that it's often impossible for legacy media companies to keep up. Banning someone from one or more of these 24-7, nonstop platforms deprives them of information they need to make decisions about whom to vote for, what policies to support, or even who is running. You're also taking away their ability to contribute to those conversations, which are migrating online in larger numbers than ever before.

Charlie Kirk, a young activist and founder of Turning Point USA, a conservative movement on over 1,400 college campuses across the country, has frequently appeared on *Justice*. He is a warrior who fights in the trenches every day to make sure that free speech is alive and well on college campuses, and in virtual spaces like Facebook and Twitter.

When asked about what a digital ban might mean, he compared Twitter to a small airline. If one airline has a complete monopoly on a small town in Montana, he said—meaning it's the only airline that flies in or out, so you have no other options—and that airline bans someone, the airline has effectively cut off that person's access to an entire town.

This is what is happening in the United States today. Social media companies—the airlines—get to decide who they want to let on their planes and who they don't, and there is really nothing any of us can do about it. This means that our access to the various "small towns" of the Internet, whether it's a discussion on an issue that matters greatly to us or just the Twitter feed of a presidential candidate, can be restricted at any moment. The irony here is Google started out with the motto, "Don't be evil." They've recently removed that in an apparent acknowledgment of their evil ways.[15] God, I love the truth!

It might not be so bad if the people who made decisions about what is "offensive" or "inflammatory" did so in a rational, unbiased way. But clearly, they don't. In an investigation done in 2017, three professors at the Stanford Graduate School of Business studied the political leanings of people who work in Silicon Valley. What they found should surprise no one. On almost every issue, the respondents leaned far to the left. They supported welfare and opposed gun rights; they are pro-globalism and favor wealth redistribution.[16] Oddly enough, the single issue on which they are *not* liberal is their view of monopolies. None of these Big Tech founders seemed to believe that the government should be allowed to step in and break up companies when they got too big.

Gee. I wonder why they think that.

It's not like the founders of these companies don't know what's going on. In several interviews conducted in early 2019, Jack Dorsey, the founder of Twitter, admitted publicly that the workforce at his company is overwhelmingly liberal. He tried to make the case that this liberal bias doesn't affect the platform and talked about the few conservatives who work there. "We have a lot of conservative-leaning folks in the company as well," he said. "And to be honest, they don't feel safe to express their opinions at the company. They do feel silenced by just the general swirl of what they perceive to be the broader percentage of leanings within the company, and I don't think that's fair or right."

Maybe Jack is being sincere, but when you catch employees of these tech giants speaking off the cuff, when their guards are down, the answers you get are much less carefully worded. That's just what Project Veritas found out when they secretly recorded senior Google executive Jen Gennai with a hidden camera, who had this to say on video:

We all got screwed over in 2016, again it wasn't just us, it was, the people got screwed over, the news media got screwed over, like, everybody got screwed over so we've rapidly been like, what happened there and how do we prevent it from happening again.

We're also training our algorithms, like, if 2016 happened again, would we have, would the outcome be different?[17]

Gennai says Elizabeth Warren's desire to break up big companies like Google would be counterproductive because, "smaller companies don't have the resources" to "prevent the next Trump situation."[18]

It doesn't get any plainer than that, folks. This is real meddling in an election and Project Veritas has sent a letter to eleven members of Congress expressing concern over that and Google's possible violation of federal laws like the Federal Election Campaign Act (FECA).[19] We'll have to see how concerned the Left really is with "saving democracy" from potential foreign intervention, given that Google is a multinational corporation with plenty of foreign stockholders.

Google's Gennai makes one thing very clear. When someone is banned or disciplined because they have said something liberal activists have deemed "offensive" (which, these days, is pretty much everything), it is really because they have dared to stray from the Left's radical agenda or because they support the traditional, conservative values held by the people who voted for Donald Trump. They are determined Trump or anyone like him is never elected again. Fortunately, Americans are catching on.

Lo and behold, as we go to publication, Twitter announced it would make some of President Trump's tweets harder to see by making users click through a "public service announcement" warning about "abusive behavior" before seeing the content.[20]

According to a study conducted in 2018 by the Pew Research Center, 72 percent of Americans believe that social media companies "censor views they don't like," and people are four times more likely to believe that these companies censor conservatives over liberals.[21] This belief doesn't come from nowhere. Another investigation by a research fellow at Columbia University reports that out of the twenty-two major political accounts that have been permanently banned since 2005, twenty-one belonged to conservatives.[22] The one outlier, by the way, was the actress Rose McGowan, who was suspended merely because one of her posts contained a private phone number, which is an actual violation of Twitter's terms of service.[23] She was quickly reinstated after the tweet in question was removed.

Democrats have little to fear in terms of being banished from social media, no matter how extreme their views or whom they harass. Op-ed writer Sarah Jeong was hired by the *New York Times* despite several openly racist, hateful, and possibly threatening tweets. Among them were, "Oh man it's kind of sick how much joy I get out of being cruel to old white men," "Dumbass f****** white people marking up the internet with their opinions like dogs pissing on fire hydrants," and "#CancelWhitePeople."[24]

What exactly does it mean to "cancel" a whole race of people? Can any reasonable person conclude James Woods "#HangThemAll" hashtag was more threatening than this? Honestly, neither Woods nor Jeong likely intended their hyperbolic tweets to be taken literally but look at the clear double standard. When Candace Owens, a black conservative activist, posted the same message but swapped out the word *white* for *Jewish*, she was banned for racism.

Twitter verified Jeong with its blue check mark after this controversy was publicized.[25] For anyone not familiar with what this means, Twitter verifies the accounts of public figures whose identities might be used for fan or parody accounts with a blue check mark next to the person's screen name. This gives the verified account advantages in Twitter's algorithms. While Twitter denies the blue check mark is an endorsement, it removed Laura Loomer's status for promoting "hateful content."[26]

When a liberal engages in racism, it's just good fun and irony. But when a conservative merely *points out* racism, she gets banned for hate speech. This double standard shows up all the time, and it's disgusting. When conservatives push the envelope, they're purged. Liberals, on the other hand, are defended.

Shadow-Banning

The bias on web search and social media platforms isn't limited to outright bans. These Left-leaning corporations also have more surreptitious means for eliminating conservative speech. One is called "shadow-banning," wherein giant tech companies like Google, Facebook, and Twitter filter out content from prominent conservatives, meaning their websites don't show up on web searches or their social media posts don't reach their followers on social media platforms. This truly Orwellian practice allows these companies to make conservatives "disappear" online, as if they don't exist. President Trump himself called out the tech giants for this sinister practice, writing on Twitter that he had received "many complaints," and that the White House would be looking into the practice.[27]

If you hadn't heard about shadow-banning, you're not alone. Even most tech company employees aren't quite sure how it's done. But the main thrust of it is this: when social media platforms have an issue with someone, say a prominent conservative writer, but that person hasn't done anything that explicitly violates the platform's terms of service, the platform cannot technically ban them. So, they resort to methods that are much more difficult to detect.

This usually means fiddling with the algorithm, the computer code that decides what posts people do and do not see. If the writer uses a certain word more often than others, for example, a programmer at a social media platform could write the algorithm in such a way that it hides most mentions of that word. Then, all of a sudden, the writer effectively disappears from the timelines of his followers, and from the digital public square altogether.

As this process is highly technical and requires expertise in computer science just to understand, it can be difficult for most people to detect. Think about it. Even if you or I were sitting at Facebook's headquarters looking at an account we know was being "shadow-banned," we likely wouldn't know what to look for. Luckily, there have been a few whistleblowers from inside who understand how it's done and they have come forward to expose this.

One of them, who chose to remain anonymous, spoke to the *Washington Examiner* in 2018, just a few weeks after he left his job at Facebook. This was just one year after Mark Zuckerberg had famously defended the rights of all people on his platform to express their views without censorship, regardless of whether those views were "deeply offensive." Even Holocaust deniers, according to Zuckerberg, should be allowed to express their opinions because, in his words, "they're not intentionally getting it wrong."[28]

According to his former employee, however, Zuckerberg and his team at Facebook were not willing to extend that same benefit of the doubt to the average conservative. He described a kind of digital tool kit he often came across on accounts he monitored for Facebook. Inside this tool kit were a series of digital commands that could make a Facebook account behave differently.

One of these tools, he said, was a line of code called "ActionDeboostLiveDistribution." When applied to the live-stream of a video on Facebook, this code would drastically reduce the number of people who saw the video.[29] A video that would normally get hundreds of thousands of views would suddenly receive far fewer. The former employee said he only saw this tool being used on the accounts of prominent conservatives such as Mike Cernovich, Steven Crowder, and the Daily Caller website. As far as he could tell, it was never used against liberal accounts. So, conservatives were being secretly filtered out of existence online, often without knowing why their audiences no longer seemed to see them or their content.

What's no secret is that just about everyone who works at these major platforms is liberal, but the leaders of these companies still maintain that having entire staffs of young, brainwashed liberals does *not* lead to biased editorial decisions on the parts of these companies.

Some of them may actually believe this. Thanks to Project Veritas, we know for certain that the liberal bias of companies like Facebook is so entrenched that most people probably don't even realize it. In 2018, the organization obtained a presentation given by two Facebook engineers named Seiji Yamamoto and

Eduardo Arino de la Rubia called "Coordinating Trolling on FB." Trolling, in case you don't know, is the practice of saying something inflammatory just to get a reaction out of someone.

Both liberals and conservatives do it all the time, and it's generally accepted as part of online conversation. In the presentation, however, these two engineers outlined the steps that engineers at Facebook could take to suppress content that didn't align with their views. In one scenario, they gave a list of terms that are often used by conservatives—from *MSM* for "mainstream media" to *SJW* for "social justice warrior"—and then described a whole cache of special tools to censor accounts that use those terms. There was even a system for rating how dangerous these accounts were called the "troll score." According to a former Facebook employee interviewed by Project Veritas, "they created the troll score so they could help identify, using words they would post, pictures . . . to determine whether this person should be on the platform or not."

In September 2018, Twitter CEO Jack Dorsey testified before the House Committee on Energy and Commerce to discuss shadow-banning and other alleged political biases.[30] While he categorically denied that his company intentionally engaged in such a practice, he would later admit that the company had been "way too aggressive" in banning the accounts of conservatives or people who defined themselves as "right-wing."[31] Dorsey did admit to Congress that employees at Twitter had "failed [their] intended impartiality." Apparently, in trying to crack down on what liberals often call "hate speech," the engineers at Twitter made it so that about 600,000 accounts were "filtered" out—meaning hidden, or shadow-banned—from the feeds of

Twitter users all over the world.[32] Some of these accounts, he said, belonged to Republican members of Congress. Most of them belonged to conservatives.

Regardless of how we solve this problem, one thing is clear: the Left has an agenda to silence conservative voices, to ensure to the extent they can that no one sees or hears any alternative view to their twisted, un-American agenda. Donald Trump took advantage of a relatively free marketplace of ideas to get his message out without obfuscation, distortion, or spin by the liberal media. That played a large part in the most shocking political victory in American history. They want to make it impossible for something like that to ever happen again.

This is not a two-way battle. There is no movement, online or off, to silence liberal speech. You don't see conservatives storming lecture halls on campuses to prevent liberal speakers from having their say. You don't see conservative media outlets, few as they are, trying to destroy the careers of liberal media figures. There is no conservative equivalent to Media Matters. And no conservatives are trying to make liberals disappear online. It's just not in our DNA.

There are reasons for that. First, conservatives are committed to a free society, where even controversial or offensive speech is tolerated, so that productive conversations occur. We know the importance of the First Amendment and would rather tolerate the Left's hate than call in the government to ban anything just because it makes us feel uncomfortable.

Second, we know our ideas will win, as long as they get a fair hearing. Just take a look around, less than three years after Donald Trump's inauguration. The economy is booming, ISIS is destroyed, international rivals are on their heels, and America has retaken its place as the preeminent leader of the free world. The only way for the Left to fight results like that is to silence anyone who talks about them. We cannot allow ourselves to be gagged and bound by these maniacs. This is a fight for the God-given right of free speech. It's a fight for the soul of America. It's time to go to war and fight for the right to say whatever we damn well please.

Chapter Fourteen

In Closing

I imagine every generation thinks things are worse than ever and, for some, rightfully so.

The generations that lived through the Civil War, the Great Depression, and World War II are among those who lived through extremely grueling times. I'm sure that during the worst of it they wished they could go back in time to the way things used to be.

As I think about these difficult times when brother fought brother, times when there wasn't enough food on the table, and times where every day was fraught with the possibility of hearing a loved one would not be coming home, fear, anxiety, and desperation were the norm every day.

But when I think about distressing periods in our history, I am always reminded of America's resilience, her ability to fight through our darkest days and come out better, stronger, and more determined. Like the phoenix, we rise from the proverbial ashes time after time. The dawn always does follow the night.

What is it about America that makes her so resilient and able to withstand these difficult hardships? Maybe it's in our DNA, or maybe it's in our history. Our forefathers were willing to give up everything—fame, fortune, even family—to start a new nation free of British rule. The houses of twelve of the signers of the Declaration of Independence were burnt to the ground. Nine signers died of wounds during the Revolutionary War.

These were not power-hungry people. They were willing to put everything on the line. They were willing to work as hard as needed for their new country. There were no demands. There was no arrogance. They were willing to logically explain why they wanted to be free and why they wanted to start their own country. There was no ambivalence, and there was certainly no political correctness. They spoke their minds and put all they had behind their words. They were clear and unashamed in their convictions.

In 1776, the Founding Fathers were prescient enough to state that all men are created equal and possess certain unalienable rights, among them life, liberty, and the pursuit of happiness. There was no doubt that it was our Creator, not any government, that endowed us with these natural rights. They understood that government does not give us rights, but rather we give our consent to be governed.

Here we are on the eve of the 2020 presidential election, and the campaigns have already begun. It's been a whirlwind two and a half years since Donald Trump became president. Since I started this book talking about the nonstop news cycle, I'd like to end it noting that so much has happened it's almost impossible to keep up, let alone record it all. Suffice it to say things are drastically different than when President Donald Trump took office.

ISIS seemed to be everywhere, not just in the Middle East massacring Christians and Muslims, but lone wolves were slaughtering Americans while they shouted "Allahu Akbar." Not only has ISIS been defeated in the Middle East, but thank God we have not experienced a lone wolf attack since Donald Trump has become president. These attacks were hard for ordinary Americans to understand when the FBI would refer to slaughters such as these as workplace violence, denying the reality of what they were. But then again Obama had a habit of calling Muslim slaughters workplace violence.

We were told manufacturing jobs were a thing of the past when Obama lost over 200,000 manufacturing jobs. Obama even made fun of Donald Trump, asking if he would wave his magic wand and create manufacturing jobs. Apparently, he did, because under Donald Trump, we have gained 600,000 new manufacturing jobs.

We were told that 1 percent growth was the new normal GDP, and yet Donald Trump has shown that a consistent 3 percent plus GDP growth is not only a possibility, but a reality.

We all have a tax cut because of the tax reform bill, although the Democrats try to deny it. But just look at your paycheck and you'll see there's a difference. We have more money in our pockets and in our 401(k)s. Unemployment is at a 50 year low.

The Left refuses to give the president credit for any of this. The Left no longer stands for anything but hate. They hate us, they hate America, and they hate the president we elected. How many of you have lost friends because they have deleted you from Facebook, Twitter, and Instagram—literally deleted you from their lives? There is no tolerance, no room for dialogue. The radicals simply don't care what you think. If you are not like them, watch out.

In their effort to remake America, they are trying to banish conservatives from the public square, both online and in person, rioting at university campuses whenever a conservative is scheduled to speak. And as we approach the 2020 election, you can bet they will continue their efforts to curb the speech of anyone who disagrees with their narrative. If you are not for reparations, you are a racist. If you don't agree with any one of their beliefs, you're a racist or a fascist. Be wary. If you're a fascist in their minds, they will tell law enforcement to stand down while Antifa is allowed to attack you. The justification for their verbal and physical hatred is that you are a racist or a fascist, which they assume simply because you're a Trump supporter wearing a red MAGA hat.

They want late-term abortion rights. They want sanctuary cities so that illegals who are criminals are protected from our legal process.

They are angry and they are jealous. They want what you have, but they're not willing to make it for themselves. They want the government to take it from you and give it to them and to illegals who have no right to be here to begin with. Illegals simply walk into our country, claiming they want asylum, and then don't show up for scheduled court hearings. They just expect us to provide for them and give them de facto amnesty.

These angry Democrats say that Donald Trump colluded with the Russians, who supposedly put their fingers on the scale and got him elected, even after it's been proven categorically false. Yet they won't bother to look at whether any Americans had their fingers on the scale to tip it against Donald Trump. They won't acknowledge either the Deep State or their illegal actions to spy on and attempt to take down the President of the United States.

They say our president is a warmonger, that he can't wait to pull the trigger, when the truth is he has exhibited restraint when it comes to our enemies. When Iran shot down one of our unmanned military drones over international waters, the president didn't overreact. He was thoughtful and decisive. His response was to put additional sanctions on Iran. Unlike the past two presidents, he wants to keep us out of unnecessary military conflicts. He's pursuing peace through strength, the same strategy that won the Cold War.

Donald Trump loves America. His Fourth of July celebration on the National Mall before a cheering crowd chanting "USA! USA!" celebrated America while the radical Left was busy denigrating the Betsy Ross flag, the same flag flown during Obama's second inauguration ceremony in 2013, calling it offensive because of its connection to an era of slavery. President Trump's Fourth of July celebration on the mall was the first in almost seventy years. He recounted great moments in our history: the Revolutionary War, the fight by the suffragettes to get the vote, and the work of the civil rights movement. Donald Trump doesn't just believe America is great; he believes America is the most exceptional nation in history. He has built our military back to being number one. He displayed military tanks, stealth bombers, and F-22 Raptor stealth fighters, but it was the flyovers, including Air Force One (although he wasn't on it), that brought thunderous applause from the massive crowd.

But it wasn't just military might the president was showcasing. He highlighted the innovation of the moon landing and the NASA space program. He lauded the development of an effective treatment for childhood leukemia and honored Clarence Henderson, who took part in the 1960 civil rights sit-in at the Woolworth lunch counter in Greensboro, North Carolina.

The Left was apoplectic days before the holiday, comparing his patriotic celebration to a North Korean military display. How ludicrous. It was nothing of the sort. It was vintage Donald Trump, the man who came from the outside, selected by the forgotten men and women of America, reminding us that American success is a choice worth celebrating, that American innovation is worth encouraging, and that America's military is always worth honoring.

As we approach 2020 you have a decision to make. You can sit back and hope that the radical Left, committed to remaking America, doesn't succeed. Or you can do something about it. Donald Trump was elected to do something about it. We need to give the man the opportunity to continue his mission, fighting to keep America on its path back to greatness. We need to elect a Congress that will work with him rather than resist him. And we need to continue to speak out, despite the Left's efforts to silence us. We cannot allow them to destroy the truth nor the America we love.

Acknowledgments

I told you the man moves faster than the speed of light, so I needed a few people to help create some cosmic interruption.

My thanks to Al Pirro, my lawyer, always generous with his time and ready to jump in and help, thanks for always having faith in me.

As we embark on our second book together, I want to express my deep gratitude to the team at Hachette led by publisher Rolf Zettersten and marketing and sales VPs Patsy Jones and Billy Clark. I thank them and everyone in sales, marketing, publicity and production for all their support. I am truly proud to be one of your authors.

To Editorial Director Kate Hartson, thanks for always being available and willing to work above and beyond what's needed, and always with a smile. Your support and enthusiasm are bright lights for me.

To Tom Mullen, thanks for your research and fastidious attention to detail as well as your availability, given both our crazy schedules.

And finally, to the newest member of my family, Stella, who like Sir Lancelot, huddles with me whenever I sit to write, providing unending warmth and loyalty. Although they are standard poodles, in spite of their size, they are really lap dogs. But don't tell anyone!

Endnotes

CHAPTER ONE: HERE'S MY OPEN

1. John Solomon, "Lisa Page bombshell: FBI couldn't prove Trump-Russia collusion before Mueller appointment." *The Hill*, September 16, 2018. https://thehill.com/hilltv/rising/406881-lisa-page-bombshell-fbi-couldnt-prove-trump-russia-collusion-before-mueller.

2. Ian Schwartz, "Brennan: I Smell More Indictments Coming from Mueller, I Hope He Uncovers More," RealClear Politics, March 8, 2019, https://www.realclearpolitics.com/video/2019/03/08/brennan_i_smell_more_indictments_coming_from_mueller_i_hope_he_uncovers_more.html.

3. Paul Krugman, "Days of Greed and Desperation," *New York Times*, November 17, 2017, https://krugman.blogs.nytimes.com/2017/11/17/days-of-greed-and-desperation/.

4. Daniel K. Williams, "What Happened on Election Day," *New York Times*, November 9, 2016, https://www.nytimes.com/interactive/projects/cp/opinion/election-night-2016.

5. John Bresnahan and Seung Min Kim, "Holder Held in Contempt," Politico, June 28, 2012, https://www.politico.com/story/2012/06/holder-held-in-contempt-of-congress-077988.

6. John Solomon and Alison Spann, "FBI Uncovered Russian Bribery Plot Before Obama Administration Approved Controversial Nuclear Deal with Moscow," *The Hill*, October 17, 2017, https://thehill.com/policy/national-security/355749-fbi-uncovered-russian-bribery-plot-before-obama-administration.

7. Andrew Prokop, "Obama Mocks Trump's Conspiracy Theory That the Election Will Be 'Rigged,'" Vox, August 4, 2016, https://www.vox.com/2016/8/4/12382282/obama-trump-election-rigged.

8. 18 US Code § 3322, Disclosure of Certain Matters Occurring Before Grand Jury, Legal Information Institute, https://www.law.cornell.edu/uscode/text/18/3322.

9. Jeremy Herb, "House Intelligence Republicans Call on Chairman Adam Schiff to Resign," CNN, March 28, 2019, https://www.cnn.com/2019/03/28/politics/adam-schiff-call-resign-republicans-house-intelligence-committee/index.html.

10. Kevin Breuninger, "House Intel Chairman Adam Schiff Bites Back After Republicans Push Him to Resign Over Russia Probe," CNBC, March 28, 2019,

https://www.cnbc.com/2019/03/28/house-intel-chairman-adam-schiff-bites-back-amid-pressure-to-resign.html.

CHAPTER TWO: THEY CAN LIE, BUT THEY CAN'T STOP TRUMP FROM WINNING

1. Abigail Tracy, "Robert Mueller Is Officially Closing in on Trump," *Vanity Fair*, September 20, 2017, https://www.vanityfair.com/news/2017/09/robert-mueller-donald-trump-white-house-documents?verso=true.

2. "Remarks by President Trump to the 72nd Session of the United Nations General Assembly," White House, September 19, 2017, https://www.whitehouse.gov/briefings-statements/remarks-president-trump-72nd-session-united-nations-general-assembly/.

3. Ibid.

4. Michael Kranz, "The Russia Investigation Is Reaching a Pivotal Moment and It Looks Like It's Closing in on Trump," Business Insider, January 24, 2018, https://www.businessinsider.com/the-russia-investigation-is-closing-in-on-trump-2018-1/.

5. Zeeshan Aleem, "Donald Trump Has Finally Dealt His First Blow to China's Economy," Vox, January 23, 2018, https://www.vox.com/world/2018/1/23/16920984/solar-panel-china-trump-tariff-washers-south-korea.

6. Scott Horsley, "Trump Aims to Play Salesman During Davos Economic Forum," NPR, January 23, 2018, https://www.npr.org/2018/01/23/580101123/trump-aims-to-play-salesman-during-davos-economic-forum.

7. Greg Price, "Is Mueller Closing in on Trump? Incidents Involving President's Lawyer and Russia Under Scrutiny, Report Says," *Newsweek*, March 6, 2018, https://www.newsweek.com/mueller-cohen-russia-trump-ukraine-833237.

8. Chad P. Brown, "Trump Has Announced Massive Aluminum and Steel Tariffs. Here Are 5 Things You Need to Know," *Washington Post*, March 1, 2018, https://www.washingtonpost.com/news/monkey-cage/wp/2018/03/01/trump-has-announced-massive-aluminum-and-steel-tariffs-here-are-5-things-you-need-to-know/?utm_term=.e6e8c260f2a7.

9. Caitlyn Oprysko, "Trump Threatens Border Shutdown If Mexico Doesn't Remove Migrants," Politico, November 26, 2018, https://www.politico.com/story/2018/11/26/trump-border-close-mexico-caravan-1014701.

10. Bill Chappell and Tom Bowman, "Trump Is Expected to Extend U.S. Troops' Deployment to Mexico Border into January," NPR, November 28, 2018, https://www.npr.org/2018/11/28/671472765/trump-is-expected-to-extend-u-s-troops-deployment-to-mexico-border-into-january.

11. John Nichols, "The Mueller Investigation Is Closing in on Trump—and the Next Congress Won't Protect Him," *The Nation*, November 29, 2018, https://www.thenation.com/article/trump-mueller-cohen-nadler/.

12. Tom Rogan, "Trump's Recognition of Juan Guaido Is Bold

Moral Leadership on Venezuela," *Washington Examiner*, January 23, 2019, https://www.washingtonexaminer.com/opinion/trumps-recognition-of-juan-guaido-is-bold-moral-leadership-on-venezuela.

13. Amy MacKinnon, "Maduro vs. Guaidó: A Global Scorecard," *Foreign Policy*, February 6, 2019, https://foreignpolicy.com/2019/02/06/maduro-vs-guaido-a-global-scorecard-map-infographic/.

14. James Kirchick, "Remember All Those Left-Wing Pundits Who Drooled Over Venezuela?" *Los Angeles Times*, August 2, 2017, https://www.latimes.com/opinion/op-ed/la-oe-kirchick-venezuela-pundits-20170802-story.html.

15. Daniel Di Martino, "Venezuela Was My Home, and Socialism Destroyed It. Slowly, It Will Destroy America, Too," *USA Today*, February 15, 2019, https://www.usatoday.com/story/opinion/voices/2019/02/15/donald-trump-venezuela-socialism-bernie-sanders-ilhan-omar-column/2861461002/.

16. Ryan Cooper, "The Mueller Investigation Is Closing in on Trump," *The Week*, January 25, 2019, https://theweek.com/articles/819785/mueller-investigation-closing-trump.

17. Brian Stetler, "Debunking Roger Stone's Anti-CNN Conspiracy Theory," CNN, February 13, 2019, https://www.cnn.com/2019/02/13/media/roger-stone-cnn-conspiracy-theory/index.html.

18. Sean Rossman, "Nearly 500 Witnesses, 675 Days: The Mueller Investigation by the Numbers," *USA Today*, March 24, 2019, https://www.usatoday.com/story/news/politics/2019/03/24/mueller-report-trump-campaign-investigation-numbers/3263353002/.

CHAPTER THREE: REVENGE OFF THE RAILS

1. Brooke Singman, "Senate Judiciary Committee narrowly advances Barr nomination; moves on to full Senate for confirmation vote," Fox News, February 7, 2019. https://www.foxnews.com/politics/senate-judiciary-committee-narrowly-advances-barr-nomination-moves-on-to-full-senate-for-confirmation-vote.

2. John Nichols, "William Barr Is Acting as Trump's Defense Lawyer, Not Attorney General," *The Nation*, May 1, 2019, https://www.thenation.com/article/william-barr-attorney-general-hearing/.

3. Josh Gerstein, "Eric Holder: 'I'm Still the President's Wingman,'" Politico, April 4, 2013, https://www.politico.com/blogs/politico44/2013/04/eric-holder-im-still-the-presidents-wingman-160861.

4. Thomas B. Langhorne, "Campaign cash trumps work in Congress, ex-members say | Secrets of the Hill," Courier and Press, October 12, 2018, https://www.courierpress.com/story/news/2018/10/12/campaign-cash-trumps-work-congress-ex-members-say-secrets-hill/1457433002/.

5. "Election Overview." Open Secrets. https://www.opensecrets.org/overview/index.php?cycle=2020&display=T&type=R.

6. Emily Tillett, Stefan Becket, and Camilo Montoya-Galvez, "Top Democrats Demand Barr Turn Over Full Mueller Report, Materials by April 2," CBS News, March 24, 2019, https://www.cbsnews.com/live-news/mueller-report-trump-russia-investigation-william-barr-summary-latest-updates-today-2019-03-25/.

7. "Rod Rosenstein's Letter Recommending Comey Be Fired," BBC News, May 10, 2017, https://www.bbc.com/news/world-us-canada-39866767.

8. Philip Ewing, "If the Full Mueller Report Were Ever Released, What Might It Reveal?" NPR, May 17, 2019, https://www.npr.org/2019/05/17/722901976/if-the-full-mueller-report-were-ever-released-what-might-it-reveal.

9. Joe Fox, John Muyskens, and Danielle Rindler, "Mueller report offers clues to what's behind the redactions," *Washington Post*, April 19, 2019, https://www.washingtonpost.com/graphics/2019/politics/mueller-report-redactions/?utm_term=.ad23f70275c5.

10. Elizabeth Vaughn, "Volume II of Sealed Version of Mueller Report Is 99.9% Unredacted; Guess How Many House Democrats Have Read It?" RedState, May 11, 2019, https://www.redstate.com/elizabeth-vaughn/2019/05/11/guess-many-house-democrats-read-minimally-redacted-copy-mueller-report/.

11. Madison Gesiotto, "Do Democrats Really Want to See the Unredacted Special Counsel Report?" *The Hill*, May 6, 2019, https://thehill.com/opinion/judiciary/442329-do-democrats-really-want-to-see-the-unredacted-special-counsel-report.

12. Tim Hains, "Mazie Hirono to Bill Barr: 'You Lied to Congress... And Now We Know,'" RealClear Politics, May 1, 2019, https://www.realclearpolitics.com/video/2019/05/01/mazie_hirono_to_bill_barr_you_lied_to_congress_and_now_we_know.html.

13. "Kamala Harris Questions William Barr: Full Video on May 1, 2019," News 19 WLTX, YouTube, May 1, 2019, https://www.youtube.com/watch?v=wZICLS7Avio.

14. Matt Zapotosky, "Trump Said Mueller's Team Has '13 Hardened Democrats.' Here Are the Facts," *Washington Post*, March 18, 2018, https://www.washingtonpost.com/news/post-politics/wp/2018/03/18/trump-said-muellers-team-has-13-hardened-democrats-here-are-the-facts/?utm_term=.957feb4f1c14.

15. Laura Jarrett, "Former Acting FBI Director: Rosenstein 'Offered to Wear a Wire into the White House,'" CNN, February 17, 2019, https://www.cnn.com/2019/02/17/politics/mccabe-fbi-rosenstein-wire/index.html.

16. Bess Levin, "Kamala Harris Guts Barr Like a Fish, Leaves Him Flopping on the Deck," *Vanity Fair*, May 1, 2019, https://www.vanityfair.com/news/2019/05/kamala-harris-william-barr?verso=true.

17. Greg Sargent, "Kamala Harris Zeroes in on the Big Problem with William Barr," *Washington Post*, May 1, 2019. https://www.washingtonpost.com/opinions/2019/05/01/kamala-harris-pinpoints-big-problem-with-william-barr/?utm_term=.290987d61343.

18. NR Symposium, "Conservatives Against Trump," *National Review*, January 22, 2016, https://www.nationalreview.com/2016/01/donald-trump-conservatives-oppose-nomination/.

19. Andrew C. McCarthy, "The Big Lie That Barr Lied," *National Review*, May 3, 2019, https://www.nationalreview.com/2019/05/the-big-lie-that-barr-lied/.

20. Andrew Desiderio, "Barr's FBI 'Spying' Claim Amps Up Fight Over Mueller Probe," Politico, April 10, 2019, https://www.politico.com/story/2019/04/10/barr-fbi-spying-trump-campaign-1266531.

21. Associated Press, "Barr Appoints Prosecutor to Examine Russia Probe Origins," Politico, May 14, 2019, https://www.politico.com/story/2019/05/14/barr-prosecutor-russia-probe-origins-1319878.

22. Ibid.

23. Marshall Cohen, "US Attorney's 'Apolitical' Reputation on the Line as He Helps Barr Review the Russia Probe," CNN, May 14, 2019, https://www.cnn.com/2019/05/14/politics/john-durham-barr-russia-probe/index.html.

CHAPTER FOUR: RATS DESERT THE SHIP

1. Luke Barr and Lee Ferran, "Trump Gives Attorney General Barr Sweeping Power to Declassify Intelligence in Russia Probe Review," ABC News, May 24, 2019, https://abcnews.go.com/Politics/trump-directs-intelligence-community-cooperate-attorney-general-investigation/story?id=63244302.

2. Andrew McCarthy, "The Steele Dossier and the 'Verified Application' That Wasn't," *National Review*, May 18, 2019. https://www.nationalreview.com/2019/05/the-steele-dossier-and-the-verified-application-that-wasnt/.

3. Matt Zapotosky, "Inspector General Report Faults Andrew McCabe for Unauthorized Disclosure of Information, Misleading Investigators," *Washington Post*, April 13, 2018, https://www.washingtonpost.com/world/national-security/justice-department-inspector-general-provides-report-to-congress-on-andrew-mccabe/2018/04/13/ce367c4c-3f36-11e8-974f-aacd97698cef_story.html?utm_term=.32fc258ed543.

4. Caitlin Oprysko, "Barr Forcefully Defends DOJ Probe into Origin of the Russia Investigation," Politico, May 17, 2019, https://www.politico.com/story/2019/05/17/william-barr-investigation-russia-1330008.

5. Katie Galioto, "Comey Has Harsh Words for Barr and Rosenstein: Trump Has 'Eaten Your Soul,'" Politico, May 1, 2019, https://www.politico.com/story/2019/05/01/james-comey-william-barr-rod-rosenstein-1296662.

6. Ibid.

7. Chris Smith, "Mr. Comey Goes to Washington," *New York*, October 10, 2003, http://nymag.com/nymetro/news/politics/n_9353/.

8. Gregg Re. "Rosenstein unloads on Comey, says he broke 'bright lines that should never be crossed." Fox News, May 13, 2019. https://www.foxnews.com/politics/rosenstein-comey-broke-bright-lines-that-should-never-be-crossed

9. Virginia Kruta, "Swalwell Blows Off Mueller, Says He Knows Trump Colluded with Russia," Daily Caller, May 26, 2019, https://dailycaller.com/2019/05/26/swalwell-trump-colluded-russia/.

10. Katie Pavlich, "John Brennan Tries to Explain: It's Not My Fault I Called Trump a Russian Traitor, I Got Bad Information," Town Hall, March 25, 2019, https://townhall.com/tipsheet/katiepavlich/2019/03/25/john-brennan-tries-to-explain-its-not-my-fault-i-was-wrong-on-russia-i-got-bad-information-n2543697.

11. Michael Isikoff, "Top FBI Officials Were 'Quite Worried' Comey Would Appear to Be Blackmailing Trump," Yahoo! News, May 15, 2019, https://news.yahoo.com/top-fbi-officials-were-quite-worried-comey-would-appear-to-be-blackmailing-trump-132955356.html.

12. Gregg Re, "Loretta Lynch Accuses Comey of Misrepresenting Key Clinton Probe Conversation, Was 'Quite Surprised' by His Testimony," Fox News, May 20, 2019, https://www.foxnews.com/politics/loretta-lynch-james-comey-contradition-clinton-probe-matter-investigation.

13. Joseph Weber, "Lynch used email alias 'Elizabeth Carlisle' to write about Clinton tarmac meeting." Fox News, August 7, 2017, https://www.foxnews.com/politics/lynch-used-email-alias-elizabeth-carlisle-to-write-about-clinton-tarmac-meeting.

14. Justin Worland, "U.S. Intelligence Chief James Clapper to Donald Trump: We Didn't Leak Russia Documents," Time, January 12, 2017, https://time.com/4632743/james-clapper-donald-trump-russia/.

15. Jonathan Easley, "GOP Report: Clapper Told CNN Host About Trump Dossier in 2017," The Hill, April 27, 2018. https://thehill.com/policy/national-security/385278-gop-report-clapper-told-cnn-host-about-trump-dossier-in-2017.

16. Ron DeSantis et al., letter from members of Congress to Jeff Sessions, Christopher Wray, and John Huber, April 18, 2018, https://gosar.house.gov/uploadedfiles/criminal-referral.pdf.

17. Brooke Singman, "Comey Admits Drafting Clinton Exoneration Before Interview, Defends Move as Routine," Fox News, April 17, 2018, https://www.foxnews.com/politics/comey-admits-drafting-clinton-exoneration-before-interview-defends-move-as-routine.

18. Ibid.

19. Pete Kasperowicz, "'Growing Body of Evidence' James Comey Lied to Congress," Washington Examiner, April 19, 2018, https://www.washingtonexaminer.com/news/growing-evidence-that-james-comey-lied-to-congress-says-mark-meadows.

20. Eric Tucker, "Lawyer: Ex-FBI Official McCabe Still Facing Investigation," Associated Press, February 22, 2019, https://www.apnews.com/8ee9211c06ca440abf80fddb1272b331.

21. Katie Pavlich, "Pavlich: When Will McCabe Face Prosecution for Lying?" The Hill, April 17, 2018, https://thehill.com/opinion/criminal-justice/383644-pavlich-when-will-mccabe-face-prosecution-for-lying.

22. Dan McLaughlin, "The FBI Inspector General Report Directly Criticized President Obama." *National Review*, June 15, 2018. https://www.nationalreview.com/corner/fbi-inspector-general-report-directly-criticized-president-obama/.

23. Brian Jacobs, "Why Do Federal Agents Still Take Interview Notes by Hand?" *Forbes*, April 4, 2016, https://www.forbes.com/sites/insider/2016/04/04/why-do-federal-agents-still-take-notes-by-hand/#37ce2bea41af.

24. "Judicial Watch: New Strzok-Page Emails Reveal FBI Gave Special Treatment to Hillary Clinton's Demands for Email Investigation Information Just Before Election," Judicial Watch, June 3, 2019, https://www.judicialwatch.org/press-room/press-releases/judicial-watch-new-strzok-page-emails-reveal-fbi-gave-special-treatment-to-hillary-clintons-demands-for-email-investigation-information-just-before-election/.

25. "Grassley Wants 'Gag Order' Lifted for FBI Informant Allegedly 'Threatened' by Obama DOJ," Fox News, October 19, 2017, https://www.foxnews.com/politics/grassley-wants-gag-order-lifted-for-fbi-informant-allegedly-threatened-by-obama-doj.

26. Alex Pappas, "Dossier Author Christopher Steele Will Be Questioned by US Investigators: Report," Fox News, June 4, 2019, https://www.foxnews.com/politics/dossier-author-christopher-steele-will-be-questioned-by-us-investigators-report-says.

CHAPTER FIVE: OPEN SEASON ON CONSERVATIVES

1. John McCormack, "Blasey Ford's Female Classmate, Her Last Named Witness, Doesn't Recall Ever Attending Party With Kavanaugh," The Weekly Standard, September 22, 2018, https://web.archive.org/web/20180923043101/https://www.weeklystandard.com/john-mccormack/blasey-fords-female-classmate-her-last-alleged-witness-denies-ever-attending-party-with-kavanaugh.

2. David French, "Christine Blasey Ford Refuses to Turn Over Her Therapy Notes—Here's Why That's a Problem," *National Review*, October 3, 2018, https://www.nationalreview.com/corner/christine-blasey-ford-therapy-notes/.

3. Rebecca Hagelin, "Christine Blasey Ford Just Democrats' Pawn to Kill Brett Kavanaugh Nomination," *Washington Times*, September 30, 2018, https://www.washingtontimes.com/news/2018/sep/30/christine-blasey-ford-just-democrats-pawn-to-kill-/.

4. Jim Geraghty, "'Innocent Until Proven Guilty' Doesn't Apply to Conservatives," *National Review*, September 24, 2018, https://www.nationalreview.com/the-morning-jolt/innocent-until-proven-guilty-doesnt-apply-to-conservatives/.

5. John Nolte, "Rap Sheet: ***639*** Acts of Media-Approved Violence and Harassment Against Trump Supporters," Breitbart, July 5, 2018, https://www.breitbart.com/the-media/2018/07/05/rap-sheet-acts-of-media-approved-violence-and-harassment-against-trump-supporters/.

6. Brett Samuels, "Boulder Thrown Through McCarthy's Office Window," *The Hill*, October 23, 2018, https://thehill.com/homenews/house/412675-boulder-thrown-through-mccarthys-office-window?amp.

7. Joshua Caplan, "Shots Fired into South Daytona Republican Party Office: 'Obviously Politically Motivated,'" Breitbart, October 29, 2018, https://www.breitbart.com/politics/2018/10/29/photos-south-daytona-republican-party-office-shot-up/.

8. "Republican Candidate for Minnesota House Seat Punched in the Face," KMSP-TV Fox9, October 15, 2018, http://www.fox9.com/news/republican-candidate-for-minnesota-house-seat-punched-in-face.

9. Laurie Everett, "Blackburn Backlash Shocks Mt. Juliet Restaurant Owner," *Wilson Post*, October 17, 2018, https://www.wilsonpost.com/community/blackburn-backlash-shocks-mt-juliet-restaurant-owner/article_313833ee-d226-11e8-9d8e-d386ca26eea3.html?fbclid=IwAR199ogdNXEdpWsbv60FCtam350NBFQbwMlfuPF6ePg2_sFCiWjrQ9MEtlU.

10. Ian Schwartz, "FNC's Kat Timpf: I Ran Out of Bar After Harassed for Working at FOX News," RealClear Politics, November 13, 2018, https://www.realclearpolitics.com/video/2018/11/13/fnc_kat_timpf_i_ran_out_of_bar_after_harassed_for_working_at_fox_news.html.

11. Brian Stetler, "How leaks and Investigative Journalists Led to Flynn's Resignation," CNN, February 14, 2017, https://money.cnn.com/2017/02/14/media/michael-flynn-investigative-journalism/index.html.

12. Susan Jones, "Ex-FBI Director Comey Explains How He Took Advantage of Fledgling Trump Administration," CNS News, December 14, 2018, https://www.cnsnews.com/news/article/susan-jones/ex-fbi-director-comey-explains-how-he-took-advantage-fledgling-trump.

13. Any Chozick, "F.B.I. Interviews Hillary Clinton Over Private Email Server," *New York Times*, July 2, 2016, https://www.nytimes.com/2016/07/03/us/politics/hillary-clinton-fbi-emails.html.

14. "Statement by FBI Director James B. Comey on the Investigation of Secretary Hillary Clinton's Use of a Personal E-Mail System," Federal Bureau of Investigation, July 5, 2016, https://www.fbi.gov/news/pressrel/press-releases/statement-by-fbi-director-james-b-comey-on-the-investigation-of-secretary-hillary-clinton2019s-use-of-a-personal-e-mail-system.

15. Andrew C. McCarthy, "FBI Rewrites Federal Law to Let Hillary Off the Hook," *National Review*, July 5, 2016, https://www.nationalreview.com/corner/fbi-rewrites-federal-law-let-hillary-hook/.

CHAPTER SIX: THE DEMOCRAT CLOWN CAR

1. John Gage, "'If only they had a uterus': Bill Maher rips Julián Castro for remark about abortion for trans women." *The Washington Examiner*, June 29, 2019, https://www.washingtonexaminer.com/news/if-only-they-had-a-uterus-bill-maher-rips-julian-castro-for-remark-about-abortion-for-trans-women.

2. Greg Robb, "Ocasio-Cortez says debate reminded her of high school class where some students didn't do their homework," Marketwatch, June 27,

2019, https://www.marketwatch.com/story/ocasio-cortez-says-debate-reminded-her-of-high-school-classroom-where-some-students-didnt-do-their-homework-2019-06-27.

3. Ian Schwartz. "Flashback: Rep. Joe Wilson Yells 'You Lie' When President Obama Said Illegals Will Not Get Health Insurance," RealClear Politics, June 28, 2019, https://www.realclearpolitics.com/video/2019/06/28/flashback_rep_joe_wilson_yells_you_lie_when_president_obama_said_illegals_will_not_get_health_insurance.html.

4. Hollie McKay, "Thousands of Trump Supporters Cheerfully Wait Days in Sweltering Temps to See Him Launch Campaign," Fox News, June 18, 2019, https://www.foxnews.com/politics/thousands-of-trump-supporters-cheerfully-wait-days-in-sweltering-temps-to-see-him-launch-campaign.

5. Caroline Glenn and David Harris, "Trump's Orlando Supporters Line Grows for Tonight's Rally at Amway Center," *Orlando Sentinel*, June 18, 2019, https://www.orlandosentinel.com/politics/os-ne-trump-orlando-campaign-line-20190617-wzvk4htrnndyfj4xuun34tvqo4-story.html.

6. Quint Forgey, "Trump Raises $24.8 Million in Less Than 24 Hours, RNC Says," Politico, June 19, 2019, https://www.politico.com/story/2019/06/19/trump-campaign-contributions-rnc-1369896.

7. Kate Rooney, "Black Unemployment Rate Falls to 5.9%, Ties Record Low Hit Earlier This Year," CNBC, December 7, 2018, https://www.cnbc.com/2018/12/07/black-unemployment-rate-falls-to-5point9percent-ties-record-low-hit-this-year.html.

8. Jeff Cox, "Workers at the Lower End of the Pay Scale Finally Are Getting the Most Benefit from Rising Wages," CNBC, March 13, 2019, https://www.cnbc.com/2019/03/13/workers-at-lower-end-of-pay-scale-getting-most-benefit-from-rising-wages.html.

9. Bo Erickson, "Biden: Trump Is an 'Existential Threat' to the U.S.," CBS News, June 11, 2019, https://www.cbsnews.com/news/biden-trump-existential-threat-to-us/.

10. Jamie Ehrlich, "Congressman Proposes Eliminating Electoral College, Preventing Presidents from Pardoning Themselves," CNN, January 5, 2019, https://www.cnn.com/2019/01/04/politics/constitutional-amendments-steve-cohen-electoral-pardon/index.html.

11. Jose A. Del Real and Julie Turkewitz, "Should the Electoral College Be Eliminated? 15 States Are Trying to Make It Obsolete," *New York Times*, May 22, 2019, https://www.nytimes.com/2019/05/22/us/electoral-college.html.

12. Lukas Mikelionis, "Ocasio-Cortez Calls to Abolish ICE, Says Latinos Must Be Exempt from Immigration Laws Because They Are 'Native' to US," Fox News, February 8, 2019, https://www.foxnews.com/politics/ocasio-cortez-calls-to-abolish-ice-says-latinos-must-be-exempt-from-immigration-laws-because-they-are-native-to-us.

13. Sheryl Gay Stolberg, "House Democrats, with Pelosi's Support, Will Consider a Commission on Reparations," *New York Times*, June 18, 2019, https://www.nytimes.com/2019/06/18/us/politics/house-democrats-reparations.html.

14. "Quick Facts," United States Census Bureau, July 1, 2018, https://www.census.gov/quickfacts/fact/table/US/PST045218.

15. Henry Louis Gates, Jr., "Did Black People Own Slaves?" The Root, March 4, 2013, https://www.theroot.com/did-black-people-own-slaves-1790895436.

16. Victoria Bekiempis, "Four in 10 Americans Prefer Socialism to Capitalism, Poll Finds," *The Guardian*, June 10, 2019, https://www.theguardian.com/us-news/2019/jun/10/america-socialism-capitalism-poll-axios.

17. Peter Hasson, "70% of Democrats Say Socialism Would Be Good for America: Survey," Daily Caller, May 21, 2019, https://dailycaller.com/2019/05/21/poll-democrats-socialism-good/.

18. Jeffery C. Mays, "De Blasio's 'Ban' on Glass and Steel Skyscrapers Isn't a Ban at All," *New York Times*, April 25, 2019, https://www.nytimes.com/2019/04/25/nyregion/glass-skyscraper-ban-nyc.html.

19. Jeff Daniels, "Cattle Industry Blasts NYC Mayor's Green New Deal Plan to Reduce Beef Purchases," CNBC, May 2, 2019, https://www.cnbc.com/2019/05/02/cattle-industry-blasts-nyc-mayors-initiative-to-reduce-beef-buying.html.

20. Sandy Fitzgerald, "De Blasio's Presidential Ambitions Ridiculed in New York City," Newsmax, May 17, 2019, https://www.newsmax.com/newsfront/bill-deblasio-nyc-presidential-run/2019/05/17/id/916419/.

21. Ibid.

22. *New York Post* (@nypost), "Today's cover: Bill de Blasio official launches 2020 presidential campaign," Twitter, May 16, 2019, https://twitter.com/nypost/status/1128979869726121985.

23. CBS News (@CBSNews), "I'm gonna get me a beer," Twitter, January 2, 2019, https://twitter.com/CBSNews/status/1080554654352793609.

24. Jeva Lange, "The Democrats' Presidential Keg Stand," *The Week*, February 27, 2019, https://theweek.com/articles/825889/democrats-presidential-keg-stand.

25. Behind 2020 (@Behind2020), "Kirsten Gillibrand relaxes after working a gay bar in Iowa," Twitter, June 8, 2019, https://twitter.com/Behind2020/status/1137294170392080384.

26. Katie Glueck, "Joe Biden Denounces Hyde Amendment, Reversing His Position," *New York Times*, June 6, 2019, https://www.nytimes.com/2019/06/06/us/politics/joe-biden-hyde-amendment.html.

27. Kate Glueck, "Biden, Recalling 'Civility' in Senate, Invokes Two Segregationist Senators," *New York Times*, June 19, 2019, https://www.nytimes.com/2019/06/19/us/politics/biden-segregationists.html.

28. Alex Thompson (@AlxThomp), "Biden hits back at Booker over segregationist senator," Twitter, June 19, 2019, https://twitter.com/AlxThomp/status/1141496692015083528.

29. Tim Hains, "Cory Booker on Biden 'Boy' Flap: 'Deeply Disappointing,' 'Vice President Biden Shouldn't Need This Lesson,'" RealClear Politics, June 20, 2019, https://www.realclearpolitics.com/video/2019/06/20/cory_booker_on_biden_boy_flap_deeply_disappointing_vice_president_biden_shouldnt_need_this_lesson.html.

30. Evans Witt, "Biden Claimed He Was in Top Half of Law Class," Associated Press, September 21, 1987, https://www.apnews.com/cd977f7ff301993f7976974ba07c5495.

31. Ian Schwartz, "Biden Launches 2020 Campaign: 'Everything That Has Made America America Is at Stake,'" RealClear Politics, April 25, 2019, https://www.realclearpolitics.com/video/2019/04/25/biden_launches_2020_campaign_america_is_at_stake.html.

32. Steve Cortes, "Trump Didn't Call Neo-Nazis 'Fine People.' Here's Proof," RealClear Politics, March 21, 2019, https://www.realclearpolitics.com/articles/2019/03/21/trump_didnt_call_neo-nazis_fine_people_heres_proof_139815.html.

33. Emily Ward, "Trump Has More Women as Top Advisers Than Obama, Bush, or Clinton," Washington Examiner, March 22, 2019, https://www.washingtonexaminer.com/news/trump-has-more-women-as-top-advisers-than-obama-bush-or-clinton.

34. Zack Colman and Natasha Korecki, "Plagiarism Charge Hits Biden Climate Change Plan," Politico, June 4, 2019, https://www.politico.com/story/2019/06/04/plagiarism-biden-climate-change-plan-1504950.

35. "'Creepy!' Joe Biden: Hands-on Moment with Defense Secretary's Wife," Inside Edition, February 18, 2015, https://www.insideedition.com/headlines/9746-creepy-joe-biden-hands-on-moment-with-defense-secretarys-wife.

36. Elise Viebeck, Colby Itkowitz, Michael Scherer, and Matt Viser, "Joe Biden's Affectionate, Physical Style with Women Comes Under Scrutiny," Washington Post, March 31, 2019, https://www.washingtonpost.com/politics/joe-bidens-affectionate-physical-style-with-women-comes-under-scrutiny/2019/03/31/a41a81d0-5275-11e9-8d28-f5149e5a2fda_story.html?utm_term=.2d4736f9dd3e.

37. James Bickerton, "Joe Biden Accused of Being 'CREEPY' with Girl, 10, After Telling Her 'You're Good Looking,'" Express, May 31, 2019, https://www.express.co.uk/news/world/1134287/Joe-Biden-news-Democrat-Presidential-Donald-Trump-republican-US-election-2020.

38. Christina Zhao, "2020 Candidate Joe Biden Backs Medicare Public Option: 'You All Should Have a Choice,'" Newsweek, April 29, 2019, https://www.newsweek.com/2020-candidate-joe-biden-backs-medicare-all-policy-you-all-should-have-choice-1409332.

39. "Remarks by the President to a Joint Session of Congress on Health Care," White House, September 9, 2009, https://obamawhitehouse.archives.gov/the-press-office/remarks-president-a-joint-session-congress-health-care.

40. Timothy Meads, "Will Bernie Sanders Quote Hugo Chavez While Defending Democratic Socialism Next Week?" Townhall, June 9, 2019, https://townhall.com/tipsheet/timothymeads/2019/06/09/bernie-sanders-to-give-speech-defending-democratic-socialism-next-week-n2547800.

41. Ira Stoll, "Biden Backs Two Years of 'Free' Community College," *Education Next*, May 14, 2019, https://www.educationnext.org/biden-backs-two-years-free-community-college/.

42. Eric Morath, "Wages Rise at Fastest Rate in Nearly a Decade as Hiring Jumps," *Wall Street Journal*, November 2, 2018, https://www.wsj.com/articles/wages-rise-at-fastest-rate-in-nearly-a-decade-as-hiring-jumps-in-october-1541161920.

43. John Solomon, "Joe Biden's 2020 Ukrainian Nightmare: A Closed Probe Is Revived," *The Hill*, April 1, 2020, https://thehill.com/opinion/white-house/436816-joe-bidens-2020-ukrainian-nightmare-a-closed-probe-is-revived.

44. Kenneth P. Vogel and Iuliia Mendel, "Biden Faces Conflict of Interest Questions That Are Being Promoted by Trump and Allies," *New York Times*, May 1, 2019, https://www.nytimes.com/2019/05/01/us/politics/biden-son-ukraine.html.

45. VP Biden (Archived) (@VP44), "Happy 55th, Barack. A brother to me, a best friend forever," Twitter, August 4, 2016, https://twitter.com/VP44/status/761253705341480962.

46. "The State of the Democratic Primary," Morning Consult, June 3, 2019, https://morningconsult.com/2020-democratic-primary/.

47. Graham Vyse, "Democratic Socialists Rack Up Wins in States," *Governing*, November 9, 2018, https://www.governing.com/topics/politics/gov-ocasio-cortez-tlaib-Democratic-Socialists-state-level.html.

48. Emily Shugerman, "Ex-Staffers: Bernie 'Struggles' with Women's Issues," Daily Beast, June 7, 2019, https://www.thedailybeast.com/bernie-sanders-has-a-blind-spot-on-womens-issues-ex-staffers-say.

49. "Issues," Bernie 2020, https://berniesanders.com/issues/.

50. Adam Shaw, "Lifestyles of the Rich and Socialist: Bernie Sanders Has 3 Houses, Makes Millions," Fox News, February 21, 2019, https://www.foxnews.com/politics/lifestyles-of-the-rich-and-socialist-bernie-sanders-has-3-houses-makes-millions.

51. Kristin Tate, "Millions of Taxpayer Dollars Fueled Bernie Sanders to Wealth Success," *The Hill*, May 26, 2019, https://thehill.com/opinion/campaign/445619-millions-of-taxpayer-dollars-fueled-bernie-sanders-to-wealth-success.

52. "Social Security Act Fact Sheet," Bernie Sanders: U.S. Senator for Vermont, https://www.sanders.senate.gov/download/social-security-expansion-act-2019-summary?id=4C5A8DAF-5840-452B-AAFF-D2652867C095&download=1&inline=file.

53. Thomas Kaplan and Jim Tankersley, "Elizabeth Warren Has Lots of Plans. Together, They Would Remake the Economy," *New York Times*, June 10, 2019, https://www.nytimes.com/2019/06/10/us/politics/elizabeth-warren-2020-policies-platform.html.

54. "Issues: Rebuild the Middle Class," Warren for President, https://elizabethwarren.com/issues#rebuild-the-middle-class.

55. Elizabeth Warren, "I'm Proposing a Big New Idea: The Real Corporate Profits Tax," Medium, April 11, 2019, https://medium.com/@teamwarren/im-proposing-a-big-new-idea-the-real-corporate-profits-tax-29dde7c960d.

56. Tyler Cowen, "Why Does Amazon Pay $0 in Federal Income Taxes?" Foundation for Economic Education, February 20, 2019, https://fee.org/articles/why-does-amazon-pay-0-in-federal-income-taxes/?gclid=EAIaIQobChMI2sTVqt_s4gIVTi2GCh0oNQ2kEAAYASAAEgIEUvD_BwE.

57. Bill George, "The Fallacy of Medicare for All," *Fortune*, April 24, 2019, http://fortune.com/2019/04/24/medicare-for-all-plan-costs/.

58. John Daniel Davidson, "50 Years Later, Medicaid and Medicare Still Spend Us into Oblivion," The Federalist, July 31, 2015, https://thefederalist.com/2015/07/31/medicare-medicaid-same-problems-50-years-ago/.

59. "A Budget for a Better America: Fiscal Year 2020 Budget of the U.S. Government," White House, https://www.whitehouse.gov/wp-content/uploads/2019/03/budget-fy2020.pdf.

60. Eliza Relman, "Alexandria Ocasio-Cortez Says Her Green New Deal Climate Plan Would Cost at Least $10 Trillion," Business Insider, June 5, 2019, https://www.businessinsider.com/alexandria-ocasio-cortez-says-green-new-deal-cost-10-trillion-2019-6.

61. Gregg Re, "Green New Deal Would Cost Up to $93 Trillion, or $600G per Household, Study Says," Fox News, February 25, 2019, https://www.foxnews.com/politics/green-new-deal-would-cost-93-trillion-or-600g-per-household-study-says.

62. Alex Muresianu, "Elizabeth Warren's Budget Math Still Doesn't Work," *Reason*, June 3, 2019, https://reason.com/2019/06/03/elizabeth-warrens-budget-math-still-doesnt-work/.

63. "Latest 2020 Democratic Presidential Primary Polls," RealClear Politics, June 11, 2019, https://www.realclearpolitics.com/epolls/latest_polls/democratic_nomination_polls/.

64. Scott Detrow and Clay Masters, "Harris: Justice Dept. 'Would Have No Choice' But to Prosecute Trump After Presidency," NPR Politics Podcast, June 12, 2019, https://www.npr.org/2019/06/08/730941386/harris-justice-dept-would-have-no-choice-but-to-prosecute-trump-after-presidency.

65. "Issues," Pete for America, https://peteforamerica.com/issues/.

66. Ibid.

67. Trudy Ring, "Buttigieg Endorses Reparations, Ending Electoral College," *Advocate*, May 16, 2019, https://www.advocate.com/politics/2019/5/16/buttigieg-endorses-reparations-ending-electoral-college.

CHAPTER SEVEN: HOME ALONE IN THE WHITE HOUSE

1. Alex Pappas, "Nancy Pelosi Is Vacationing at Hawaii Resort During Shutdown," Fox News, December 28, 2018, https://www.foxnews.com/politics/nancy-pelosi-is-vacationing-at-hawaii-resort-during-shutdown.

2. "Remarks by President Trump on the Humanitarian Crisis on Our Southern Border and the Shutdown," White House, January 19, 2019, https://www.whitehouse.gov/briefings-statements/remarks-president-trump-humanitarian-crisis-southern-border-shutdown/.

3. Sophie Tatum, "Lawmakers Reject Trump's Latest Immigration Proposal," CNN, January 21, 2019, https://www.cnn.com/2019/01/19/politics/trump-border-wall-shutdown-congress-reaction/index.html.

4. Ian Schwartz, "CNN Instant Poll: 76% Of Viewers Approved Of Trump State Of The Union," CNN, February 5, 2019, https://www.realclearpolitics.com/video/2019/02/05/cnn_instant_poll_76_of_viewers_approved_of_trump_state_of_the_union.html.

5. Quinn Scanlan and Roey Hadar, "Democrats Will Not Agree to Any Funding for US-Mexico Border Wall: Senator Jeff Merkley," ABC News, December 23, 2018, https://abcnews.go.com/beta-story-container/Politics/democrats-agree-funding-us-mexico-border-wall-senator/story?id=59977718.

6. Sophie Brickman, "Nancy Pelosi on Her New Role, Trump's Manhood, and *That* Red Max Mara Coat," *Elle*, January 2, 2019, https://www.elle.com/culture/career-politics/a25725869/nancy-pelosi-house-speaker-interview/.

7. Mike DeBonis, "'It's like a manhood thing for him': Pelosi's power play with Trump serves as message to opponents." *Washington Post*, December 11, 2018, https://www.washingtonpost.com/powerpost/pelosi-questions-trumps-manhood-after-confrontational-white-house-meeting/2018/12/11/2b2111be-fd79-11e8-862a-b6a6f3ce8199_story.html?utm_term=.39402df6c485.

8. Michael Rubin, "The Places Where Walls Work," American Enterprise Institute, January 27, 2017, http://www.aei.org/publication/the-places-where-walls-work/.

9. Kim Hjelmgaard, "From 7 to 77: There's Been an Explosion in Building Border Walls Since World War II," *USA Today*, May 24, 2018, https://www.usatoday.com/story/news/world/2018/05/24/border-walls-berlin-wall-donald-trump-wall/553250002/.

10. William J. Bennett, "Bill Bennett: Democrats Have Made a Sharp Left Turn—Here's What's Behind It," Fox News, February 3, 2019, https://www.foxnews.com/opinion/bill-bennett-democrats-have-made-a-sharp-left-turn-heres-whats-behind-it.

11. Stephen Dinan, "Border Agents: Steel Fence Not Impenetrable But Still Needed," *Washington Times*, January 10, 2019, https://www.washingtontimes.com/news/2019/jan/10/border-agents-steel-fence-not-impenetrable/.

12. Tal Kopan, "Trump Ends DACA But Gives Congress Window to Save It," CNN, September 5, 2017, https://www.cnn.com/2017/09/05/politics/daca-trump-congress/index.html.

13. Jonathan Allen, "When Trump Doesn't Want to Decide, He Punts to Congress," NBC News, October 21, 2017, https://www.nbcnews.com/politics/white-house/when-trump-doesn-t-want-decide-he-punts-congress-n812591.

14. Tal Kopan, "White House Lays Out DACA Deal Asks," CNN, October 9, 2017, https://www.cnn.com/2017/10/08/politics/white-house-daca-deal-principles/index.html.

15. Jake Novak, "Democrats Would Be Crazy to Reject Trump's DACA Deal," CNBC, January 26, 2018, https://www.cnbc.com/2018/01/26/trump-daca-deal-is-a-dream-come-true-for-democrats-commentary.html.

16. Jill Colvin and Catherine Lucey, "Democrats Dismiss President Trump's Shutdown-Ending DACA Deal as a 'Non-Starter,'" *Time*, January 19, 2019.

17. Matthew Sheffield, "Poll Shows Voters Blame Trump More Than Dems for Government Shutdown," *The Hill*, January 2, 2019, https://thehill.com/hilltv/what-americas-thinking/423513-democrats-facing-little-blame-from-public-over-partial.

18. "Immigration Update: Voters Don't Think Government's Doing Enough to Stop Illegal Immigration," Rasmussen Reports, January 11, 2019, http://www.rasmussenreports.com/public_content/politics/current_events/immigration/immigration_update_jan11.

19. Nicholas Fandos, Sheryl Gay Stolberg, and Peter Baker, "Trump Signs Bill Reopening Government for 3 Weeks in Surprise Retreat From Wall," *New York Times*, January 25, 2019, https://www.nytimes.com/2019/01/25/us/politics/trump-shutdown-deal.html.

20. Erica Werner, Mike DeBonis, and John Wagner, "Trump Signs Bill to Open the Government, Ending the Longest Shutdown in History," *Washington Post*, January 25, 2019, https://www.washingtonpost.com/politics/senate-leaders-continue-to-seek-a-deal-to-end-shutdown-that-will-satisfy-trump/2019/01/25/09c898dc-20ad-11e9-8e21-59a09ff1e2a1_story.html.

21. Brian Flood, "Nancy Pelosi Praised by Liberals for 'Exquisite Shade' of SOTU Applause," Fox News, February 6, 2019, https://www.foxnews.com/politics/liberals-praise-nancy-pelosi-for-exquisite-shade-of-nancy-pelosis-sotu-applause.

22. Patton Oswalt (@pattonoswalt), "Congrats to @SpeakerPelosi for inventing the 'f--- you' clap," Twitter, February 5, 2019, https://twitter.com/pattonoswalt/status/1092984227623141377.

23. "State of the Union 2019: Read the Full Transcript," CNN, February 6, 2019, https://www.cnn.com/2019/02/05/politics/donald-trump-state-of-the-union-2019-transcript/index.html.

24. Julie Hirschfeld Davis and Nicholas Fandos, "Pelosi and Trump Agree on Something: She Should Be Speaker," *New York Times*, November 7, 2018, https://www.nytimes.com/2018/11/07/us/politics/pelosi-trump-house-speaker.html.

25. Caitlin Oprysko, "Trump: 'I Like Bernie' but He May Have Missed His Shot," Politico, February 19, 2019, https://www.politico.com/story/2019/02/19/trump-bernie-sanders-1175611.

26. "State of the Union 2019: Read the Full Transcript," CNN, February 6, 2019, https://www.cnn.com/2019/02/05/politics/donald-trump-state-of-the-union-2019-transcript/index.html.

27. Ian Schwartz, "CNN Instant Poll: 76% Of Viewers Approved of Trump State of the Union," CNN, February 5, 2019, https://www.realclearpolitics.com/video/2019/02/05/cnn_instant_poll_76_of_viewers_approved_of_trump_state_of_the_union.html.

CHAPTER EIGHT: INVASION AT THE BORDER

1. Allyson Chiu, "'He's running for embarrassing dad at a Mexican restaurant': Democrats debate in Spanish, to mixed reviews/. *Washington Post*, June 27, 2019, https://www.washingtonpost.com/nation/2019/06/27/hes-running-embarrassing-dad-mexican-restaurant-democrats-debate-spanish-mixed-reviews/?utm_term=.c4fd4dd0ae32.

2. Daniel Horowitz, "Why Aren't We Deporting Illegal Aliens Who Already Have Deportation Orders?" Conservative Review, March 19, 2019, https://www.conservativereview.com/news/arent-deporting-illegal-aliens-already-deportation-orders/.

3. Nick Miroff and Maria Sacchetti, "Burgeoning court backlog of more than 850,000 cases undercuts Trump immigration agenda," *Washington Post*, May 1, 2019, https://www.washingtonpost.com/immigration/burgeoning-court-backlog-of-more-than-850000-cases-undercuts-trump-immigration-agenda/2019/05/01/09c0b84a-6b69-11e9-a66d-a82d3f3d96d5_story.html?utm_term=.6270f60d75a6.

4. "HHS Secretary Azar: We are running out of money to take care of migrant children." Fox News, June 24, 2019.

5. https://twitter.com/AOC/status/1140968240073662466.

6. Doree Lawark, "'Nobel Prize in stupidity': Holocaust survivor wants AOC out of Congress." *New York Post*, June 29, 2019, https://nypost.com/2019/06/29/nobel-prize-in-stupidity-holocaust-survivor-wants-aoc-out-of-congress/.

7. Nick Givas, "Holocaust survivors respond to AOC's 'concentration camp' comments in new video," Fox News, June 23, 2019, https://www.foxnews.com/politics/.aoc-holocaust-survivors-respond-to-aocs-concentration-camp-comments

8. "The Crisis at the Southern Border Is Too Urgent to Ignore," White House, January 10, 2019, https://www.whitehouse.gov/briefings-statements/crisis-southern-border-urgent-ignore/.

9. Mary Plummer, "Automatic Voter Registration Could Have a Big Impact By 2020 Election," NPR, April 18, 2018, https://www.npr.org/2018/04/18/603693118/automatic-voter-registration-could-have-a-big-impact-by-2020-election.

10. Alex Pappas, "House Dems Overwhelmingly Reject Motion to Condemn Illegal Immigrant Voting," Fox News, March 8, 2019, https://www.foxnews.com/politics/democrats-vote-against-motion-condemning-illegal-immigrant-voting.

11. "Statement from the President Regarding Emergency Measures to Address the Border Crisis," White House, May 30, 2019, https://www.whitehouse.gov/briefings-statements/statement-president-regarding-emergency-measures-address-border-crisis/.

12. Ibid.

13. Ibid.

14. Annie Karni, Ana Swanson, and Michael D. Shear, "Trump Says U.S. Will Hit Mexico With 5% Tariffs on All Goods," *New York Times,* May 30, 2019, https://www.nytimes.com/2019/05/30/us/politics/trump-mexico-tariffs.html.

15. Josh Katz, "Who Will Be President," *New York Times*, November 8, 2016, https://www.nytimes.com/interactive/2016/upshot/presidential-polls-forecast.html.

16. Peter Baker, Sheryl Gay Stolberg, and Nicholas Fandos, "Christine Blasey Ford Wants F.B.I. to Investigate Kavanaugh Before She Testifies," *New York Times,* September 18, 2018, https://www.nytimes.com/2018/09/18/us/politics/christine-blasey-ford-kavanaugh-senate-hearing.html?rref=collection%2Fsectioncollection%2Fcorrections.

17. Kimberly Amadeo, "Mexico's Economy Facts, Opportunities, and Challenges," *The Balance,* January 22, 2019, https://www.thebalance.com/mexico-s-economy-facts-opportunites-challenges-3306351.

18. Patti Domm, "Why Trump's Pivot To Using Tariffs as a Political Weapon Is So Dangerous for the Economy," CNBC, June 5, 2019, https://www.cnbc.com/2019/06/05/trump-policy-domm-190604-ec.html.

19. Michael Bloomberg, "Stop Trump on Trade," *Bloomberg Opinion*, May 31, 2019, https://www.bloomberg.com/opinion/articles/2019-05-31/mexico-tariffs-trump-s-latest-move-on-trade-is-dangerous.

20. Nathan Bomey, "State of the Union Fact Check: Trump's U.S. Job Growth Claims Generally Accurate," *USA Today,* January 30, 2018, https://www.usatoday.com/story/money/2018/01/30/state-union-president-trump/1081452001/.

21. Kayla Tausche and Tucker Higgins, "Mnuchin and Lighthizer opposed Trump Tariffs on Mexico, source says," CNBC, May 31, 2019, https://www.cnbc.com/2019/05/31/mnuchin-and-lighthizer-were-opposed-to-trump-tariffs-on-mexico-source-says.html.

22. "U.S. Immigrant Population and Share Over Time, 1850–Present," Migration Policy Institute, https://www.migrationpolicy.org/programs/data-hub/charts/immigrant-population-over-time.

23. Jason Lemon, "DEPORTATIONS UNDER TRUMP STILL LAG FAR BEHIND THOSE CARRIED OUT BY THE OBAMA ADMINISTRATION," Newsweek, December 18, 2018, https://www.newsweek.com/trump-still-deports-less-people-obama-1269962.

24. "Fact Sheet: The Dream Act, DACA, and Other Policies Designed to Protect Dreamers," https://www.americanimmigrationcouncil.org/research/dream-act-daca-and-other-policies-designed-protect-dreamers.

25. https://www.nytimes.com/2014/10/01/us/obama-approves-plan-to-let-children-apply-for-refugee-status-in-central-america.html.

26. Ryan Lovelace, "Teenage Latin Border Horde," *National Review*, June 13, 2019, https://www.nationalreview.com/2014/06/teenage-latin-border-horde-ryan-lovelace/.

27. Azam Ahmed, "Mexico Sets Domestic Priorities Aside to Meet Terms of U.S. Trade Deal," *New York Times*, June 8, 2019, https://www.nytimes.com/2019/06/08/world/americas/mexico-tariffs-migration.html.

28. Julie Hirschfield Davis, "House Votes to Give 'Dreamers' a Path to Citizenship," *New York Times*, June 4, 2019, https://www.nytimes.com/2019/06/04/us/politics/dream-promise-act.html.

29. Cristina Marcos, "House Dems move to give lawmakers a pay increase," *The Hill*, June 4, 2019, https://thehill.com/homenews/house/446946-house-dems-move-to-give-lawmakers-a-pay-increase.

30. Laurie Kellman and Zeke Miller, "Trump, Pelosi trade insults as their feud heats up," *AP*, May 24, 2019, https://www.apnews.com/ce08485cee37470db8983b8bd06c40a0.

31. Harry Enten, "Congress' Approval Rating Hasn't Hit 30% in 10 Years. That's a Record," CNN, June 1, 2019, https://www.cnn.com/2019/06/01/politics/poll-of-the-week-congress-approval-rating/index.html.

32. Robert E. Kessler, "MS-13 member sentenced to 55 years in machete quadruple murder," *Long Island Newsday*, June 12, 2019, https://www.newsday.com/long-island/crime/ms-13-machete-murders-central-islip-1.32294790

33. Nicole Fuller, "MS-13 murders down on LI, but gang is trying to rebuild," *Long Island Newsday*, May 12, 2019, https://www.newsday.com/long-island/crime/ms13-murders-fbi-1.30900131.

34. Gate Miskimen, "New court filing gives rare glimpse into Mollie Tibbetts investigation," *Des Moines Register*, May 31, 2019, https://www.desmoinesregister.com/story/news/crime-and-courts/2019/05/31/mollie-tibbetts-iowa-university-of-iowa-cristhian-bahena-rivera-investigation-murder-poweshiek-trial/1301865001/.

35. Victims of Illegal Aliens Memorial, http://www.ojjpac.org/memorial.asp.

36. Joshua Caplan, "Nancy Pelosi Refuses to Meet with Angel Moms Protesting Inside Her Office," Breitbart, January 15, 2019, https://www.breitbart.com/politics/2019/01/15/nancy-pelosi-refuses-to-meet-with-angel-moms-protesting-inside-her-office/.

37. Cat Cardenas, "Border Patrol Leaves San Antonio to Sort Out Surge of African Migrants." *Texas Monthly*, July 2, 2019, https://www.texasmonthly.com/news/border-patrol-leaves-san-antonio-to-sort-out-surge-of-african-migrants/.

38. Josh Gerstein, "Judge Rejects Trump Request to Alter Agreement on Release of Immigrant Kids," Politico, July 9, 2019, https://www.politico.com/story/2018/07/09/judge-rejects-trump-request-flores-immigrant-children-704019.

39. Jack Crowe, "DHS Secretary: 90 Percent of Recent Asylum-Seekers Skipped Their Hearings," *National Review*, June 11, 2019, https://www.nationalreview.com/news/dhs-secretary-90-percent-of-recent-asylum-seekers-skipped-their-hearings/.

40. Jake Tapper, "Nancy Pelosi called Trump Friday night asking him to call off ICE raids," CNN, June 22, 2019, https://www.cnn.com/2019/06/22/politics/nancy-pelosi-ice-raids-house-speaker-called-donald-trump/index.html.

CHAPTER NINE: THE RADICALS' REVENGE

1. Veronica Stracqualursi, "New House Democrat Rashida Tlaib: 'We're Gonna Impeach the Motherf****r,'" CNN, January 4, 2019, https://www.cnn.com/2019/01/04/politics/rashida-tlaib-trump-impeachment-comments/index.html.

2. Avie Schneider, "U.S. Unemployment Rate Drops to 3.7 Percent, Lowest in Nearly 50 Years," NPR, October 5, 2018, https://www.npr.org/2018/10/05/654417887/u-s-unemployment-rate-drops-to-3-7-percent-lowest-in-nearly-50-years.

3. Rami Ayyub, Ali Sawafta, "West Bank kin cheer first Palestinian-American woman in U.S. Congress," Reuters, November 7, 2018. https://www.reuters.com/article/us-usa-election-michigan-palestinians/west-bank-kin-cheer-first-palestinian-american-woman-in-u-s-congress-idUSKCN1NC1HL.

4. Jeremy Herb and Manu Raju, "House Democrat Reintroduces Impeachment Articles Against Trump," CNN, January 3, 2019, https://www.cnn.com/2019/01/03/politics/impeachment-house-democrats-brad-sherman-trump/index.html.

5. Paul Davidson, "December Jobs Report: 312,000 Added, Easing Recession Fears Amid Stock Turmoil," January 4, 2019, https://www.usatoday.com/story/money/2019/01/04/jobs-report-booming-312-000-were-added-last-month-economists-expected-181-000/2477547002/.

6. Aris Folley, "Pelosi on Tlaib 'Impeach the Motherf---Er' Comment: 'I'm Not in the Censorship Business,'" *The Hill*, January 4, 2019, https://thehill.com/homenews/house/423882-pelosi-on-tlaib-impeach-the-motherf-er-comment-im-not-in-the-censorship.

7. David Harsanyi, "First on Nancy Pelosi's Agenda: Attacking Free Expression," Reason, January 4, 2019, https://reason.com/archives/2019/01/04/first-on-nancy-pelosis-agenda-attacking.

8. "CITIZENS UNITED, APPELLANT v. FEDERAL ELECTION COMMISSION." Supreme Court of the United States, January 21, 2010. https://www.supremecourt.gov/opinions/09pdf/08-205.pdf.

9. Rebecca Ballhaus and Brody Mullins, "Donors in Most Industries Back Hillary Clinton," *Wall Street Journal*, September 9, 2016, https://www.wsj.com/articles/donors-in-most-industries-back-hillary-clinton-1473462212.

10. Patrick Svitek, "Nancy Pelosi Escalates Call for Citizens United Constitutional Amendment," HuffPost, July 26, 2012, https://www. huffingtonpost.com/2012/07/26/nancy-pelosi-citizens-united-constitutional-amendment_n_1708114.html.

11. Peter Overby, "House Democrats Introduce Anti-Corruption Bill as Symbolic 1st Act," NPR, January 5, 2019, https://www.npr.org/2019/01/05/682286587/house-democrats-introduce-anti-corruption-bill-as-symbolic-first-act.

12. Emily Birnbaum, "Dem Introduces Bills to Eliminate Electoral College, Stop Presidents from Pardoning Themselves," The Hill, January 3, 2019, https://thehill.com/homenews/house/423810-dem-introduces-bills-to-eliminate-electoral-college-stop-presidents-from.

13. Jenna Johnson, "Beto O'Rourke's immigration plan: No wall, few specifics." Washington Post, January 15, 2019, https://www.washingtonpost.com/politics/beto-orourkes-immigration-plan-no-wall-but-no-specifics/2019/01/15/f6e36fac-15ea-11e9-90a8-136fa44b80ba_story.html?noredirect=on&utm_term=.b89d7bbeb2b3.

14. Felicia Sonmez, "Nancy Pelosi Will 'Cut Your Head Off and You Won't Even Know You're Bleeding,' Daughter Alexandra Pelosi Says," CNN, January 2, 2019, https://www.washingtonpost.com/politics/nancy-pelosi-will-cut-your-head-off-and-you-wont-even-know-youre-bleeding-daughter-alexandra-pelosi-says/2019/01/02/959ea7da-0ebe-11e9-84fc-d58c33d6c8c7_story.html?noredirect=on&utm_term=.a0b21ad26969.

15. Caitlin Yilek, "Kathy Griffin Photoshoot Features Beheaded Trump," Washington Examiner, May 30, 2017, https://www.washingtonexaminer.com/kathy-griffin-photoshoot-features-beheaded-trump.

16. Matt Wilstein, "Kathy Griffin Takes Back Trump Apology on 'The View': 'F*ck Him,'" Daily Beast, April 30, 2018, https://www.thedailybeast.com/kathy-griffin-takes-back-trump-apology-on-the-view-fuck-him.

17. Press Association, "Johnny Depp Jokes about Killing Donald Trump in Glastonbury Appearance," The Guardian, June 23, 2017, https://www.theguardian.com/film/2017/jun/23/johnny-depp-jokes-about-killing-trump-in-glastonbury-appearance.

18. Travis M. Andrews, "Trump-like 'Julius Caesar' Assassinated in New York Play. Delta, Bank of America Pull Funding," Washington Post, June 12, 2017, https://www.washingtonpost.com/news/morning-mix/wp/2017/06/12/trump-like-julius-caesar-assassinated-in-new-york-play-delta-bank-of-america-pull-funding/?utm_term=.402c60b8cfb4.

19. Adam Andrzejewski, "Julius Caesar's Parent Company—The New York Shakespeare Festival—Received $30M from Taxpayers," Forbes, June 13, 2017, https://www.forbes.com/sites/adamandrzejewski/2017/06/13/the-new-york-shakespeare-festival-received-30-million-in-government-grants-since-2009/#579220c3eb35.

20. Sopan Deb, "Actress Carole Cook Jokes about a Trump Assassination," *New York Times*, September 10, 2018, https://www.nytimes.com/2018/09/10/arts/carole-cook-john-wilkes-booth.html.

21. Ellen Barkin (@EllenBarkin), "this man should be removed . . . and not just from office," Twitter, October 1, 2018, https://twitter.com/EllenBarkin/status/1046808065008447488.

22. Christian Toto, "Ellen Barkin Wants Louis C.K. Raped, Shot," Hollywood in Toto, January 1, 2019, https://www.hollywoodintoto.com/ellen-barkin-louis-c-k-raped-shot/.

23. Mairead McArdle, "Kamala Harris Jokes about Killing Trump, Pence, Sessions," *National Review*, April 6, 2018, https://www.nationalreview.com/news/kamala-harris-jokes-about-killing-trump-pence-sessions/.

24. Maya Oppenheim, "Missouri State Senator Says She Hopes Donald Trump Is Assassinated Sparking Secret Service Investigation," *The Independent*, August 18, 2017, https://www.independent.co.uk/news/world/americas/maria-chappelle-nadal-donald-trump-missouri-state-senator-assassination-us-president-secret-service-a7900151.html.

25. Dom Calicchio and Gregg Re, "GOP's Steve Scalise Shuts Down Twitter Debate on Taxes with Ocasio-Cortez After 'Radical Followers' Allude to Virginia Shooting," Fox News, January 6, 2019, https://www.foxnews.com/politics/gops-steve-scalise-shuts-down-twitter-debate-on-taxes-with-ocasio-cortez-after-radical-followers-allude-to-virginia-shooting.

26. Tribune News Services, "Punches, Eggs Thrown as Protesters Attack Trump Supporters Outside San Jose Rally," *Chicago Tribune*, June 3, 2016, https://www.chicagotribune.com/news/nationworld/politics/ct-trump-rally-california-20160602-story.html.

27. Randy Roguski, "Trump Supporter Clobbered for His Allegiance to the President," *Sun Sentinel*, July 6, 2018, https://www.sun-sentinel.com/local/palm-beach/boynton-beach/fl-pn-trump-flag-attack-20180706-story.html.

28. Amy B. Wang, "A Truck with 'Trump 2020' Bumper Stickers Was Left at a Bar Overnight. Someone Set It on Fire," *Washington Post*, October 11, 2018, https://www.washingtonpost.com/nation/2018/10/10/truck-with-trump-bumper-stickers-was-left-bar-overnight-someone-set-it-fire/?utm_term=.bd50fc3ed555.

29. Katie Mettler, "She knocked a MAGA hat off a man's head in a Mexican restaurant. Now she could be deported," *Washington Post*, February 28, 2019, https://www.washingtonpost.com/nation/2019/02/28/she-knocked-maga-hat-off-mans-head-mexican-restaurant-now-she-could-be-deported/?utm_term=.b6d6be7286fd.

30. Ian Schwartz, "Sen. Kamala Harris vs. ICE Nominee: Are You Aware of Parallels Between ICE and KKK?" RealClear Politics, November 15, 2018, https://www.realclearpolitics.com/video/2018/11/15/kamala_harris_ice_nominee_ronald_vitiello_are_you_aware_of_parallels_between_ice_kkk.html.

31. Julia Cohen, "Antifa Escalates Doxxing ICE Employees by Publishing Home Addresses," Daily Caller, June 21, 2018, https://dailycaller.com/2018/06/21/antifa-doxxing-home-addresses-oregon/.

32. Kyle Perisic, "The Person Doxxing Ice Employees Is a Professor at NYU," *Daily Caller*, June 20, 2018, https://dailycaller.com/2018/06/20/antifa-doxxing-professor-nyu-ice/.

33. Mitchell Gunter, "Student Antifa organizations Dox, Protest ICE Agents," *Washington Examiner*, July 16, 2018, https://www.washingtonexaminer.com/red-alert-politics/student-antifa-organizations-dox-protest-ice-agents.

34. Lucia I. Suarez Sang, "Marines Testify about Antifa Mob Attack in Philadelphia, Fox News, December 17, 2018, https://www.foxnews.com/us/marines-testify-about-antifa-mob-they-say-attacked-them-in-philadelphia.

35. Kevin D. Williamson, "Whose Streets, Indeed?" *National Review*, December 20, 2018, https://www.nationalreview.com/magazine/2018/12/31/whose-streets-indeed/.

CHAPTER TEN: RESISTING REALITY: *MEDIA MADNESS*

1. Katelyn Polantz and Caroline Kelly, "Mueller's Office Disputes BuzzFeed Report That Trump Directed Michael Cohen to Lie to Congress," CNN, January 19, 2019, https://www.cnn.com/2019/01/18/politics/mueller-statement-buzzfeed/index.html.

2. Jason Leopold and Anthony Cormier, "President Trump Directed His Attorney Michael Cohen to Lie to Congress about the Moscow Tower Project," BuzzFeed, January 17, 2019, https://www.buzzfeednews.com/article/jasonleopold/trump-russia-cohen-moscow-tower-mueller-investigation.

3. "BuzzFeed News: Trump Ordered Michael Cohen to Lie to Congress," MSNBC, January 17, 2019, https://www.msnbc.com/brian-williams/watch/buzzfeed-news-trump-ordered-michael-cohen-to-lie-to-congress-1428069443571.

4. Michael Brice-Saddler, "BuzzFeed's Trump-Cohen Bombshell Dominated the Morning News Shows—Except on 'Fox & Friends,'" January 18, 2019, https://www.washingtonpost.com/politics/2019/01/18/buzzfeeds-trump-cohen-bombshell-dominated-morning-news-shows-except-fox-friends/?utm_term=.176b0b9b655d.

5. Justin Caruso, "Trevor Noah on Covington Teenager: Everyone 'Wants to Punch That Kid,'" Breitbart, January 22, 2019, https://www.breitbart.com/entertainment/2019/01/22/trevor-noah-on-covington-teenager-everyone-wants-to-punch-that-kid/.

6. Matt Wolking (@MattWolking), screenshot of "He is a deplorable. Some ppl can also be punched in the face," Twitter, January 21, 2019, https://twitter.com/MattWolking/status/1087327139937030144.

7. Brian Stetler, "CNN cancels Reza Aslan's show 'Believer' after profane anti-Trump tweets," CNN, June 9, 2017, https://money.cnn.com/2017/06/09/media/cnn-reza-aslan-decision/index.html.

8. Reza Aslan (@rezaaslan), "Honest question. Have you ever seen a more punchable face than this kid's?" Twitter, January 19, 2019, https://twitter.com/rezaaslan/status/1086806539552284672.

9. Max Londberg and Sarah Brookbank, "NKY Catholic School Faces Backlash After Video of Incident at Indigenous Peoples March Surfaces," *Cincinnati Enquirer*, January 19, 2019, https://www.cincinnati.com/story/news/2019/01/19/video-shows-apparent-incident-indigenous-peoples-march/2623820002/.

10. Adam Beam and Brian Melley, "Catholic High School Students in 'MAGA' Hats Mock Native American After D.C. Rally, Could Face Expulsion," *Chicago Tribune*, January 19, 2019, https://www.chicagotribune.com/news/nationworld/ct-kentucky-students-in-maga-hats-mock-native-american-20190119-story.html.

11. Cleve R. Wootson, Jr., Antonio Olivo, and Joe Heim, "'It Was Getting Ugly': Native American Drummer Speaks on His Encounter with MAGA-Hat-Wearing Teens," *Washington Post*, January 22, 2019, https://www.washingtonpost.com/nation/2019/01/20/it-was-getting-ugly-native-american-drummer-speaks-maga-hat-wearing-teens-who-surrounded-him/?utm_term=.5fd37124cee4.

12. Michael E. Miller, "Viral Standoff Between a Tribal Elder and a High Schooler Is More Complicated Than It First Seemed," *Washington Post*, January 22, 2019, https://www.washingtonpost.com/local/social-issues/picture-of-the-conflict-on-the-mall-comes-into-clearer-focus/2019/01/20/c078f092-1ceb-11e9-9145-3f74070bbdb9_story.html?utm_term=.78b6b013253b.

13. Robby Soave, "The Media Wildly Mischaracterized That Video of Covington Catholic Students Confronting a Native American Veteran," *Reason*, January 20, 2019. https://reason.com/blog/2019/01/20/covington-catholic-nathan-phillips-video.

14. "Statement of Nick Sandmann, Covington Catholic High School Junior, Regarding Incident at the Lincoln Memorial," CNN, January 23, 2019, https://www.cnn.com/2019/01/20/us/covington-kentucky-student-statement/index.html.

15. Johsua Gill, "Nathan Phillips' Military Record Reveals He Was Not a Vietnam Combat Veteran," Daily Caller, January 23, 2019, https://dailycaller.com/2019/01/23/nathan-phillips-not-vietnam-veteran/.

16. See note 11 above.

17. Peter Hasson, "Nathan Phillips Keeps Changing His Story, Still Keeps Getting It Wrong," Daily Caller, January 22, 2019, https://dailycaller.com/2019/01/22/nathan-phillips-story-covington/.

18. Matt Richardson, "Washington Post Publishes Editor's Note on Covington Controversy Coverage," Fox News, March 2, 2019, https://www.foxnews.com/us/washington-post-publishes-editors-note-on-covington-controversy-coverage.

19. Ibid.

20. "Nick Sandmann Speaks Out on Viral Encounter with Nathan Phillips," *Today*, January 23, 2019, https://www.today.com/video/nick-sandmann-speaks-out-on-viral-encounter-with-nathan-phillips-1430461507922.

21. Eun Kyung Kim, "Nathan Phillips on Viral Encounter with Nick Sandmann: 'I Forgive Him,'" *Today*, January 24, 2019, https://www.today.com/news/nathan-phillips-talks-today-show-s-savannah-guthrie-about-viral-t147369.

22. Keith Coffman, "CNN hit with $275 million defamation suit by Kentucky student," Reuters, March 13, 2019. https://www.reuters.com/article/us-usa-nativeamerican/cnn-hit-with-275-million-defamation-suit-by-kentucky-student-idUSKBN1QU0BY.

23. Merriam-Webster Online Dictionary. https://www.merriam-webster.com/dictionary/racism.

24. Hunter Walker, "Donald Trump just released an epic statement raging against Mexican immigrants and 'disease'," July 6, 2015, https://www.businessinsider.com/donald-trumps-epic-statement-on-mexico-2015-7.

25. Elizabeth Weise, "Assault on 'Empire' Actor Jussie Smollett Serves as Reminder—Lynching, Noose Symbolism Still Prevalent," *USA Today*, January 31, 2019, https://www.usatoday.com/story/news/2019/01/31/attack-empire-star-jussie-smollett-shows-rise-lynching-symbolism/2719869002/.

26. Peter Hasson, "Here's a List of Hoax 'Hate Crimes' in the Trump Era," Daily Caller, February 18, 2019, https://dailycaller.com/2019/02/18/hoax-hate-crimes-list/.

27. Laura Bradley, "Ellen Page Tearfully Condemns Jussie Smollett Attack—And the Trump Administration," *Vanity Fair*, February 1, 2019, https://www.vanityfair.com/hollywood/2019/02/ellen-page-jussie-smollett-colbert-late-show?verso=true.

28. Julia Manchester, "Pollster Says Past Obama, Clinton Views on Same-Sex Marriage Would Be 'Disqualifying' Today," *The Hill*, March 18, 2019, https://thehill.com/hilltv/what-americas-thinking/434578-pollster-says-past-obama-clinton-views-on-same-sex-marriage.

29. Bethonie Butler and Elahe Izadi, "Jussie Smollett Speaks Out After Alleged Attack: 'My Body Is Strong But My Soul Is Stronger," *Washington Post*, February 1, 2019, https://www.washingtonpost.com/arts-entertainment/2019/01/31/this-was-racial-homophobic-hate-crime-jussie-smolletts-family-speaks-out-after-alleged-assault/?utm_term=.03c5ab0f61c9.

30. Jennifer Smith, "Chicago Police Say Jussie Smollett Gave 'Insufficient' Phone Records That Were Heavily Redacted and Do Not Prove He Was Talking To His Manager At The Time Of Racist, Homophobic Attack," *Daily Mail*, February 12, 2019, https://www.dailymail.co.uk/news/article-6695695/Chicago-police-say-Jussie-Smollett-gave-insufficient-redacted-phone-records.html.

31. Sopan Deb and Jack Healy, "Jussie Smollett Rehearsed His Own Assault, Prosecutors Say," *New York Times*, February 21, 2019, https://www.nytimes.com/2019/02/21/arts/television/jussie-smollett-arrest-salary-letter.html.

32. Amadna Seitz and Michael Tarm, "Prosecutors Dismiss Charges Against Smollett, Draw Backlash," Associated Press, March 26, 2019. https://www.apnews.com/1cb151c45b714a749ebadf8e50910a0d.

33. Phil Helsel, "City of Chicago Sues Jussie Smollett For Investigation Costs," NBC News, April 11, 2019, https://www.nbcnews.com/news/us-news/city-chicago-sues-jussie-smollett-investigation-costs-n993676.

34. Kim Foxx, "Commentary: Kim Foxx: I welcome an outside review of how we handled the Jussie Smollett case," *Chicago Tribune*, March 29, 2019.

35. Sandra E. Garcia, "Jussie Smollett Charges Were Dropped Because Conviction Was Uncertain, Prosecutor Says," *New York Times*, March 30, 2019, https://www.nytimes.com/2019/03/30/us/kim-foxx-chicago-smollett.html.

36. Robert Chiarito and Julia Jacobs, "Jussie Smollett Case to Be Investigated by Special Prosecutor," *New York Times*, June 21, 2019. https://www.nytimes.com/2019/06/21/arts/television/jussie-smollett-special-prosecutor.html?searchResultPosition=1&module=inline.

37. Elizabeth Drew, "The Danger in Not Impeaching Trump," *New York Times*, April 25, 2019, https://www.nytimes.com/2019/04/25/opinion/trump-impeachment.html.

38. Kevin Townsend, "Radio Atlantic: To Impeach or Not to Impeach?" *The Atlantic*, April 26, 2019, https://www.theatlantic.com/politics/archive/2019/04/to-impeach-or-not-to-impeach/588019/.

39. David Bauder, "Fake news? No, Mueller Report Shows Journalists Mostly Got It Right on Trump, Russia," *Chicago Tribune*, April 19, 2019, https://www.chicagotribune.com/news/nationworld/politics/ct-trump-russia-mueller-report-mainstream-media-20190419-story.html.

40. Ibid.

41. Chuck Ross, "Jake Tapper: CNN Didn't Get 'Anything' Wrong in Russiagate Reporting," Daily Caller, March 31, 2019, https://dailycaller.com/2019/03/31/jake-tapper-cnn-trump-russia/.

42. Marshall Cohen, "Analysis: Unredacted Paul Manafort Filing Hints at Collusion," CNN, January 8, 2019, https://www.cnn.com/2019/01/08/politics/unredacted-manafort-filing-analysis/index.html.

43. Max Boot, "The Collusion Case Against Trump Just Got a Lot Stronger," *Washington Post*, January 9, 2019, https://www.washingtonpost.com/opinions/2019/01/09/collusion-case-against-trump-just-got-lot-stronger/?utm_term=.9e45640de849.

44. Stephen Collinson, "Trump Tries to Change the Story, but Russia Cloud Darkens," CNN, December 10, 2018, https://www.cnn.com/2018/12/08/politics/donald-trump-robert-mueller-john-kelly-russia-emmanuel-macron/index.html.

45. Glenn Greenwald, "Robert Mueller Did Not Merely Reject the Trump-Russia Conspiracy Theories. He Obliterated Them," The Intercept, April 18, 2019, https://theintercept.com/2019/04/18/robert-mueller-did-not-merely-reject-the-trumprussia-conspiracy-theories-he-obliterated-them/.

46. Matt Taibbi, "The Press Will Learn Nothing From the Russiagate Fiasco," *Rolling Stone*, April 23, 2019, https://www.rollingstone.com/politics/politics-features/russiagate-fiasco-taibbi-news-media-826246/.

CHAPTER ELEVEN: THE RADICALS' ATTACK ON LIFE ITSELF

1. Valerie Richardson, "Virginia Republicans defeat Democratic bill allowing abortions up until birth," *Washington Times*, January 30, 2019, https://www.washingtontimes.com/news/2019/jan/30/va-gop-defeats-bill-allowing-abortions-until-birth/.

2. "Failed Virginia Bill Sparks National Debate About Abortion," NPR, January 31, 2019, https://www.npr.org/2019/01/31/690468965/failed-virginia-bill-sparks-national-debate-about-abortion.

3. Devan Cole, "Virginia Governor Faces Backlash Over Comments Supporting Late-Term Abortion Bill," CNN, January 31, 2019, https://www.cnn.com/2019/01/31/politics/ralph-northam-third-trimester-abortion/index.html.

4. Sean Moran, "Ralph Northam Got Nearly $2 Million in Donations from Planned Parenthood," Breitbart News, February 1, 2019, https://www.breitbart.com/politics/2019/02/01/ralph-northam-got-nearly-2-million-in-donations-from-planned-parenthood/.

5. Samantha Schmidt, "'Not a Scintilla of Evidence' of Wrongdoing by Planned Parenthood: Federal Judge Blocks Texas Defunding Effort," *Washington Post*, February 22, 2017, https://www.washingtonpost.com/news/morning-mix/wp/2017/02/22/not-a-scintilla-of-evidence-of-wrongdoing-by-planned-parenthood-federal-judge-blocks-texas-defunding-effortar-medicaid-funds-to-the-organization/?utm_term=.3c2271256df3.

6. Christopher Mele, "Judge Blocks Medicaid Cuts to Planned Parenthood in Texas," *New York Times*, February 21, 2017, https://www.nytimes.com/2017/02/21/us/texas-planned-parenthood-medicaid.html.

7. Alexandra DeSanctis, "Fifth Circuit Ruling Dismantles Planned Parenthood Talking Points," *National Review*, January 17, 2019, https://www.nationalreview.com/corner/fifth-circuit-ruling-dismantles-planned-parenthood-talking-points/.

8. Ibid.

9. Jon Campbell, "Abortion Law in New York: What the Reproductive Health Act Does and Doesn't Do," *The Democrat & Chronicle*, February 6, 2019, https://www.democratandchronicle.com/story/news/politics/albany/2019/02/01/abortion-law-ny-what-reproductive-health-act-does-and-doesnt-do/2743142002/.

10. *Doe v. Bolton* (No. 70-40), January 22, 1973, Legal Information Institute, https://www.law.cornell.edu/supremecourt/text/410/179.

11. Caleb Parke, "New York 'Celebrates' Legalizing Abortion Until Birth as Catholic Bishops Question Cuomo's Faith," Fox News, January 23, 2019, https://www.foxnews.com/politics/new-york-celebrates-legalizing-abortion-until-birth-as-catholic-bishops-question-cuomos-faith.

12. "An Act Relating to Health and Safety—The Reproductive Health Care Act," introduced January 19, 2019, http://webserver.rilin.state.ri.us/BillText/BillText19/HouseText19/H5127.pdf.

13. Bill Rappleye and Sam Read, "Advocates Converge at RI State House for Abortion Bills," WJAR NBC 10, January 29, 2019, https://turnto10.com/politics/advocates-converge-at-ri-state-house-for-abortion-bills.

14. Jessica A. Botelho, "Woman Creates 'Me, Still Me' Movement as RI Lawmakers Mull Abortion Bills," WJAR NBC 10, January 28, 2019, https://turnto10.com/politics/woman-creates-me-still-me-movement-as-ri-lawmakers-mull-abortion-bill-01-28-2019.

15. "Homicide, Abortion and Related Offenses," Article 125, NY Penal Law, http://ypdcrime.com/penal.law/article125.htm.

16. Ibid.

17. Assembly Bill A1748, 2017–2018 Legislative Session, New York State Senate, https://www.nysenate.gov/legislation/bills/2017/a1748.

18. Joshua Gill, "Catholics Demand Governor Cuomo's Excommunication Over NY Abortion Law," Daily Caller, January 24, 2019, https://dailycaller.com/2019/01/24/catholics-cuomo-excommunication-abortion/.

19. Rev. Edward B. Scharfenberger, "Bishop Writes Open Letter to Gov. Cuomo," *The Evangelist*, January 19, 2019, https://evangelist.org/Content/Default/Homepage-Rotator/Article/Bishop-writes-open-letter-to-Gov-Cuomo-/-3/141/27245.

20. Caleb Parke, "Catholic Leaders Call for Gov. Cuomo to Be Excommunicated for 'Flagrant Celebration of Pro-Abortion Bill,'" Fox News, January 28, 2019, https://www.foxnews.com/faith-values/catholics-call-for-new-york-gov-andrew-cuomo-to-be-excommunicated-for-abortion-bill.

21. Ibid.

22. Eric J. Lyman, "Pope: Abortion Is 'White Glove' Equivalent to Nazi Crimes." *USA Today*, June 16, 2018, https://www.usatoday.com/story/news/world/2018/06/16/pope-francis-abortion-equivalent-nazi-eugenics-crimes/707661002/.

23. Angela Giuffrida, "Pope Francis Compares Abortion to Hiring a Hitman," *The Guardian*, October 10, 2018, https://www.theguardian.com/world/2018/oct/10/pope-francis-compares-abortion-hiring-hitman.

24. Vincenzo Pinto, "Pope Francis, asked about Trump's border wall, says fear of migration is 'making us crazy,'" CBS News, January 23, 2019, https://www.cbsnews.com/news/pope-francis-donald-trump-mexico-border-wall-fear-of-migration-making-us-crazy/.

25. Courtney Grogan, "Pope Francis: Pray with St. Bakhita for the End of Human Trafficking," Catholic News Agency, February 10, 2019, https://www.catholicnewsagency.com/news/pope-francis-pray-with-st-bakhita-for-the-end-of-human-trafficking-75927.

26. Marjorie Dannenfelser, "The Democratic Party Is More Extreme on Abortion Than Ever," *Time*, July 26, 2016, http://time.com/4424971/democrats-extreme-abortion/.

27. "1996 Democratic Party Platform," *The American Presidency Project*, August 26, 1996, https://www.presidency.ucsb.edu/documents/1996-democratic-party-platform.

28. https://shoutyourabortion.com/.

29. Nicole Russell, "Abortion Is a Celebration Now. That's Insanely Wrong," The Federalist, September 15, 2017, http://thefederalist.com/2017/09/15/abortion-celebration-now-thats-insanely-wrong/.

30. Annie Linskey and Ariana Eunjung Cha, "Battle Over Virginia Abortion Measure Roils Multistate Plans by Advocates to Lock in Rights Protections," *Washington Post*, February 2, 2019, https://www.washingtonpost.com/politics/battle-over-virginia-abortion-measure-roils-multistate-plans-by-advocates-to-lock-in-rights-protections/2019/02/02/01283f36-2637-11e9-90cd-dedb0c92dc17_story.html?utm_term=.b8d28d772267.

31. Phillip Wegmann, "Late-Term Abortion Stance May Be Trump Card in 2020," RealClear Politics, February 8, 2019, https://www.realclearpolitics.com/articles/2019/02/08/late-term_abortion_stance_may_be_trump_card_in_2020_139409.html.

32. "State of the Union 2019: Read the Full Transcript," CNN, February 6, 2019, https://www.cnn.com/2019/02/05/politics/donald-trump-state-of-the-union-2019-transcript/index.html.

CHAPTER TWELVE: THE DEMOCRATS' SIREN SONG OF SOCIALISM

1. Ryan Saavedra, "WATCH: Ocasio-Cortez Proves She Has No Idea What Congress Does," The Daily Wire, October 2, 2018, https://www.dailywire.com/news/36604/watch-ocasio-cortez-proves-she-has-no-idea-what-ryan-saavedra.

2. Eliza Relman, "Alexandria Ocasio-Cortez says the theory that deficit spending is good for the economy should 'absolutely' be part of the conversation," Business Insider, January 7, 2019, https://www.businessinsider.com/alexandria-ocasio-cortez-ommt-modern-monetary-theory-how-pay-for-policies-2019-1?r=US&IR=T.

3. Alexander Tanzi, "Top 3% of U.S. Taxpayers Paid Majority of Income Tax in 2016," Bloomberg, October 14, 2018, https://www.bloomberg.com/news/articles/2018-10-14/top-3-of-u-s-taxpayers-paid-majority-of-income-taxes-in-2016

4. "Building a Stronger America: President Donald J. Trump's American Infrastructure Initiative," The White House, February 12, 2018, https://www.whitehouse.gov/briefings-statements/building-stronger-america-president-donald-j-trumps-american-infrastructure-initiative/.

5. Doyle McManus, "Most 2020 Democrats Say Capitalism Is a System That Needs Fixing," *Los Angeles Times*, March 20, 2019, https://www.latimes.com/politics/la-na-pol-democrats-socialism-capitalism-20190320-story.html.

6. Maxim Lott, "Americans Warming to Socialism Over Capitalism, Polls Show," Fox News, January 4, 2019, https://www.foxnews.com/politics/americans-warming-to-socialism-over-capitalism-polls-show.

7. Rachel Frazin, "Kamala Harris: 'I Am Not a Democratic Socialist,'" *The Hill*, February 19, 2019, https://thehill.com/homenews/campaign/430554-kamala-harris-i-am-not-a-democratic-socialist.

8. Matt Welch, "Can a Self-Described 'Capitalist' Win the 2020 Democratic Primary?" *Reason*, March 1, 2019, https://reason.com/2019/03/01/can-a-self-described-capitalist-win-the/.

9. Mike Brest, "Cory Booker: 'I Am Not a Socialist,'" Daily Caller, March 18, 2019, https://dailycaller.com/2019/03/18/cory-booker-socialist-capitalism/.

10. "Town Hall with Bernie Sanders: Part 1," Fox News Show Clips, April 15, 2019, https://video.foxnews.com/v/6026527843001/#sp=show-clips.

11. Raymond J. Keating, "Original Intent and the Income Tax," Foundation for Economic Freedom, February 1, 1996, https://fee.org/articles/original-intent-and-the-income-tax/.

12. Joseph Simonson, "Bernie Sanders: Soviet Socialism 'Not My Thing' but 'Denmark and Sweden Do Very Well,'" *Washington Examiner*, April 6, 2019, https://www.washingtonexaminer.com/news/bernie-sanders-says-soviet-socialism-is-not-my-thing-but-denmark-and-sweden-do-very-well.

13. Adam Shaw, "Vintage Bernie Footage Shows Now-Presidential Candidate Praising Breadlines, Communist Nations," Fox News, February 22, 2019, https://www.foxnews.com/politics/vintage-bernie-footage-shows-now-presidential-candidate-praising-breadlines-communist-nations.

14. Frank Dikötter, "The Disappeared," *Foreign Policy*, January 2, 2013, https://foreignpolicy.com/2013/01/02/the-disappeared-mao/.

15. James A. Levine, "Poverty and Obesity in the U.S.," American Diabetes Association, November 2011, http://diabetes.diabetesjournals.org/content/60/11/2667.

16. *Valley News* Editorial Board, "Close the Gaps: Disparities That Threaten America," *Valley News*, August 5, 2011, https://www.sanders.senate.gov/newsroom/must-read/close-the-gaps-disparities-that-threaten-america.

17. Flora Charner, Paula Newton, and Natalie Gallón, "Opponents Slam Venezuelan President Nicolas Maduro's Election Victory as a Sham," CNN, May 21, 2018, https://edition.cnn.com/2018/05/20/americas/venezuela-elections/index.html.

18. Matthew Yglesias, "Denmark's Prime Minister Says Bernie Sanders Is Wrong to Call His Country Socialist," Vox, October 31, 2015, https://www.vox.com/2015/10/31/9650030/denmark-prime-minister-bernie-sanders.

19. Claire Boyte-White, "5 Developed Countries without Minimum Wages," Investopedia, August 5, 2015, https://www.investopedia.com/articles/investing/080515/5-developed-countries-without-minimum-wages.asp.

20. "2019 Index of Economic Freedom," Heritage Foundation, https://www.heritage.org/index/ranking.

21. Brian Darling, "Trump Regulatory Reform Saved Taxpayers $23 Billion," Townhall, October 19, 2018, https://townhall.com/columnists/briandarling/2018/10/19/trump-regulatory-reform-saved-taxpayers-23-billion-n2530055.

22. "Corporate Tax Rates Table," KPMG, https://home.kpmg/vg/en/home/services/tax1/tax-tools-and-resources/tax-rates-online/corporate-tax-rates-table.html.

23. Kyle Pomerleau, "Corporate Income Tax Rates Around the World, 2015," Tax Foundation, October 1, 2015, https://taxfoundation.org/corporate-income-tax-rates-around-world-2015/.

24. Mahdi Barakat, "No, It's Actually the Rich Who Deserve a Tax Break," Foundation for Economic Education, December 15, 2017, https://fee.org/articles/no-it-s-actually-the-rich-who-deserve-a-tax-break/.

25. Justin Fox, "How High-Tax Countries Tax," Bloomberg, February 19, 2019, https://www.bloomberg.com/opinion/articles/2019-02-19/high-tax-countries-make-more-people-pay-taxes.

26. Elke Asen, "VAT Rates in Europe," Tax Foundation, February 28, 2019, https://taxfoundation.org/vat-rates-europe-2019/.

27. Mark J. Perry, "Quotations from Thomas Sowell—One of the Greatest Living Economists," American Enterprise Institute, January 7, 2016, http://www.aei.org/publication/quotations-from-thomas-sowell-one-of-the-greatest-economists-alive-today/.

28. Fred Bergsten, "The Swedish Model for Economic Recovery," Petersen Institute for International Economics, August 30, 2013, https://piie.com/commentary/op-eds/swedish-model-economic-recovery.

29. Ibid.

30. "Sweden Corporate Tax Rate," Trading Economics, https://tradingeconomics.com/sweden/corporate-tax-rate.

31. "Sweden Government Spending to GDP," Trading Economics, https://tradingeconomics.com/sweden/government-spending-to-gdp.

32. "Denmark Government Spending to GDP," Trading Economics, https://tradingeconomics.com/denmark/government-spending-to-gdp.

33. Amanda Billner, Rafaela Lindeberg, and Niklas Magnusson, "Now Even Swedes Are Questioning the Welfare State," Bloomberg, June 26, 2018, https://www.bloomberg.com/news/articles/2018-06-26/now-even-swedes-are-questioning-the-welfare-state.

34. Daniel Chaitin, "AOC to critics of Green New Deal: 'I'm the boss' until you try," *The Washington Examiner*, February 24, 2019, https://www.washingtonexaminer.com/news/aoc-to-critics-of-green-new-deal-im-the-boss-until-you-try.

35. Ian Schwartz, "Full Video: FOX News Town Hall with Bernie Sanders," RealClear Politics, April 15, 2019, https://www.realclearpolitics.com/video/2019/04/15/full_video_fox_news_town_hall_with_bernie_sanders.html.

36. Meera Senthilingam, "After 70 Years of Universal Health Care, Is the NHS at a Crisis Point?" CNN, February 13, 2018, https://www.cnn.com/2018/02/10/health/uk-nhs-universal-health-coverage-crisis-point-intl/index.html.

37. Alanna Petroff, "U.K. hospital crisis: Why can't a rich economy fund its health care?" CNN, January 12, 2018, https://money.cnn.com/2018/01/12/news/nhs-health-care-doctors-hospitals/index.html.

38. Brett J. Skinner and Mark Rovere, "Canada's Health Care Crisis Is an Economics Problem, Not a Management Problem," Fraser Institute, https://www.fraserinstitute.org/article/canadas-health-care-crisis-is-an-economics-problem-not-a-management-problem.

CHAPTER THIRTEEN: GHOSTING CONSERVATIVES

1. Andrew McCarthy, "In Europe, Free Speech Bows to Sharia," *National Review*, October 27, 2019, https://www.nationalreview.com/2018/10/free-speech-sharia-european-court-of-human-rights-ruling/.

2. Martin Niemöller, United States Holocaust Memorial Museum, https://encyclopedia.ushmm.org/content/en/photo/quotation-from-martin-niemoeller.

3. Tom McKay, "YouTube: No, We Won't Remove These Videos of Racist, Anti-Gay Harassment Because It's Just 'Debating'," Gizmodo, June 5, 2019, https://gizmodo.com/youtube-no-we-wont-remove-these-videos-of-racist-ant-1835259054.

4. "PragerU Takes Legal Action Against Google and YouTube for Discrimination," PragerU, https://www.prageru.com/press-release/prageru-takes-legal-action-against-google-and-youtube-for-discrimination/.

5. Anna Hopkins, "PragerU Accuses Twitter, YouTube of Censoring Ads and Videos, Founder Calls Out 'Assault' on Free Speech," Fox News, June 26, 2019, https://www.foxnews.com/tech/prageru-founder-accuses-twitter-youtube-of-censoring-advertisements-and-videos.

6. Ibid.

7. David Schultz, "Marketplace of Ideas," Encyclopedia of the First Amendment, June 2017, https://www.mtsu.edu/first-amendment/article/999/marketplace-of-ideas.

8. Joseph Curl, "New York Times Editor Admits Paper Is Very, Very (Very) Biased," *Washington Times*, October 17, 2017, https://www.washingtontimes.com/news/2017/oct/17/new-york-times-editor-admits-paper-is-very-very-ve/.

9. Chris Cillizza, "Just 7 Percent of Journalists Are Republicans. That's Far Fewer Than Even a Decade Ago," *Washington Post*, May 6, 2014, https://www.washingtonpost.com/news/the-fix/wp/2014/05/06/just-7-percent-of-journalists-are-republicans-thats-far-less-than-even-a-decade-ago/?utm_term=.c4bb4b576282.

10. "Obama, Democrats Got 88 Percent of 2008 Contributions by TV Network Execs, Writers, Reporters UPDATED!" *Washington Examiner,* August 27, 2010, https://www.washingtonexaminer.com/obama-democrats-got-88-percent-of-2008-contributions-by-tv-network-execs-writers-reporters-updated.

11. "Indicators of News Media Trust," Knight Foundation, September 11, 2018, https://www.knightfoundation.org/reports/indicators-of-news-media-trust.

12. Oren Tsur, "The Data Behind Donald Trump's Twitter Takeover," *Politico Magazine,* April 29, 2016, https://www.politico.com/magazine/story/2016/04/donald-trump-2016-twitter-takeover-213861.

13. Jaclyn Peiser, "New York Times Tops 4 Million Mark in Total Subscribers," *New York Times,* November 1, 2018, https://www.nytimes.com/2018/11/01/business/media/new-york-times-earnings-subscribers.html.

14. Tony Romm and Elizabeth Dwoskin, "Facebook, Google and other tech giants to face antitrust investigation by House lawmakers," *Washington Post,* June 3, 2019, https://www.washingtonpost.com/technology/2019/06/03/facebook-google-other-tech-giants-face-antitrust-investigation-by-house-lawmakers/?utm_term=.7782b39ddfd6.

15. Kate Conger, "Google Removes 'Don't Be Evil' Clause From Its Code of Conduct," Gizmodo, May 18, 2018, https://gizmodo.com/google-removes-nearly-all-mentions-of-dont-be-evil-from-1826153393.

16. David E. Broockman, Gregorgy Ferenstein, and Neil Malhotra, "The Political Behavior of Wealthy Americans: Evidence from Technology Entrepreneurs," Stanford Graduate School of Business, September 5, 2017, https://www.gsb.stanford.edu/gsb-cmis/gsb-cmis-download-auth/441556.

17. "Insider Blows Whistle & Exec Reveals Google Plan to Prevent 'Trump situation' in 2020 on Hidden Cam," Project Veritas, June 24, 2019, https://www.projectveritas.com/2019/06/24/insider-blows-whistle-exec-reveals-google-plan-to-prevent-trump-situation-in-2020-on-hidden-cam/.

18. Ibid.

19. "Project Veritas Sends Google Letters to Congress," Project Veritas, June 28, 2019, https://www.projectveritas.com/2019/06/28/project-veritas-sends-google-letters-to-congress/.

20. Theodore Schleifer, "Twitter Won't Censor Trump's Rule-Breaking Tweets, But It Will Make Them Harder to Find," Vox, June 27, 2019, https://www.vox.com/recode/2019/6/27/18761360/donald-trump-twitter-policy-censorship-rules.

21. Aaron Smith, "Public Attitudes Toward Technology Companies," Pew Research Center, June 28, 2018, https://www.pewinternet.org/2018/06/28/public-attitudes-toward-technology-companies/?utm_source=adaptivemailer&utm_medium=email&utm_campaign=18-06-28%20views%20of%20tech%20companies&org=982&lvl=100&ite=2793&lea=618395&ctr=0&par=1&trk=.

22. Richard Hanania, "It Isn't Your Imagination: Twitter Treats Conservatives More Harshly Than Liberals," Quillette, February 12, 2019, https://quillette.

com/2019/02/12/it-isnt-your-imagination-twitter-treats-conservatives-more-harshly-than-liberals/.

23. Andrew Griffin, "Twitter Explains Why It Banned Rose McGowan After She Spoke Out About Hollywood Abuse," *The Independent*, October 13, 2017, https://www.independent.co.uk/life-style/gadgets-and-tech/news/twitter-rose-mcgowan-harvey-weinstein-ben-affleck-tweets-account-boycott-women-a7998996.html.

24. Ian Schwartz, "Tucker Carlson on Sarah Jeong: Left Thinks Racism Against White People 'Impossible,'" RealClear Politics, August 3, 2018, https://www.realclearpolitics.com/video/2018/08/03/tucker_carlson_on_sarah_jeong_left_thinks_racism_against_white_people_impossible.html.

25. Jon Levine, "Twitter Verifies NY Times Writer Sarah Jeong After Outrage Over Old Tweets," The Wrap, August 16, 2018, https://www.thewrap.com/twitter-verifies-sarah-jeong-after-outrage-over-old-tweets/.

26. Ibid.

27. Donald Trump (@realDonaldTrump), "Twitter 'SHADOW BANNING' prominent Republicans. Not good. We will look into this discriminatory and illegal practice at once! Many complaints," Twitter, July 26, 2018, https://twitter.com/realdonaldtrump/status/1022447980408983552?lang=en.

28. Sam Levin and Olivia Solon, "Zuckerberg Defends Facebook Users' Right to Be Wrong—Even Holocaust Deniers," *The Guardian,* July 18, 2018, https://www.theguardian.com/technology/2018/jul/18/zuckerberg-facebook-holocaust-deniers-censorship.

29. Brian Robertson, "Facebook Censorship Fast Becoming an Enemy of Free Speech for Conservatives," *Washington Examiner*, March 6, 2019, https://www.washingtonexaminer.com/opinion/op-eds/facebook-censorship-fast-becoming-an-enemy-of-free-expression-for-conservatives.

30. "Read CEO Jack Dorsey's Full Testimony on Twitter and Political Bias," PBS, September 4, 2018, https://www.pbs.org/newshour/politics/read-ceo-jack-dorseys-full-testimony-on-twitter-and-political-bias.

31. Andrew Griffin, "Twitter CEO Jack Dorsey Says He Was Probably Too Aggressive in Banning Right-Wing Activists," *The Independent,* March 6, 2019, https://www.independent.co.uk/life-style/gadgets-and-tech/news/twitter-ban-conservatives-right-wing-jack-dorsey-joe-rogan-interview-a8809866.html.

32. Katy Clifton, "Twitter boss Admits Algorithms Unfairly Hid 600,000 Accounts," *Evening Standard,* September 6, 2018, https://www.standard.co.uk/front/twitter-boss-admits-algorithms-unfairly-hid-600000-accounts-a3929286.html.

Index

McCabe and, 49, 59
multiple investigations into, 45
of Steele dossier, 55
life, attack on. *See* abortion;
abortion, late-term
Lightfoot, Lori, 76
Lincoln Memorial, fake news from,
175–184
Loomer, Laura, 236–237, 250
Lynch, Loretta
confidence of conspirators and, 4
conflicting stories with Comey,
53–54, 58–59
Hillary planning to keep as AG,
54
investigation/accountability
needed, 6, 24–26, 45
in jeopardy, 53–55, 61–62
John Durham and, 54–55
meeting Bill Clinton on tarmac,
then letting Hillary off, 30, 54,
56–57
as Obama ally, 29
Uranium One deal and threat by,
61–62
"lynching," fake, 184–191

M

Maduro, Nicholas, 16, 221
MAGA hat wearers, actions against,
168–169, 175–184
mainstream media and fake news.
See also censoring conservatives
Barr's Senate testimony and,
38–39
bypassing, 242–243
Catholic boys/Native American
fake news, 175–184
enabling corrupt investigation
into Trump, 47–48
evolution of how we get news
and, 239–243
Greenwald comments on, 193,
194
journalists' political affiliations
and donations, 241
Krugman claims, 7
Mueller correcting false BuzzFeed
report, 173–174
new "public square" and, 239–243

objectivity lost, 239–241
The Post movie and, 11–12
post–no collusion self-delusion,
191–194
relationship with the Left, 12, 240
Smollett fake "lynching," 184–191
suspicious "closing in" pattern,
12–17
Trump bypassing on Twitter,
242–243
trust (lack of) in, 241–242
writers on Left recognizing
situation, 193–194
Manafort, Paul, 10, 55, 192
manufacturing jobs, resurgence of,
259
McCabe, Andrew
FISA court conspiracy, 63–64
investigation/accountability
needed, 24–26, 38
investigations underway, 48–49, 59
lying under oath, 49, 59
Michael Flynn set-up, 79–80, 81
McCabe, Kevin, 76
McCarthy, Andrew, 40, 80
McGowan, Rose, 249
media. *See* censoring conservatives;
free speech; mainstream media and
fake news
Medicare for All, 101–102, 105, 107,
108, 110, 211, 216, 224
Mekeland, Shane, 76
Mexico, helping control border,
137–141, 142–144. *See also* border;
immigration
Modern Monetary Theory (MMT),
211–215
Morgan, Mark, 121–122, 155
MS-13, 136, 141, 142, 148–149,
150–151
Mueller investigation. *See also*
FBI investigation of Trump;
investigation of Trump
investigators
breadth and depth of, 6, 7, 21, 44
"closing in" pattern of media,
12–17
duration and timing of, 4–5
indictments from, 5–6
justification for. *See* Steele dossier
Roger Stone raid and, 17–18